Prentice Hall *LITERATURE*

PENGUIN EDITION

D1605126

Unit Three
Resources

Grade Eight

PEARSON

Upper Saddle River, New Jersey
Boston, Massachusetts
Chandler, Arizona
Glenview, Illinois

BQ Tunes Credits
Keith London, Defined Mind, Inc., Executive Producer
Mike Pandolfo, Wonderful, Producer
All songs mixed and mastered by Mike Pandolfo, Wonderful
Vlad Gutkovich, Wonderful, Assistant Engineer
Recorded November 2007 – February 2008 in SoHo, New York City, at
Wonderful, 594 Broadway

ISBN–13: 978-0-13-366445-4
ISBN–10: 0-13-366445-7

3 4 5 6 7 8 9 10   12 11 10 09

CONTENTS

For information about the Unit Resources, assessing fluency, and teaching with BQ Tunes, see the opening pages of your Unit One Resources.

AIO/All-in-One Workbook; UR/Unit Resources   AIO   UR

BQ Tunes Lyrics: "Quality Over Quantity" . . . . 115 ix

Big Question Vocabulary—1 . . . . 117 1

Big Question Vocabulary—2 . . . . 118 2

Big Question Vocabulary—3 . . . . 119 3

Applying the Big Question 120 4

Unit 3 Skills Concept Map 1 5

"Making Tracks on Mars" by Andrew Mishkin

Vocabulary and Reading Warm-ups 7

Listening and Viewing . . . . 121 . . . 11

Learning About Nonfiction . . . . 122 . . . 12

Model Selection: Nonfiction . . . . 123 . . . 13

Open-Book Test 14

Selection Test A 17

Selection Test B 20

"Baseball" by Lionel G. García

Vocabulary and Reading Warm-ups 23

Writing About the Big Question . . . . 124 . . . 27

Reading: Use Details to Identify the Main Idea . . . . 125 . . . 28

Literary Analysis: Narrative Essay . . . . 126 . . . 29

Vocabulary Builder . . . . 127 . . . 30

Enrichment: Outlining 31

Open-Book Test 32

Selection Test A 35

Selection Test B 38

"Harriet Tubman: Conductor on the Underground Railroad" by Ann Petry

Vocabulary and Reading Warm-ups 41

Writing About the Big Question . . . . 128 . . . 45

Reading: Use Details to Identify the Main Idea . . . . 129 . . . 46

Literary Analysis: Narrative Essay . . . . 130 . . . 47

Vocabulary Builder . . . . 131 . . . 48

Enrichment: Defining by Example 49

	AIO	UR

"Baseball" and "Harriet Tubman: Conductor on the Underground Railroad"
- Integrated Language Skills: Grammar . . . . 132. . . 50
- Integrated Language Skills: Support for Writing a Biographical Sketch . . . . 133. . . 51
- Integrated Language Skills: Listening and Speaking 52

"Harriet Tubman: Conductor on the Underground Railroad"
- Open-Book Test 53
- Selection Test A 56
- Selection Test B 59

"Always to Remember: The Vision of Maya Ying Lin"
by Brent Ashabranner
- Vocabulary and Reading Warm-ups 62
- Writing About the Big Question . . . . 134. . . 66
- Reading: Making Connections Between Supporting Paragraphs
         and the Main Idea . . . . 135. . . 67
- Literary Analysis: Biography and Autobiography . . . . 136. . . 68
- Vocabulary Builder . . . . 137. . . 69
- Enrichment: Memorial Design 70
- Open-Book Test 71
- Selection Test A 74
- Selection Test B 77

from I Know Why the Caged Bird Sings by Maya Angelou
- Vocabulary and Reading Warm-ups 80
- Writing About the Big Question . . . . 138. . . 84
- Reading: Making Connections Between Supporting Paragraphs
         and the Main Idea . . . . 139. . . 85
- Literary Analysis: Biography and Autobiography . . . . 140. . . 86
- Vocabulary Builder . . . . 141. . . 87
- Enrichment: Mentoring 88

"Always to Remember: The Vision of Maya Ying Lin"
and from I Know Why the Caged Bird Sings
- Integrated Language Skills: Grammar . . . . 142. . . 89
- Integrated Language Skills: Support for Writing a Reflective Essay . . . . 143. . . 90
- Integrated Language Skills: Research and Technology 91

from I Know Why the Caged Bird Sings
- Open-Book Test 92
- Selection Test A 95
- Selection Test B 98

"Forest Fire" by Anaïs Nin

"Why Leaves Turn Color in the Fall" by Diane Ackerman

"The Season's Curmudgeon Sees the Light" by Mary C. Curtis

Vocabulary and Reading Warm-ups 101

Writing About the Big Question . . . . 144 . . 105

Literary Analysis: Comparing Types of Organization . . . . 145 . . 106

Vocabulary Builder . . . . 146 . . 107

Support for Writing to Compare Essay Organization . . . . 147 . . 108

Open-Book Test 109

Selection Test A 112

Selection Test B 115

Writing Workshop: Exposition—How to Essay **118**

Writing Workshop: Comparative and Superlative Forms **119**

Benchmark Test 5 . . . . **120**

Skills Concept Map 2 . . . . **126**

"The Trouble With Television" by Robert MacNeil

Vocabulary and Reading Warm-ups 127

Writing About the Big Question . . . . 148 . . 131

Reading: Use Clue Words to Distinguish Fact From Opinion. . . . . 149 . . 132

Literary Analysis: Persuasive Techniques . . . . 150 . . 133

Vocabulary Builder . . . . 151 . . 134

Enrichment: Television and Society 135

Open-Book Test 136

Selection Test A 139

Selection Test B 142

"On Woman's Right to Suffrage" by Susan B. Anthony

Vocabulary and Reading Warm-ups 145

Writing About the Big Question . . . . 152 . . 149

Reading: Use Clue Words to Distinguish Fact From Opinion. . . . . 153 . . 150

Literary Analysis: Persuasive Techniques . . . . 154 . . 151

Vocabulary Builder . . . . 155 . . 152

Enrichment: Community Action 153

"The Trouble With Television" and "On Woman's Right to Suffrage"

Integrated Language Skills: Grammar . . . . 156. . 154

Integrated Language Skills: Support for Writing an Evaluation . . . . 157. . 155

Integrated Language Skills: Research and Technology 156

"On Woman's Right to Suffrage"

Open-Book Test 157

Selection Test A 160

Selection Test B 163

From **"Sharing in the American Dream"** by Colin Powell

Vocabulary and Reading Warm-ups 166

Writing About the Big Question . . . . 158. . 170

Reading: Use Support for Fact and Opinion . . . . 159. . 171

Literary Analysis: Use Word Choice to Convey Ideas. . . . . 160. . 172

Vocabulary Builder . . . . 161. . 173

Enrichment: Community Service Opportunities 174

Open-Book Test 175

Selection Test A 178

Selection Test B 181

"Science and the Sense of Wonder" by Isaac Asimov

Vocabulary and Reading Warm-ups 184

Writing About the Big Question . . . . 162. . 188

Reading: Use Support for Fact and Opinion . . . . 163. . 189

Literary Analysis: Use Word Choice to Convey Ideas. . . . . 164. . 190

Vocabulary Builder . . . . 165. . 191

Enrichment: Basic Questions of Astronomy 192

From **"Sharing in the American Dream"**
and "Science and the Sense of Wonder"

Integrated Language Skills: Grammar . . . . 166. . 193

Integrated Language Skills: Support for Writing a Response to Literature. . . . . . . 167. . 194

Integrated Language Skills: Listening and Speaking. 195

"Science and the Sense of Wonder"

Open-Book Test 196

Selection Test A 199

Selection Test B 202

"Emancipation" *from* **Lincoln: A Photobiography by Russell Freedman**

"Brown vs. Board of Education" by Walter Dean Myers

Vocabulary and Reading Warm-ups 205
Writing About the Big Question . . . . 168. . 209
Literary Analysis: Comparing Tone. . . . . 169. . 210
Vocabulary Builder. . . . . 170. . 211
Support for Writing to Compare Tone . . . . 171. . 212
Open-Book Test 213
Selection Test A 216
Selection Test B 219

Writing Workshop: Persuasion: Editorial **222**

Writing Workshop: Conjunctions **223**

Vocabulary Workshop **224**

Communications Workshop **226**

Benchmark Test 6 (with Vocabulary in Context—Diagnostic) **227**

Diagnostic/Vocabulary in Context and Benchmark Test
   Interpretation Guides **236**

Answers **250**

Quality Over Quantity, performed by Nina Zeitlin

How much information do we need
To prevent **discrimination**?
That will lead to **inequality** amongst the people
No more unequal treatment of different people

In the world around you
Global issues, know about them
'Cause knowledge always gives some answers
Yeah knowledge always gives an **explanation**, yeah

What's **valuable** to me
When I think of what's worthy
It's hidden truth **revealed** for all to see
It's not how much you know
It's greatness that shows
That it's **quality** over **quantity**

Development and progress come from
Using the right information
Statistics are limited to
Sample numbers of the population
Sample numbers of the population, yeah

Accumulating over time
Thoughts in your brain
That form your mind
Follow the path of **exploration**
Follow down the path of **exploration**, yeah

What's **valuable** to me
What I deem worthy
Is hidden truth **revealed** for all to see
It's not how much you know
It's greatness that shows

Continued

That it's **quality** over **quantity**

La la la, la la la...

How much information do we need
To prevent **discrimination**?
No more **inequality** amongst the people
No more **inequality** amongst the people

The **decisions** that we make
The **challenges** we face
All depend on the **factors** in place
All depend on the **factors** in place

But what's **valuable** to me
When I think of what's worthy
It's hidden truth **revealed** for all to see
It's not how much you know
It's greatness that shows
That it's **quality** over **quantity**

Song Title: **Quality Over Quantity**
Artist / Performed by Nina Zeitlin
Guitar: Josh Green
Drums/Percussion: Vlad Gutkovich
Lyrics by Nina Zeitlin
Music composed by Nina Zeitlin
Produced by Mike Pandolfo, Wonderful
Executive Producer: Keith London, Defined Mind

x

Unit 3 Types of Nonfiction
Big Question Vocabulary—1

The Big Question: How much information is enough?

Thematic Vocabulary

accumulate: *v.* to gradually get more and more of something; other form: *accumulation*

development: *n.* the process by which someone or something grows or is built up; other forms: *develop, developing*

discrimination: *n.* the act of treating a person or group differently, in an unfair way; other forms: *discriminate, discriminating*

reveal: *v.* to uncover a secret or make something known; other forms: *revealing, revealed*

valuable: *adj.* useful, helpful, or important; other forms: *value, valued*

A. DIRECTIONS: *From the words in the box, choose the correct synonym and antonym for each Thematic Vocabulary word. You will not use every word in the box.*

hide	gather	growth	treasured	fairness	pride
prejudice	expose	deterioration	worthless	scatter	

1. accumulate   **Synonym:** _____   **Antonym:** _____

2. development   **Synonym:** _____   **Antonym:** _____

3. discrimination   **Synonym:** _____   **Antonym:** _____

4. reveal   **Synonym:** _____   **Antonym:** _____

5. valuable   **Synonym:** _____   **Antonym:** _____

B. DIRECTIONS: *Complete each sentence by writing the correct Thematic Vocabulary word on the line.*

1. The _____ of a plant begins with the sprouting of a tiny seed.

2. As a stamp collector, my goal is to _____ a large quantity of valuable stamps.

3. This beautiful portrait is _____ because it was painted by a famous artist.

4. The candidate vowed that she would rule fairly and avoid all forms of _____.

5. When will the judges _____ the identity of the new champion?

Unit 3 Types of Nonfiction
Big Question Vocabulary—2

The Big Question: How much information is enough?

Thematic Vocabulary

challenge: *n.* a task requiring great strength or effort; other forms: *challenged, challenging*

decision: *n.* a choice that is made after considering the options; other forms: *decide, deciding*

explanation: *n.* the act of making something clear and understandable; other forms: *explain, explaining, explained*

exploration: *n.* the study and observation of a location in order to find facts or make a discovery; other forms: *explore, exploring, explored*

inequality: *n.* an unfair situation in which some people have more money, opportunities, or power than others; other forms: *equal, equality*

A. DIRECTIONS: *Complete the passage by inserting the correct Thematic Vocabulary word on each line.*

In 1620, the Pilgrims faced the mighty (1) _____ of crossing the Atlantic Ocean in the *Mayflower*, a small wooden ship. They suffered greatly along the way, and many died. However, they had great determination. They had left home due to the (2) _____ they faced due to the unfair laws of the British king. He had thrown many Pilgrims into jail because they held religious beliefs that were different from his. Therefore, the Pilgrims' (3) _____ was firm; they would not turn back, despite the suffering. Finally, their battered ship reached the calm waters of Massachusetts Bay, and they dropped anchor. After a small group went ashore for a thorough (4) _____ of the thickly wooded land, they returned and gave the others the following (5) _____ of their settlement plans: They would build a small village, and they would name it Plymouth, after the British port city from which they had sailed.

B. DIRECTIONS: *Answer this question:* If you were President of the United States, what would you do to solve the problem of inequality? *Use as many vocabulary words as you can.*

_____

_____

_____

_____

2

Name _____ Date _____

The Big Question: How much information is enough?

Thematic Vocabulary

challenge: *v.* to question, oppose, or confront in order to dispute a viewpoint; other forms: *challenged, challenging*

global: *adj.* affecting or including the entire world; other forms: *globe, globally*

quality: *n.* the degree to which something is good or bad
  adj. having good qualities

quantity: *n.* an amount of something that can be counted or measured; other form: *quantities*

statistics: *n.* a set of numbers that represent facts or measurements; other forms: *statistical, statistically*

Before the voyage of Christopher Columbus, many people believed that the Earth was flat. Columbus set out to prove them wrong.

A. DIRECTIONS: *Write a proposal that he might have made, trying to persuade King Ferdinand and Queen Isabella to fund his voyage. Use facts about the good qualities of your crew and stress that you will keep a log of facts and measurements throughout the voyage. Use all five Thematic Vocabulary words.*

_____

_____

_____

_____

_____

_____

B. DIRECTIONS: *Okay, Columbus. Now answer these questions. Use the words in parentheses.*

1. Queen Isabella: Tell me, Mr. Columbus, how many ships do you need?

   Answer: (***quantity***): _____

2. King Ferdinand: People say that you'll fall off the edge of the world. What about that?

   Answer: (***challenge***): _____

3. Queen Isabella: Well, why will history ever think this voyage is important?

   Answer: (***global***): _____

Name _____ Date _____

Unit 3 Types of Nonfiction
Applying the Big Question

How much information is enough?

DIRECTIONS: *Complete the chart below to apply what you have learned about quality and quantity of information. One row has been completed for you.*

Example	Type of Information	Useful	Not Useful	What I Learned
From Literature	What Harriet Tubman told the fugitive slaves	Information about success stories	Information that she had never been to Canada	Some information is best left unsaid.
From Literature				
From Science				
From Social Studies				
From Real Life				

Name _____

Unit 3: Types of Nonfiction Skills Concept Map—1
How much information is enough?

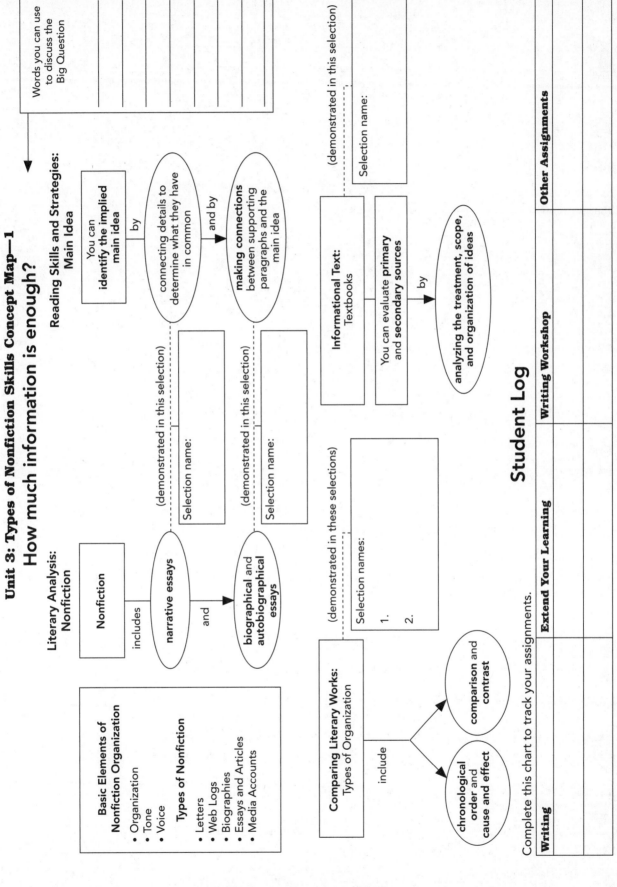

Literary Analysis: Nonfiction

Reading Skills and Strategies: Main Idea

Words you can use to discuss the Big Question

You can **identify the implied main idea**

by

connecting details to determine what they have in common

and by

making connections between supporting paragraphs and the main idea

(demonstrated in this selection)

Selection name:

Informational Text: Textbooks

You can evaluate **primary** and **secondary** sources

by

analyzing the treatment, scope, and organization of ideas

Nonfiction

includes

narrative essays

and

biographical and autobiographical essays

(demonstrated in this selection)

Selection name:

(demonstrated in this selection)

Selection name:

Basic Elements of Nonfiction Organization
- Organization
- Tone
- Voice

Types of Nonfiction
- Letters
- Web Logs
- Biographies
- Essays and Articles
- Media Accounts

Comparing Literary Works: Types of Organization

include

comparison and contrast

chronological order and cause and effect

(demonstrated in these selections)

Selection names:
1.
2.

Student Log

Complete this chart to track your assignments.

Writing	Extend Your Learning	Writing Workshop	Other Assignments

5

Study these words from the "Making Tracks on Mars." Then, complete the activities that follow.

Word List A

critical [KRIT i kuhl] *adj.* very serious or very dangerous
The situation was <u>critical</u>, and we could do nothing to fix it.

exploration [ek spluh RAY shuhn] *n.* an examination of an unknown place
Thorough <u>exploration</u> of the cave took a total of three days.

meteor [MEE tee uhr] *n.* a chunk of rock or metal from space
The <u>meteor</u> streaked through the sky and crashed on Earth.

operations [ahp uh RAY shuhnz] *n.* the managing and running of something
Mr. Phillips is in charge of <u>operations</u> monitoring at the plant.

panels [PAN uhlz] *n.* flat pieces of material
We installed plywood <u>panels</u> on the walls of the basement.

software [SAWFT wair] *adj.* having to do with computer programs
Jones, a <u>software</u> engineer, revised the computer payroll program.

solar [SOH ler] *adj.* having to do with the sun or its power
In a <u>solar</u> eclipse, the moon moves between the Earth and the sun.

spacecraft [SPAYS kraft] *n.* vehicle that goes into space
The United States launched a <u>spacecraft</u> to explore the outer planets.

Word List B

alternatives [awl TER nuh tivz] *n.* other choices
Sidney was afraid to fly, so he explored the <u>alternatives</u>.

collapsed [kuh LAPSD] *v.* fell apart; lost force
The explosion rocked the building, and the walls <u>collapsed</u>.

confirmation [kahn fer MAY shuhn] *n.* a statement that something is true
Anna wanted <u>confirmation</u> that she had given the right answer.

diagnosis [dy uhg NOH sis] *n.* the result of finding the cause of a problem
The <u>diagnosis</u> of the computer glitch was discouraging.

director [di REK ter] *n.* a person in charge
The program <u>director</u> decided to change the class schedule.

incredulous [in KREJ uh luhs] *adj.* being unable or unwilling to believe something
Clyde wrote an <u>incredulous</u> article about the sightings of Bigfoot.

regain [ree GAYN] *v.* to get something back again
The Yankees hope to <u>regain</u> their first-place position this year.

transmitter [TRANS mit er] *n.* a device that sends out signals
The radio <u>transmitter</u> could send signals for two hundred miles.

"Making Tracks on Mars" by Andrew Mishkin
Vocabulary Warm-up Exercises

Exercise A *Fill in each blank in the paragraph below with an appropriate word from Word List A. Use each word only once.*

[1] _____ of the moon's surface began on the second day following the landing of the newly designed [2] _____. The robotic surveyor, which would do the work, depended on energy from [3] _____ [4] _____ that captured sunlight. In case of a system failure, the [5] _____ programmers had built a backup system. If both energy sources failed, however, the situation would become [6] _____. On Earth, the people in charge of [7] _____ control had to hope that wouldn't happen. Luckily, the surveyor completed its investigation with no problems. It took rock samples from a crater formed when a [8] _____ crashed on the surface. These samples were the first from this particular bowl-shaped hollow.

Exercise B *Revise each sentence so that the underlined vocabulary word(s) is used in a logical way. Be sure to keep the vocabulary word in your revision.*

Example: Stories of ghosts have never seemed <u>incredulous</u> to me.
Stories of ghosts have always seemed <u>incredulous</u> to me.

1. The <u>diagnosis</u> was great; Sam would never <u>regain</u> his health.

    _____

2. The program <u>director</u> took orders from the office workers.

    _____

3. I received written <u>confirmation</u> that my application had not arrived.

    _____

4. In the juice department of the supermarket, there are no <u>alternatives</u> to orange juice.

    _____

5. When the radio station's roof <u>collapsed</u>, the <u>transmitter</u> that had been positioned there was stronger than ever.

    _____

Name _____ Date _____

"**Making Tracks on Mars**" by Andrew Mishkin
Reading Warm-up A

Read the following passage. Pay special attention to the underlined words. Then, read it again, and complete the activities. Use a separate sheet of paper for your written answers.

In 1965, we got our first close-up picture of the planet Mars. Since then, <u>spacecraft</u> traveling by and landing on the red planet have shown us an amazing world. <u>Exploration</u> of Mars has brought us increasing knowledge of this cold, rocky wasteland.

Clues hint at past conditions quite different from those today. For example, at one time, volcanoes erupted on Mars. Many a <u>meteor</u>, streaking through the sky, crashed and left deep craters.

The big question today for most scientists is whether life ever existed on Mars. To find out, <u>operations</u> managers at the U.S. space agency have developed a strategy called "follow the water." Scientists gather data from features such as the polar ice caps and dry riverbeds. They hope this work will show that water once may have covered parts of the planet. They also hope to find hot springs or pockets of water beneath the Martian surface.

Advances in computers have been a huge help in studying Mars. Here on Earth, scientists can receive data from a Mars explorer that moves along the surface. If the explorer stops working properly, they can correct its programs.

One problem that equipment on Mars has had is dust from the planet's surface. Dust forms a layer on the spacecraft's <u>solar</u> <u>panels</u>. These collect sunlight and change it to the electricity the spacecraft needs. If the spaceship does not get enough power, the situation could become <u>critical</u>. A mission might have to end early unless <u>software</u> engineers can develop a computer program to fix the problem.

Will people ever travel to Mars? Scientists need to know a lot more than they do now to send humans there. If humans do walk on Mars, might they be able to discover more than any robot can? Perhaps in your lifetime you'll find out!

1. Circle the words that tell where <u>spacecraft</u> have landed. Explain whether you would like to travel on a *spacecraft*.

2. Circle the words that tell what <u>exploration</u> has resulted in. Tell about an *exploration* of your own.

3. Underline the words that help explain what a <u>meteor</u> is. Write about what could happen if a *meteor* crashed on Earth.

4. Circle what <u>operations</u> managers have done. Describe what *operations* managers might do in an ice-cream factory.

5. Underline the sentence that tells what <u>solar panels</u> do. Explain what *solar panels* are.

6. Circle the sentence that tells what might happen if a mission becomes <u>critical</u>. Describe what might happen if a hospital patient becomes *critical*.

7. Circle the words that tell you what a <u>software</u> engineer works with. Describe some *software* that you have used.

Name _____   Date _____

"**Making Tracks on Mars**" by Andrew Mishkin
Reading Warm-up B

Read the following passage. Pay special attention to the underlined words. Then, read it again, and complete the activities. Use a separate sheet of paper for your written answers.

On April 11, 1970, Apollo 13 was headed to the moon. It would be the third manned moon landing of the U.S. space program. Astronauts James Lovell, John Swigert, and Fred Haise were aboard. Two days into the mission, they heard a loud bang. An oxygen tank had exploded, and a second tank was damaged. A whole section of the wall of the service module, one of three sections of their spacecraft, had <u>collapsed</u>.

The astronauts analyzed the situation, and their <u>diagnosis</u> was not encouraging. Luckily, the command module, which they occupied, was unharmed. It was no longer a question of completing the mission. Now, the question was would they have enough power to get home?

Everyone working for the U.S. space agency, NASA, from the <u>director</u> down to the lowest-level worker, was <u>incredulous</u> over the unbelievable turn of events. Scientists who studied the situation knew that the mission could not <u>regain</u> its course to the moon. The goal now was to bring back the astronauts safely to Earth.

NASA engineers looked for <u>alternatives</u> to the damaged power supply. They figured out that a control system in the lunar module, which was in one piece, could remove dangerous carbon dioxide gas from the astronauts' cabin. Its engine could help steer them home.

<u>Confirmation</u> that their idea worked came when the astronauts safely splashed down in the Pacific Ocean. The television <u>transmitter</u> from NASA headquarters gave an anxious public something to cheer for. The public could see and hear that despite the danger the astronauts had been in, things had turned out all right for them.

Many people think of Apollo 13 as a disaster, as a failure. Still, it is amazing that the astronauts were rescued more than 200,000 miles from Earth. From that point of view, the mission was a great success!

1. Underline the words that tell what <u>collapsed</u>. Tell about something you know that *collapsed*.

2. Underline the words that suggest the meaning of <u>diagnosis</u>. Describe another situation in which a *diagnosis* is important.

3. Circle the words that suggest the opposite of a <u>director</u>. Describe another place that has a *director*.

4. Underline the word that is similar in meaning to <u>incredulous</u>. Tell about something else that is *incredulous*.

5. Circle the words that tell what the mission could not <u>regain</u>. Explain *regain*.

6. Circle the words that name one of the <u>alternatives</u> to the power supply. Name some *alternatives* you've had.

7. Underline the words that suggest the meaning of <u>confirmation</u>. When is a written *confirmation* necessary?

8. Circle the word that identifies a kind of <u>transmitter</u>. Write a sentence using *transmitter*.

Name _____ Date _____

Andrew Mishkin
Listening and Viewing

Segment 1: Meet Andrew Mishkin
- Andrew Mishkin uses his experiences as an engineer as the basis for his writing. How does he accomplish this? In your opinion, what aspect of writing might Mishkin find most challenging?

_____

_____

_____

_____

Segment 2: Nonfiction
- Why did Mishkin decide to write a book about the project he worked on? Why was his daily essay writing important to the development of his book?

_____

_____

_____

_____

Segment 3: The Writing Process
- How does Mishkin revise his writing? Is revision important to the process of writing essays and articles? Why or why not?

_____

_____

_____

_____

Segment 4: The Rewards of Writing
- What does Mishkin hope his book conveys to readers? Do you think it is important to tell the stories behind "things of value," as Mishkin does? Why or why not?

_____

_____

_____

_____

Learning About Nonfiction

Nonfiction deals with real people, real events, real places, and ideas. A nonfiction author chooses a method of **organization.** He or she also uses a particular **tone** (his or her attitude toward the audience and the subject) and **voice** (his or her distinctive way of speaking, based on word choice, tone, sound devices, pace, and grammatical structure). This chart names and describes some common types of nonfiction writing:

Type of Nonfiction	Description and Characteristics
Letter	writing addressed to a person or organization
Memoir or journal	writing about one's life that contains thoughts and reflections
Web log (blog)	a journal posted and frequently updated online
Biography	someone's life story written by another person
Autobiography	one's own life story
Media account	writing for newspapers, magazines, television, or radio
Essay or article	a short work on a topic

A. DIRECTIONS: *Write the type of nonfiction that would be most appropriate for the item.*

_____ 1. the story of the writer's life, from childhood to the present

_____ 2. a daily online account of a writer's experiences as a restaurant chef

_____ 3. a short work meant to persuade readers to visit Australia

_____ 4. a request for information about a museum exhibit

_____ 5. a description of the causes and effects of a local fire

_____ 6. reflections on the experience of growing up on a farm

_____ 7. the story of the life of a noted jazz musician

_____ 8. a daily account of a surgeon's thoughts about his or her experiences

B. DIRECTIONS: *Read each sample of nonfiction writing. Indicate whether the author's tone is* formal *or* informal, *and give reasons for your answer.*

Over five weeks, the research team observed a variety of fossils and recorded their findings in a daily journal. The scientists used this journal as the basis for a detailed report on the area's prehistoric animal and plant life.

Tone: _____   **Explanation:** _____

Name _____ Date _____

"Making Tracks on Mars" by Andrew Mishkin
Model Selection: Nonfiction

Nonfiction writing is about real people, real events, real places, and ideas. Examples of nonfiction writing include letters, memoirs, journals, Web logs (or blogs), biographies, autobiographies, media accounts, essays, and articles.

Nonfiction writers choose the method of **organization** that best fits their purpose. Methods of organization include **chronological** (presenting details in time order), **comparison and contrast** (showing how subjects are similar and different), **cause and effect** (showing relationships between events), and **problem and solution** (identifying a problem, presenting a solution). The writer of a biography, for example, would most likely present his or her subject's life chronologically, ordering events from earliest to most recent. The writer of a book about a war might use cause-and-effect organization, showing how events led to one another and affected one another.

Nonfiction writers reveal their attitude toward their audience and their subject by using a particular **tone.** Their tone might be formal, informal, playful, or serious.

A. DIRECTIONS: *Answer the following questions about "Making Tracks on Mars."*

1. How do you know that the journal is organized chronologically?

   _____

2. What is the purpose of the journal's subheads?

   _____

3. Would you describe the author's tone as formal or informal? Why?

   _____

4. What major historical event does Mishkin's journal track?

   _____

5. What was Mishkin's job at the time of the events he writes about?

   _____

B. DIRECTIONS: *Andrew Mishkin posted a blog, in which he recorded the progress of the rovers* Spirit *and* Opportunity. *His online audience was able to keep track of the ups and downs of the crafts' experiences on Mars. Was the mission that Mishkin describes in "Making Tracks on Mars" successful? Cite two examples from the selection to support your opinion.*

_____

_____

_____

_____

Name _____ Date _____

"Making Tracks on Mars: A Journal Based on a Blog" by Andrew Mishkin
Open-Book Test

Short Answer *Write your responses to the questions in this section on the lines provided.*

1. You are reading a work of nonfiction, and you want to analyze the method of organization. You notice that the information is presented in time order. The author begins by telling the first thing that happened. Then, he tells the next thing. He continues until he has told the last thing that happened. What method of organization is the author using?

   _____

2. You are analyzing a work of nonfiction. You read the entire work. You think that the author has a serious attitude toward her subject and her readers. What element of nonfiction are you analyzing?

   _____

3. You are analyzing a work of nonfiction. You pay attention to the word choice, grammatical structures, and tone that the writer uses. What element of the work are you focusing on?

   _____

4. You are reading an essay. It presents facts and ideas without trying to convince the reader to adopt a particular point of view. What type of work are you reading?

   _____

5. In "Making Tracks on Mars," the author is at the Jet Propulsion Laboratory on "Landing Day." As he waits, the *Spirit*'s lander approaches Mars. How can you tell what mood the author is in as he waits?

   _____

   _____

   _____

6. The blog, "Making Tracks on Mars" is divided into sections. Each section contains the date and a title. What do the dates tell you about the organization of the blog?

   _____

7. Use one word to describe the author's tone in "Making Tracks on Mars." Cite three details from the blog to support your answer.

   _____

   _____

   _____

   _____

   _____

8. To understand "Making Tracks on Mars," it is important to pay attention to the order in which events happen. Number the following events from the blog from 1 to 4 to show the order in which they occurred. Then, based on the events in the chart, state what the reader is left wondering after the last event. Write your answer on the line below the chart.

Order	Event
	Spirit leaves the lander platform.
	Spirit sends photographs of Mars.
	Spirit reaches Mars.
	Spirit breaks down.

_____

9. The author of "Making Tracks on Mars" describes events that are taking place on Mars while he is in a laboratory on Earth. Yet he writes, "We were on Mars!" "We can drive here!" What do these remarks tell you about his feelings toward his job and his fellow workers?

_____

_____

_____

10. In "Making Tracks on Mars," when *Opportunity* lands on Mars, one scientist says, "Jackpot!" What does he mean by that exclamation?

_____

_____

_____

Essay

Write an extended response to the question of your choice or to the question or questions your teacher assigns you.

11. Imagine that you are going to keep a journal of an experience you expect to have or a project you will work on. In an essay, describe the journal you would keep. How would you organize it? What tone would you use? What elements would you include to make your journal reflective?

12. People write Web logs, or blogs, on a variety of topics. In an essay, explain why someone might keep a blog. Discuss the kinds of topics that are best suited to a blog. Be sure to describe the kind of information that would be included in a blog. Cite examples from "Making Tracks on Mars" to support your points.

13. It is easy for many readers to feel that they are involved with the progress of the rover *Spirit* as they follow Andrew Mishkin's journal entries in "Making Tracks on Mars." In an essay, discuss why the journal format is—or is not—an effective way to interest readers in a topic. Cite at least two details from the selection to support your main ideas.

14. **Thinking About the Big Question: How much information is enough?** Andrew Mishkin gives readers a lot of information about the exploration of Mars in "Making Tracks on Mars." Does he tell you everything you want to know? In an essay, explain whether you think the journal provided you with enough information. If not, what else do you want to know? Use details from the journal to illustrate your response.

Oral Response

15. Go back to question 5, 6, or 10 or to the question your teacher assigns you. Take a few minutes to expand your answer and prepare an oral response. Find additional details in "Making Tracks on Mars" that will support your points. If necessary, make notes to guide your oral response.

"**Making Tracks on Mars**" by Andrew Mishkin
Selection Test A

Learning About Nonfiction *Identify the letter of the choice that best answers the question.*

_____ 1. Which types of writing are examples of nonfiction?
  I. an essay
  II. a journal
  III. a novel
  IV. a biography
A. I, III, IV
B. II, III, IV
C. I, II, III
D. I, II, IV

_____ 2. Which statement defines chronological organization in a work of nonfiction?
A. The writer presents events in time order.
B. The writer compares and contrasts events.
C. The writer presents a problem and a solution.
D. The writer shows relationships among events.

_____ 3. What is the best definition of an author's tone?
A. his or her use of rhyme
B. his or her theme
C. his or her method of organization
D. his or her attitude toward the subject

_____ 4. When writers want to tell their life story, what kind of work would they most likely write?
A. a blog
B. an autobiography
C. a letter
D. an essay

_____ 5. What is the main purpose of a persuasive essay?
A. to convince the reader of something
B. to tell about a real-life experience
C. to explain a process
D. to present facts

Name _____   Date _____

Critical Reading

____ 6. According to "Making Tracks on Mars," what are the rovers meant to search for on Mars?
A. evidence of water
B. plants and animals
C. a lost spacecraft
D. the *Beagle 2*

____ 7. Who wrote "Making Tracks on Mars"?
A. a newspaper editor   C. an astronaut
B. an engineer   D. a physics professor

____ 8. According to "Making Tracks on Mars," where are the people who are controlling the rovers?
A. on Mars   C. on the landers
B. in the rovers   D. in a laboratory

____ 9. Which word best expresses the author's mood as the *Spirit*'s lander approaches Mars in "Making Tracks on Mars"?
A. confident   C. tense
B. upset   D. preoccupied

____ 10. According to "Making Tracks on Mars," what is a *sol*?
A. a rover's landing gear
B. a Martian moon
C. a Martian day
D. a rover's camera

____ 11. What problem occurs during the mission?
A. *Spirit* rolls into a crater.
B. The second rover crash-lands.
C. *Spirit* stops responding to commands.
D. The second rover's camera is damaged.

____ 12. What does the author see in *Opportunity*'s first photos?
A. deep-red soil and bedrock
B. a large pool of water
C. the rover *Spirit*
D. the spacecraft *Beagle 2*

___ 13. How can a reader tell that the author of "Making Tracks on Mars" feels emotion-
ally involved with the rover *Spirit*?
A. He signs on for a future mission to Venus.
B. He uses "we" or "us" to refer to the rover.
C. He decides to train to become an astronaut.
D. He pauses to watch the landing of *Opportunity*.

___ 14. Which of these statements from "Making Tracks on Mars" best illustrates the
author's informal tone?
A. "All the engineering data looked 'nominal.'"
B. "Everyone tensed up. Time dragged."
C. "Mars time continues to be disorienting."
D. "*Opportunity* has been falling toward Mars."

___ 15. What type of nonfiction writing does "Making Tracks on Mars" represent?
A. a journal
B. a letter
C. an essay
D. an article

Essay

16. Imagine that you were going to keep a journal of an experience you expect to have or
a project you will work on. In an essay, describe the journal you would keep. Tell
how you would write the journal. Would you write it all in one sitting? Would you
write it over the course of the experience or the project? What kinds of information
would you include? Would you write only about the experience or the project?
Would you include other information as well? If so, what might you include?

17. The author of "Making Tracks on Mars" uses a friendly and informal tone to write
about a complicated and important space mission. Readers learn about the details of
the mission as well as the emotional ups and downs of the people who are working on
it. In an essay, write about the author's tone. Cite at least two examples from the
journal to show how Mishkin creates a personal, friendly tone. To begin, you might
think about how he describes his team's reactions to the progress of the rover *Spirit*.

18. **Thinking About the Big Question: How much information is enough?** Andrew
Mishkin gives readers a lot of information about the exploration of Mars in "Making
Tracks on Mars." Does he tell you everything you want to know? In an essay, explain
whether you think the journal provided you with enough information. Use details
from the journal to support your opinion.

"**Making Tracks on Mars**" by Andrew Mishkin
Selection Test B

Learning About Nonfiction *Identify the letter of the choice that best completes the statement or answers the question.*

____ 1. Essays, articles, biographies, and journals are all examples of
    A. memoirs.
    B. nonfiction.
    C. Web logs.
    D. persuasive writing.

____ 2. When an author presents details in time order, this type of organization is called
    A. cause and effect.
    B. problem and solution.
    C. chronological.
    D. comparison and contrast.

____ 3. Which statement is true of an author's tone?
    A. It is the writer's presentation of information.
    B. It is related to the theme in a work of nonfiction.
    C. It has to do with word choice, sound devices, and pace.
    D. It is the writer's attitude toward his or her audience and subject.

____ 4. A writer's distinctive way of "speaking" in his or her writing is called
    A. tone.
    B. personality.
    C. pace.
    D. voice.

____ 5. Which of the following is an example of a persuasive essay?
    A. a newspaper editorial
    B. a media account
    C. a description of a new technology
    D. a discussion of a reality television show

____ 6. Nonfiction that presents facts, discusses ideas, or explains a process is called
    A. narrative writing.
    B. reflective writing.
    C. expository writing.
    D. factual writing.

Critical Reading

____ 7. What information does the subhead of each entry in "Making Tracks on Mars" provide?
    A. It refers readers to additional information about the mission.
    B. It introduces new information about the mission.
    C. It clarifies difficult or unusual vocabulary.
    D. It identifies the focus of each entry.

_____ 8. In "Making Tracks on Mars," what is the main mission of the exploration rovers?
   A. to search for evidence of water in Mars's ancient past
   B. to search for evidence of prehistoric animals on Mars
   C. to confirm possible similarities between Mars and Earth
   D. to find out if Mars is capable of supporting human life

_____ 9. According to "Making Tracks on Mars," what country launched the *Beagle 2*?
   A. Russia
   B. China
   C. Great Britain
   D. Australia

_____ 10. According to "Making Tracks on Mars," how long do signals take to get to Earth from the spacecraft carrying *Spirit*?
   A. ten minutes
   B. ten seconds
   C. two hours
   D. almost one day

_____ 11. In "Making Tracks on Mars," who or what controls the rovers *Spirit* and *Opportunity*?
   A. astronauts on board
   B. a remote device on a nearby planet
   C. engineers in a space station
   D. engineers on Earth

_____ 12. How would you describe the author's tone in "Making Tracks on Mars"?
   A. informal
   B. serious
   C. formal
   D. cold

_____ 13. Why does the author of "Making Tracks on Mars" sometimes use the pronouns "we" and "us" when he is writing about the rovers?
   A. He and the rovers are on the same spacecraft.
   B. There are hundreds of people involved in the mission.
   C. He and his team identify strongly with the rovers.
   D. He identifies more with Mars than with Earth.

_____ 14. In "Making Tracks on Mars," what is the author's main job at mission control?
   A. building new commands for the rover
   B. briefing visiting members of Congress
   C. sending daily commands to the rover
   D. making sure that the rover does not roll over

_____ 15. The January 15 and 22 entries of "Making Tracks on Mars" refer to *sol*. What is the most likely explanation for the inclusion of this word?
   A. The author is referring to the sun.
   B. The author is learning a new language.
   C. The author is tracking the rover's progress.
   D. The author is thinking in terms of Martian time.

___ 16. According to "Making Tracks on Mars," "drive-off day" is dangerous for the rover because on that day the rover
   A. lands on Mars.
   B. drives into a prehistoric lake.
   C. reenters Earth's atmosphere.
   D. rolls off the lander platform.

___ 17. In "Making Tracks on Mars," what event suggests that *Spirit* is having problems?
   A. Its wheels get caught in cracks on the surface of Mars.
   B. It misses preprogrammed communication times.
   C. Its camera flash does not adjust for nightfall.
   D. It does not reconnect with its lander.

___ 18. What kind of organization does Mishkin use to present the information in "Making Tracks on Mars"?
   A. comparison and contrast
   B. chronological order
   C. cause and effect
   D. problem and solution

___ 19. Which statement from "Making Tracks on Mars" is a reflection by the author?
   A. "I cannot help but hope that our own landing goes more smoothly."
   B. "*Spirit* had survived! . . . We were on Mars!"
   C. "We could see 360 degrees around the rover, to the horizon."
   D. "I just finished working the Martian night."

Essay

20. The author of "Making Tracks on Mars" uses a friendly and informal tone to write about a complicated and important space mission. Readers learn about the mission itself, as well as the emotional ups and downs of the scientists and engineers controlling the spacecraft. In an essay, give three examples of ways in which Mishkin creates this personal, friendly tone. To begin, think about how he describes his and his teammates' reactions to the progress of the rover *Spirit*.

21. People write Web logs, or blogs, on a variety of topics. In an essay, explain why someone might keep a blog, and discuss the kinds of topics that are best suited to one. Be sure to describe the kind of information that would be included in a blog. Cite two examples from "Making Tracks on Mars" to support your points.

22. It is easy for many readers to feel that they are involved with the progress of the rover *Spirit* as they follow Andrew Mishkin's journal entries in "Making Tracks on Mars." In an essay, discuss why the journal format is—or is not—an effective way to interest readers in a topic. Cite at least two details from the selection to support your main ideas.

23. **Thinking About the Big Question: How much information is enough?** Andrew Mishkin gives readers a lot of information about the exploration of Mars in "Making Tracks on Mars." Does he tell you everything you want to know? In an essay, explain whether you think the journal provided you with enough information. If not, what else do you want to know? Use details from the journal to illustrate your response.

Vocabulary Warm-up Word Lists

Study these words from "Baseball." Then, complete the activities.

Word List A

complicate [KAHM pli kayt] *v.* to make something more difficult
Don't <u>complicate</u> a simple recipe, and it will turn out well.

exception [ek SEP shuhn] *n.* someone or something not included
Today is a holiday and there is an <u>exception</u> to the no parking rules.

exhausted [eg ZAWST id] *adj.* very tired
When Ben finished his first day as a sales clerk, he was <u>exhausted</u>.

fielder [FEEL der] *n.* a baseball player other than pitcher or catcher
An all-around baseball player is a good hitter and a good <u>fielder</u>.

ignorance [IG nuhr uhns] *n.* lack of knowledge or information
Teri tried to cover her <u>ignorance</u> of history by changing subjects.

professional [pruh FESH uh nuhl] *adj.* playing a sport for money
Harry wanted to play <u>professional</u> football, but he broke his leg.

scheme [SKEEM] *n.* plan
Carrie came up with a brilliant <u>scheme</u> to raise money.

standard [STAN derd] *adj.* usual or normal
The <u>standard</u> amount for parking at the stadium is five dollars.

Word List B

erupted [i RUHP tid] *v.* suddenly broke out
The normally quiet audience <u>erupted</u> into thunderous applause.

evaded [i VAYD id] *v.* avoided something
The bank robbers <u>evaded</u> the law, and the money was never found.

expanse [ek SPANS] *n.* very large area of land, sky, and so on
The house was surrounded on all sides by a great <u>expanse</u> of lawn.

idle [EYE duhl] *adj.* having no useful purpose
The child's <u>idle</u> activity kept her busy but didn't teach her a thing.

mightily [MY tel ee] *adv.* with great strength; powerfully
At the carnival, James swung a hammer <u>mightily</u> and rang the bell.

option [AHP shuhn] *n.* a choice you can make in a situation
Denise had the <u>option</u> of taking French or German in school.

outfield [OWT feeld] *n.* the outer part of the baseball field
Rachel hit the ball deep into the <u>outfield</u>, almost to the fence.

rotate [ROH tayt] *v.* to take turns doing something; following a fixed order
Every oil change, we <u>rotate</u> the tires to prevent too much wear.

Name _____   Date _____

"Baseball" by Lionel G. García
Vocabulary Warm-up Exercises

Exercise A *Fill in each blank in the paragraph below with an appropriate word from Word List A. Use each word only once.*

All of us at training camp, without [1] _____, wanted to become

[2] _____ ballplayers. Our coach said, whether we wanted to be a

pitcher or a [3] _____, we had to be "better than good." Out of

[4] _____ about how hard we'd have to work, we all stupidly started

boasting about our great chances. Then, the daily [5] _____ began. It

seemed so simple: train, eat, sleep. There was nothing to [6] _____ our

routine, and we had no excuse for not sticking to the [7] _____ proce-

dures. We were in the middle of nowhere, far from any town. Then, one week passed and

we were feeling totally [8] _____. We could hardly move. It was then

that we began to understand what our coach meant about being "better than good."

Exercise B *Write a complete sentence to answer each question. For each answer, use a word from Word List B to replace each underlined word or group of words without changing its meaning.*

1. The kids' chatter, which was <u>without a real purpose</u>, drifted though the window making it hard for me to concentrate.

   _____

2. After the fight <u>suddenly broke out</u>, the police came, but everyone <u>escaped</u> capture.

   _____

3. We stood in the <u>huge area</u> of green that made up the <u>area beyond the infield</u>.

   _____

4. Paul Bunyan strode <u>with great force</u> through the northern forests.

   _____

5. On our mock quiz show, we decided to <u>take turns</u> being emcee and panelists.

   _____

6. My <u>choice</u> is to save all my money for college or use a part of it for a summer vacation.

   _____

24

"Baseball" by Lionel G. García
Reading Warm-up A

Read the following passage. Pay special attention to the underlined words. Then, read it again, and complete the activities. Use a separate sheet of paper for your written answers.

Girls playing baseball? That thought amazed some people in 1943. It was during World War II, and many <u>professional</u> ballplayers were on a different field—the battlefield. Too few men remained at home to fill jobs. Major league baseball was no <u>exception</u>. It, too, was in need of players.

Philip K. Wrigley, owner of the Chicago Cubs, knew that many young American women played softball and enjoyed it. He came up with a <u>scheme</u> to find players from all over the country. According to his plan, they would play in a women's league in the Midwest. He started with four teams.

Many young women tried out for the few spots on the teams. Just like the men, woman had to demonstrate skill on the field. They also had to be models of good behavior off the field. Pitcher, catcher, and <u>fielder</u>—each and every player—trained hard until they were <u>exhausted</u>. To <u>complicate</u> a busy week of training and games, they also had to travel. The distance between cities may not seem great today, but roads and vehicles were much less developed in the 1940s.

The women worked hard, and the All-American Girls Professional Baseball League became a success. <u>Standard</u> softball rules were changed to make them more like men's professional baseball.

After the war was over and the men returned, many people, perhaps out of <u>ignorance</u>, expected the league to fold, but it only grew stronger. In 1948, ten teams played in the league and almost a million fans filled the stands.

Why did the league finally end in 1954? Television was bringing baseball games into people's homes, and attendance at games dropped. As the teams lost their fans, money to advertise games and to bring on new players dried up. All the same, the All-American Girls made their mark, however brief, on the history of baseball.

1. Circle the group that is described as <u>professional</u>. Write a sentence using *professional*.

2. Underline the words that tell in what way the major league was no <u>exception</u> on the homefront. Then, use *exception* in a sentence.

3. Circle the word in the next sentence that is a synonym for <u>scheme</u>. Then, explain what Wrigley's *scheme* was.

4. Circle the names of positions played in baseball. Explain what a *fielder* is.

5. Circle the words that tell why the women were <u>exhausted</u>. Then, tell about a time you were *exhausted*.

6. Underline the words that tell what could <u>complicate</u> the women's already busy schedule. Then, write a sentence using *complicate*.

7. Circle the words that tell what was <u>standard</u>. Then, explain what *standard* means.

8. Write a sentence describing something you thought out of <u>ignorance</u> and tell why you were wrong.

"**Baseball**" by Lionel G. García
Reading Warm-up B

Read the following passage. Pay special attention to the underlined words. Then, read it again, and complete the activities. Use a separate sheet of paper for your written answers.

After school, we often didn't have enough guys or enough time for a real game of softball or baseball. The option we chose was to play one of the many strange relatives of America's popular pastime.

Box ball was a favorite. We marked home plate near the curb of the widest street in the neighborhood. We created a large area, or box, on the street. We placed first and second base across the street and third on the same side as home. Beyond the first-to-second baseline was the sidewalk, then the steps and lawns of houses. Beyond the second-to-third baseline was a huge expanse of street that served as a proper outfield.

A pitcher threw the white pimple ball or the smooth pink one to the plate on a bounce, and the "batter" had to hit it with his fist. The goal was not to just hit it mightily, as in regular baseball, but to make it land inside the box and then bounce through the hole between infielders. The outfielder could not engage in idle daydreaming. He had to be on constant lookout for cars. He also had to be ready for a ball bouncing fast and far. If it evaded his capture, it could roll all the way down the block. As you might imagine, playing outfield was rather thankless, so we would rotate positions. No one had to play outfield for long.

As usual, arguments and fights erupted during the game, mostly over fair or foul calls. Neighborhood dogs ran off with the ball, and their owners complained about trampled lawns. Two sewers lacking grates might decide the end of our game just as easily as a player's mom calling him home to supper. But unless it rained, we would be out playing box ball the next afternoon.

1. Circle the word that provides a context clue for option. Then, write your own sentence for *option*.

2. Circle the word that describes expanse and gives a clue to its meaning. Then, write about an *expanse* you know.

3. Underline the words that tell where the outfield was. Then, write your own sentence for *outfield*.

4. Circle the word that tells what a player would do mightily. Then, use *mightily* in a sentence.

5. Underline the words in the paragraph that describe what kept the outfielder from idle daydreaming. Then, explain what *idle* means.

6. Underline the word that, by contrast, gives a clue to evaded. Write about something that you *evaded* or that *evaded* you.

7. Underline the sentence that explains rotate. Then, rewrite the phrase with *rotate*, replacing it with a word or phrase that means the same thing.

8. Circle the words that tell what erupted during box ball. Write about something you know that has *erupted*.

Name _____ Date _____

Writing About the Big Question

How much information is enough?

Big Question Vocabulary

accumulate	challenge	decision	development	discrimination
explanation	exploration	factor	global	inequality
quality	quantity	reveal	statistics	valuable

A. *Use a word from list above to complete each sentence.*

1. A(n) _____ is one kind of information.

2. Computers have made information instantly _____.

3. Information can _____ more quickly than ever.

4. Computers can lessen _____.

B. *Follow the directions in responding to each of the items below.*

1. In two sentences, describe an important decision you made and explain what made that decision so important to you.

   _____

   _____

2. What was a factor that entered into your decision? Use at least two words from the list in your answer.

   _____

   _____

   _____

C. *Complete the sentence below. Then, write a short paragraph in which you connect this answer to the Big Question. In your answer, consider the kinds of information children might need to play a game.*

Children's games should be _____

_____

_____

_____

_____

_____

27

Name _____ Date _____

"**Baseball**" by Lionel G. García
Reading: Use Details to Identify the Main Idea

The **main idea** of a work of nonfiction is the central point that the author conveys. Sometimes the author states the main idea directly. More often, the author implies, or suggests, the main idea by giving you details to consider. To **identify the implied main idea,** connect the details that the author provides. The main idea you decide on should cover all the important details in the paragraph, section, or essay.

In "Baseball," the author describes how, as children, he and his friends made up their own rules for playing baseball. He includes details about specific rules, neighborhood observers, and particularly memorable incidents.

Ask: What does the author want me to think or discover as I read these details?

DIRECTIONS: *Read each excerpt from the selection, and summarize its details. The first one is done as an example. Then, add up all the details to identify the main idea of the selection.*

1. The way we played baseball was to rotate positions after every out. First base, the only base we used, was located where one would normally find second base. . . . Aside from the pitcher, the batter and the first baseman, we had a catcher. All the rest of us would stand in the outfield. After an out, the catcher would come up to bat. The pitcher took the position of catcher, and the first baseman moved up to be the pitcher. Those in the outfield were left to their own devices. I don't remember ever getting to bat.

   Summary of details: The players used only one base. Most played in the outfield and never got to bat.

2. First base was wherever Matías or Juan or Cota tossed a stone. They were the law. The distance could be long or short depending on how soon we thought we were going to be called in to eat.

   Summary of details: _____

3. To complicate matters, on the way to home plate the batter had the choice of running anywhere possible to avoid getting hit. . . . Many a time we would wind up . . . in front of the rectory half a block away.

   Summary of details: _____

4. One time we wound up all the way across town before we cornered Juan against a fence, held him down, and hit him with the ball. Afterwards, we all fell laughing in a pile on top of each other, exhausted from the run through town.

   Summary of details: _____

5. What a game! In what enormous stadium would it be played to allow such freedom over such an expanse of ground?

   Summary of details: _____

   Main idea of the selection: _____

   _____

"**Baseball**" by Lionel G. García
Literary Analysis: Narrative Essay

A **narrative essay** tells the story of real events experienced by real people in real places. Narrative essays share these features with fictional stories:

- People's traits and personalities are developed through their words, actions, and thoughts.
- The setting of the action may be an important element.

In "Baseball," Lionel G. García tells a true story about the kind of baseball he and his friends played in their neighborhood while growing up. He includes certain details about people and events during these games. The details help the reader understand the author's personality and the feelings he had about these childhood experiences.

In the essay, the author describes a particular incident in which the players chase Juan across town until they all fall into a laughing heap. These details make it clear that even though the youngsters did not belong to a formal baseball team or follow the traditional rules, they enjoyed the company of friends and playing a fast, unique version of baseball.

DIRECTIONS: *Answer the following questions. Your answers will help you identify the details that the author provides to develop his personality.*

1. Where do the baseball games take place?

   _____

   _____

2. What does the author say to describe Father Zavala's reactions to watching the games?

   _____

   _____

3. Why do you think the author played when he rarely, if ever, got to bat?

   _____

   _____

4. Why was it more interesting and fun if the fielder missed hitting the batter?

   _____

   _____

5. Based on the details the author tells about their game, how do you think the author reacted to Uncle Adolfo's negative comment?

   _____

   _____

"Baseball" by Lionel G. García
Vocabulary Builder

Word List

devices   evaded   ignorance   option   rotate   scheme   shiftless

A. DIRECTIONS: *Write the letter of the word or phrase that best defines each numbered word.*

____ 1. devices
    A. judgments
    B. duplicates
    C. schemes
    D. licenses

____ 2. evaded
    A. avoided
    B. controlled
    C. lacked
    D. envisioned

____ 3. ignorance
    A. more than enough
    B. knowledge
    C. avoidance
    D. lack of knowledge

____ 4. scheme
    A. plan
    B. problem
    C. mistake
    D. position

____ 5. option
    A. idea
    B. choice
    C. nickname
    D. transaction

____ 6. rotate
    A. turn
    B. rumble
    C. overcome
    D. break down

____ 7. shiftless
    A. tired
    B. foreign
    C. lazy
    D. strange

B. WORD STUDY The suffix *-ance* changes a verb or adjective into a noun that names a condition or state of being. For each sentence, write a synonym of the underlined word with the suffix *-ance*.

1. An excited puppy can cause quite a <u>disturbance</u>.

_____

2. He seems sincere, but do you think his <u>repentance</u> is genuine?

_____

3. <u>Resistance</u> is futile, so don't even dream of trying to escape.

_____

"Baseball" by Lionel G. García
Enrichment: Outlining

"Baseball" is based on the author's recollections of childhood. Lionel G. García describes the unique variety of baseball that he and his friends played as children. You may have childhood memories of special games you played or watched. Now that you are older, you have the opportunity to create a new game for young children to play. You can explain the game in the form of an outline.

DIRECTIONS: *Working independently or with a partner, create a new game for children. Complete the outline below with information that children will need to know in order to play the game.*

I. Name of game _____

II. Equipment or materials needed to play

    A. _____

    B. _____

    C. _____

III. Objective or goal

_____

_____

IV. Procedures (steps) for playing

    A. _____

    B. _____

    C. _____

    D. _____

    E. _____

    F. _____

V. Special rules

    A. _____

    B. _____

    C. _____

    D. _____

    E. _____

    F. _____

"Baseball" by Lionel G. García
Open-Book Test

Short Answer *Write your responses to the questions in this section on the lines provided.*

1. In "Baseball," Father Zavala reacts to the children's games by laughing with enjoyment. What does his enjoyment tell you about his personality?

   _____

   _____

2. The author of "Baseball" says that Matías, Juan, and Cota "were the law." What does he mean by this statement?

   _____

   _____

3. In "Baseball," the narrator writes that the batters sometimes "evaded being hit with the ball." What happened when the batters did not evade being hit? Base your answer on the meaning of *evaded*.

   _____

4. By noting the details in a work of nonfiction, a reader can figure out the main idea. A reader can also work backward, finding the details that support a main idea. Do that in this diagram. Write three details that support this implied main idea in "Baseball." Then, on the lines below, explain what these details tell you about Lionel García and his childhood friends.

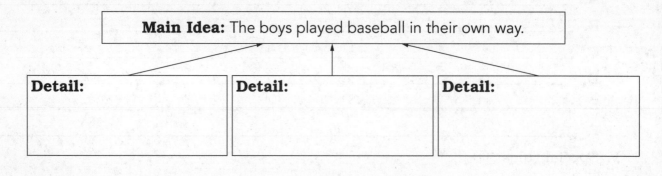

   Main Idea: The boys played baseball in their own way.

   Detail: **Detail:**   **Detail:**

   _____

   _____

5. The author of "Baseball" mentions Father Zavala's reactions several times. Why are Father Zavala's reactions important in the essay?

   _____

   _____

6. In "Baseball," the narrator's uncle Adolfo sees the children playing. Adolfo is a former professional baseball player, and he had given the boys the baseball they play with. How does he feel about their version of the game?

   _____

7. According to the narrator of "Baseball," when his uncle Adolfo sees the children playing, he marvels at their ignorance. What does the narrator mean by this statement? Base your answer on the meaning of *ignorance*.

_____

_____

_____

8. The narrator of "Baseball" is an adult writing about a game he played as a child. Although a lot of time has passed since he played the game, he recalls with clarity a set of complicated rules. What does the preciseness of his memory of those rules tell you about the narrator?

_____

_____

_____

9. Think about the information that is revealed in "Baseball." What elements of this work of nonfiction make it a narrative essay?

_____

_____

_____

10. The main idea of an essay is its most important idea. What is the main idea of "Baseball"?

_____

_____

_____

Essay

Write an extended response to the question of your choice or to the question or questions your teacher assigns you.

11. The author of "Baseball" makes a point of describing Father Zavala's reactions to the children's games, which he watches from the rectory porch. In an essay, describe Father Zavala's reactions. Then, offer an explanation for why the author included them. In writing your response, think about the main idea of the essay.

12. The narrator of "Baseball" writes that he does not remember ever getting the opportunity to bat. In an essay, explain why he kept playing anyway. Use examples from the story to support your ideas.

13. The narrator of "Baseball" says that his uncle Adolfo walked away from the children's baseball game "marveling at our ignorance." Consider what you know about the narrator's uncle, and then consider the narrator's use of the word *ignorance*. In an essay, describe how you think Uncle Adolfo viewed the children's baseball game, and comment on the children's ignorance. What were they ignorant of? What might Uncle Adolfo have been ignorant of?

14. **Thinking About the Big Question: How much information is enough?** The narrator of "Baseball" clearly enjoyed the games he and his friends played as children. In an essay, tell whether you think he gives enough information to explain why the games were fun. Think about the rules of the game, and tell whether you would have fun playing according to those rules. Support your response with details from the essay.

Oral Response

15. Go back to question 6, 9, or 10 or to the question your teacher assigns you. Take a few minutes to expand your answer and prepare an oral response. Find additional details in "Baseball" that will support your points. If necessary, make notes to guide your oral response.

"Baseball" by Lionel G. García
Selection Test A

Critical Reading *Identify the letter of the choice that best answers the question.*

___ 1. In García's essay "Baseball," what was unusual about how the author and his friends played the game?
A. They always played after dark.
B. They played without a real ball.
C. They had only five players.
D. They made up their own rules.

___ 2. How would you describe the equipment used by the author of "Baseball" and his friends?
A. They used standard baseball equipment.
B. They preferred aluminum bats.
C. They used a ball and a stick.
D. They used a stone for the ball.

___ 3. In "Baseball," who had the final word on how the game was played?
A. Father Zavala
B. Matías, Juan, and Cota
C. Uncle Adolfo
D. the author

___ 4. In "Baseball," what object served as first base?
A. a stone
B. a stick
C. a hat
D. a tree

___ 5. Why would the author of "Baseball" play if he does not remember ever getting to bat?
A. He enjoyed the game for other reasons.
B. He was bullied into playing.
C. He wanted to please Uncle Adolfo.
D. He wanted to please Father Zavala.

___ 6. What had Uncle Adolfo given the author of "Baseball"?
A. a baseball bat
B. tickets to a major league game
C. a baseball
D. an official baseball rulebook

___ 7. In "Baseball," how did Father Zavala react to the games the children played?
   A. He was upset when they ran on his lawn.
   B. He laughed with enjoyment.
   C. He asked to be the referee.
   D. He shouted at them to be quiet.

___ 8. Where do the children begin each ball game in "Baseball"?
   A. on a regulation baseball diamond
   B. in the street
   C. in the park
   D. on the school grounds

___ 9. Which of the following sentences from "Baseball" best states the main idea?
   A. "I don't remember ever getting to bat."
   B. "Father Zavala enjoyed watching us."
   C. "We loved to play baseball."
   D. "What a waste of a good ball."

___ 10. What was Uncle Adolfo's reaction to the way the children played in "Baseball"?
   A. He was surprised.
   B. He joined in the game.
   C. He urged them to learn the official rules.
   D. He yelled at them.

___ 11. What determined when the game ended in "Baseball"?
   A. It ended after nine innings.
   B. It usually ended when the players were called in to eat.
   C. Juan decided when the game should end.
   D. It ended when everyone had batted.

Vocabulary and Grammar

___ 12. Which of the following sentences does *not* contain an adjective?
   A. I saw a beautiful sunset over the lake.
   B. My aunt's paintings are colorful.
   C. He decided to make dinner.
   D. His hair is a bright red.

_____ **13.** In which of the following sentences is *evaded* used *incorrectly*?

    A. The criminal evaded the police.

    B. He evaded the question by looking away.

    C. The stray dog evaded capture for a year.

    D. My hungry friends evaded the cookie jar.

_____ **14.** Read the following sentence from "Baseball," and select the meaning that best fits the word *devices*.

    Those in the outfield were left to their own devices.

    A. ways of working things out

    B. division into teams

    C. tools for research

    D. ways to catch fly balls

_____ **15.** In the following sentence, which word is an adjective?

    The stormy clouds rolled quickly through the sky.

    A. stormy

    B. rolled

    C. quickly

    D. through

Essay

16. The author of "Baseball" clearly enjoyed the games he and his friends played as children. In a brief essay, describe some of the rules for their games. Then, explain how these rules made the games especially fun to play.

17. The author of "Baseball" makes a point of describing Father Zavala's reactions while watching the children's games from the rectory porch. Write a brief essay in which you describe Father Zavala's reactions and explain why you think the author included them. For help while you plan your essay, think about the work's main idea.

18. **Thinking About the Big Question: How much information is enough?** The narrator of "Baseball" clearly enjoyed the games he and his friends played as children. In an essay, tell whether you think he gives enough information to explain why the games were fun. Support your response with details from the essay.

Unit 3 Resources: Types of Nonfiction
37

"**Baseball**" by Lionel G. García
Selection Test B

Critical Reading *Identify the letter of the choice that best completes the statement or answers the question.*

____ 1. You can tell that "Baseball" is a narrative essay because
A. it explains the game of baseball in detail.
B. it reports events from the distant past.
C. the story is about real events and people.
D. the author includes fictional characters.

____ 2. What does the following sentence from "Baseball" tell you about the children's game?
The way we played baseball was to rotate positions after every out.
A. The children made up their own rules.
B. The author is an expert on baseball.
C. The children found the game too rough.
D. The author resented being in the outfield.

____ 3. What does the following statement from "Baseball" tell you about Matías, Juan, and Cota?
They were the law.
A. They were bullies.
B. They were best friends.
C. They made the rules.
D. They had relatives on the police force.

____ 4. According to "Baseball," what was true about first base?
A. The first-base stone was a set size.
B. First base was behind the pitcher.
C. First base was in its usual position.
D. There was no first base.

____ 5. According to "Baseball," what happened to a player who caught a ball on the fly?
A. The player would be the next catcher.
B. The player would be chased.
C. The player could move first base.
D. The player would be the next batter.

____ 6. What position does the author of "Baseball" remember playing most often?
A. outfield
B. pitcher
C. catcher
D. first base

_____ 7. What is the main idea in the following passage from "Baseball"?
   One time we wound up all the way across town before we cornered Juan against a
   fence.
     . . . Afterwards, we all fell laughing in a pile on top of each other, exhausted. . . .
   A. Running long distances is exhausting.
   B. The fastest way across town is to run.
   C. Playing baseball their own way was fun.
   D. Even a made-up game has rules.

_____ 8. Why was the setting of the game enjoyable to the author of "Baseball"?
   A. It was almost like a real baseball field.
   B. It allowed players to run far.
   C. It was close to his home.
   D. There always was an audience.

_____ 9. What can you conclude by noting that the author of "Baseball" clearly remembers
   the rules of his childhood game?
   A. He has an unusually sharp memory.
   B. He did a lot of research for this narrative.
   C. He has respect for Father Zavala.
   D. He played the game often and had fun.

_____ 10. How did the children in the essay "Baseball" get their ball?
   A. They found it in the street.
   B. They saved up to buy it.
   C. They received it as a gift.
   D. It belonged to the author's father.

_____ 11. What does the author of "Baseball" mean by writing that his uncle walked away
   "marveling at our ignorance"?
   A. The children were not very smart.
   B. The uncle was astounded at what the children did not know about baseball.
   C. Uncle Adolfo was jealous of the fun the children had.
   D. Uncle Adolfo intended to teach the children the official rules for baseball.

_____ 12. Why is Father Zavala an important person in "Baseball"?
   A. Father Zavala's enjoyment is part of the author's pleasant memories.
   B. Father Zavala is a longtime friend of the author's family.
   C. Father Zavala became the author's high school teacher.
   D. Father Zavala allowed the children to play at the rectory.

_____ 13. What did Uncle Adolfo in "Baseball" mean when he said, "What a waste of a good
   ball"?
   A. The children lost the ball.
   B. Father Zavala took the ball.
   C. The children wanted to save the major-league ball rather than use it.
   D. The children did not use the ball the way he thought they would.

____ 14. Which of the following details does *not* contribute to the main idea of "Baseball"?
   A. Uncle Adolfo returned for a visit.
   B. The pitcher decided where to stand.
   C. The batter got chased a lot.
   D. Father Zavala watched and laughed.

Vocabulary and Grammar

____ 15. Which word is the adjective in the following sentence?
   We watched the beautiful sunset as it sank slowly into the horizon.

   A. beautiful   C. sank
   B. sunset   D. slowly

____ 16. Which word is most similar in meaning to *evaded*?
   A. stunned   C. avoided
   B. entertained   D. paid

____ 17. Which word has a meaning that is the opposite of *ignorance*?
   A. dullness   C. mystery
   B. hope   D. knowledge

____ 18. Which of the following sentences contains an adjective?
   A. My brother drives cautiously.   C. She laughs often and loudly.
   B. Nate and his three sisters like to   D. His bike is locked up over there.
   knit.

Essay

19. The author of "Baseball" comments that he does not remember ever getting to bat. In a brief essay, explain why you think he kept playing anyway. Use examples from the story to support your ideas.

20. In "Baseball," the author includes Father Zavala as an observer of the games. In an essay, describe Father Zavala's reactions, according to the author. Then, explain how these details support the story's main idea.

21. The author says that Uncle Adolfo walked away from watching the children's version of playing baseball, "marveling at our ignorance." In a brief essay, describe how Uncle Adolfo probably viewed the children's version of baseball. Then, consider the author's use of the word *ignorance*. Of what things might Uncle Adolfo be ignorant?

22. **Thinking About the Big Question: How much information is enough?** The narrator of "Baseball" clearly enjoyed the games he and his friends played as children. In an essay, tell whether you think he gives enough information to explain why the games were fun. Think about the rules of the game, and tell whether you would have fun playing according to those rules. Support your response with details from the essay.

Vocabulary Warm-up Word Lists

Study these words from the excerpt from"Harriet Tubman: Conductor on the Underground Railroad" Then, complete the activities that follow.

Word List A

husky [HUHS kee] *adj.* (of a voice) deep and rough
    María's high soprano was a strong contrast to Marco's <u>husky</u> voice.

hysterical [hi STER i kuhl] *adj.* out of control because of fear, excitement, or anger
    In an emergency, it's important not to become <u>hysterical</u>.

reluctance [ri LUHK tuhns] *n.* unwillingness to do something
    The show was so wonderful that the audience had a <u>reluctance</u> to see it end.

serenity [se REN i tee] *n.* calmness or peacefulness
    Dale found a strange <u>serenity</u> even with all the noise around him.

succession [suhk SESH uhn] *n.* one thing after another
    Amanda tried on four coats in <u>succession</u>, but did not like any of them.

sufficient [suh FISH uhnt] *adj.* enough; as much as you need
    With <u>sufficient</u> preparation, you should be able to learn your lines.

underground [UN der grownd] *adj.* secret; hidden
    School officials found the <u>underground</u> newspaper annoying.

vicinity [vi SIN i tee] *n.* the area around a specific place
    If you're going to be in the <u>vicinity</u> on Sunday, stop by.

Word List B

crystallized [KRIS tuh lyzd] *adj.* clear
    With a <u>crystallized</u> plan, Aisha could begin to take action.

eloquence [EL uh kwuhns] *n.* the ability to use language well
    A speaker with his <u>eloquence</u> can change people's minds.

imprisoned [im PRIZ uhnd] *adj.* jailed
    The <u>imprisoned</u> protesters only stayed in jail for one night.

invariably [in VAIR ee uh blee] *adv.* always; with no exception
    Aunt Joan <u>invariably</u> brings potato salad to our family picnics.

lingered [LING gerd] *v.* stayed around for a while
    The smell of hot dogs on the grill <u>lingered</u> for almost an hour.

sullen [SUHL uhn] *adj.* quiet and unhappy because of anger or hurt feelings
    The toddler was <u>sullen</u> after his mother reprimanded him.

unconcealed [un kuhn SEELD] *adj.* not hidden; able to be seen
    Don and Ray's dislike for one another was <u>unconcealed</u>.

vigilance [VIJ uh luhns] *n.* the state of being watchful or alert
    Thanks to the doctor's <u>vigilance</u>, Mei's life was saved.

Name _____ Date _____

from "Harriet Tubman: Conductor on the Underground Railroad" by Ann Petry
Vocabulary Warm-up Exercises

Exercise A *Fill in each blank in the paragraph below with an appropriate word from Word List A. Use each word only once.*

During the war, unknown to many, an [1] _____ army fought bravely against the invaders. It was hard to maintain any kind of [2] _____ in the face of such danger. However, there was not a single reported occurrence of an out-of-control, [3] _____ soldier. Without [4] _____ supplies, the army struggled. Its members had a great [5] _____ to admit defeat. They freed five small towns in [6] _____, until the fighting finally reached the [7] _____ of the capital. After the battle was won, soldiers recalled the [8] _____ voice of their commander, urging them on to victory. They were proud that they freed their country from foreign rule.

Exercise B *Decide whether each statement below is true or false. Circle T or F. Then, explain your answer.*

1. If a plan is <u>crystallized</u>, it is also <u>unconcealed</u>.
   T / F _____

2. With <u>vigilance</u>, a guard can keep criminals safely <u>imprisoned</u>.
   T / F _____

3. Hosts want their party guests to be <u>sullen</u>.
   T / F _____

4. If you <u>lingered</u> at the party, you probably enjoyed yourself.
   T / F _____

5. Great speakers are <u>invariably</u> known for their <u>eloquence</u>, but not always for their politeness.
   T / F _____

Name _____ Date _____

from **"Harriet Tubman: Conductor on the Underground Railroad"** by Ann Petry
Reading Warm-up A

Read the following passage. Pay special attention to the underlined words. Then, read it again, and complete the activities. Use a separate sheet of paper for your written answers.

The four men and three women had started on their journey. Each one carried a burning desire for freedom and a strong <u>reluctance</u> to give up that dream.

They had brought <u>sufficient</u> food for only two days. Their leader, however, assured them that they would not go hungry. At a <u>succession</u> of stations on the <u>Underground</u> Railroad, the "conductors," or people helping them escape, would see that they were sheltered, fed, and clothed.

James, only fifteen, was the youngest "man" in the group. He had pictured each of the stations along the way as little depots lying below the ground alongside buried train tracks. Then, Matilda explained that *underground* meant "secret" in this case. They did have to hike under cover of the night, however. Otherwise, people looking for escaped slaves could easily spot them.

There was an unnatural <u>serenity</u> when they started out. James had expected some show of outward excitement, at least from Big Jim or Althea. If anyone felt <u>hysterical</u> inside, he or she sure hid it well.

In the <u>vicinity</u> of Howland's Mill, the group stopped and gazed at the starry sky. The nearby mill was deserted. The <u>husky</u> voices of the men who usually traveled along the mill road were now silent, replaced by high-pitched chirrups of spring frogs living in the pond.

James remembered a song he knew, "Follow the Drinking Gourd." Those words were a code for the group of stars that would guide his group north. He looked up at the patch of sky between the trees. Yes, he could make out the Big Dipper. It was just as the song had said.

James had no idea of the weariness and fear he would feel before his five-hundred-mile trek to freedom was over. For now, he was experiencing only the stillness of the spring night and the hope of a new life.

1. Underline the words that specifically tell what the people had a <u>reluctance</u> to give up. Write a sentence using *reluctance*.

2. Circle the words that tell for how long the food was <u>sufficient</u>. Write a sentence using *sufficient*.

3. Circle the word that tells what was in <u>succession</u>. Then, write your own sentence for *succession*.

4. Underline the sentence in the next paragraph that helps explain what the <u>Underground</u> Railroad was. Write a sentence about something else that can be *underground*.

5. Circle the words that mean the opposite of <u>serenity</u>. In a sentence, tell why the *serenity* seems unnatural to James.

6. Circle the words that tell what anyone who might have been <u>hysterical</u> did. Tell how a *hysterical* person might act.

7. Circle the word in the next sentence that gives a clue to the meaning of <u>vicinity</u>. Then, write your own sentence for *vicinity*.

8. Write a sentence that explains what the author contrasts with the men's <u>husky</u> voices.

Name _____   Date _____

from "Harriet Tubman: Conductor on the Underground Railroad" by Ann Petry
Reading Warm-up B

Read the following passage. Pay special attention to the underlined words. Then, read it again, and complete the activities. Use a separate sheet of paper for your written answers.

At birth, no one could have predicted that Frederick Douglass would lead a life of greatness. Born into slavery on a Maryland plantation in 1818, Frederick was sent to Baltimore at the age of eight.

Frederick might have grown into a <u>sullen</u>, illiterate young man, but an unexpected gift filled him with hope. He learned to read, something that the law did not allow. After years of being treated cruelly, Frederick, at eighteen, planned an escape. His plan was discovered, and he was <u>imprisoned</u>. Once out of jail, Frederick's dream of freedom became <u>crystallized</u>, and he fled north to New Bedford, Massachusetts.

Douglass became active in antislavery organizations. At one abolitionists' meeting, he met the great speaker William Lloyd Garrison. Garrison's <u>unconcealed</u> hatred for slavery and his fiery speech <u>invariably</u> inspired Douglass.

A few days later, Douglass himself gave a speech at an antislavery convention. One observer wrote, "Flinty [hard] hearts were pierced, and cold ones melted by his <u>eloquence</u>." Douglass's speech so stirred listeners that he became a lecturer, traveling to many places in the North and to Europe.

Douglas also published an autobiography. Because it gave details of his former life, he had to increase his <u>vigilance</u> against possible capture by his former owner. If he had <u>lingered</u> in the United States, he would always have to watch his back. So he went on a two-year speaking tour to the British Isles.

Frederick returned from Europe with enough money to buy his freedom and to start his own antislavery paper, the *North Star*. After the Civil War, he began fighting for civil rights for freed slaves and for women. He also served in several government positions. No one could have predicted a life of greatness for him, but Douglass surely stood as an example of it to all the world.

1. Underline the words that show why Frederick Douglass didn't grow up to be <u>sullen</u>. Then, write a sentence about someone you know who is *sullen*.

2. Circle the words that by contrast give a clue to the meaning of <u>imprisoned</u>. Then, write a sentence using *imprisoned*.

3. Write a sentence about something that became <u>crystallized</u> in your mind.

4. Circle the word that tells what was <u>unconcealed</u>. Then, explain how you would know it is *unconcealed*.

5. Which word could replace <u>invariably</u>: *always* or *never*? Write a sentence using *invariably*.

6. Underline the words that give a clue to the meaning of <u>eloquence</u>. Tell about a time you were moved by *eloquence*.

7. Circle the word in the paragraph that gives a clue to the meaning of <u>vigilance</u>. Then, use *vigilance* in a sentence.

8. Tell about a time you <u>lingered</u> somewhere.

from "Harriet Tubman: Conductor on the Underground Railroad" by Ann Petry

Writing About the Big Question

How much information is enough?

Big Question Vocabulary

accumulate	challenge	decision	development	discrimination
explanation	exploration	factor	global	inequality
quality	quantity	reveal	statistics	valuable

A. *Use a word from the list above to complete each sentence.*

1. Research tells us that slaves enjoyed a lesser _____
   of life than white servants did.

2. The _____ to try to escape was difficult for a
   slave to make.

3. There was _____ disapproval of slavery.

4. Documents show that many spoke out against _____
   based on race.

B. *Follow the directions in responding to each of the items below.*

1. Explain why slavery was more common in the South than in the North. Use at least
   two words from the list in your explanation.

   _____

   _____

2. Do you think slavery will ever disappear completely? Use at least two words from
   the list in your answer.

   _____

   _____

C. *Complete the sentence below. Then, write a short paragraph in which you connect this
answer to the Big Question.*

The situation of slaves in the United States was _____

_____

_____

_____

from "Harriet Tubman: Conductor on the Underground Railroad" by Ann Petry
Reading: Use Details to Identify the Main Idea

The **main idea** of a work of nonfiction is the central point that the author conveys. Sometimes the author states the main idea directly. More often, the author implies, or suggests, the main idea by giving you details to consider. To **identify the implied main idea,** connect details that the author provides. The main idea you decide upon should cover all the important details in the paragraph, section, or essay.

In "Harriet Tubman: Conductor on the Underground Railroad," the author tells how Tubman led fugitive slaves to freedom in Canada. Harriet Tubman believed strongly in the right of freedom for all. Therefore, she repeatedly risked her own freedom to gain it for others.

Ask: What does the author want me to discover about Harriet Tubman as I read the details of her efforts?

DIRECTIONS: *Read each excerpt from the selection, and summarize its details. The first one is done as an example. Then, add up all the details to identify the main idea of the selection.*

1. In December 1851, when she started out with the band of fugitives that she planned to take to Canada, she had been in the vicinity of the plantation for days, planning the trip, carefully selecting the slaves that she would take with her.

   Summary of details: Tubman planned carefully for each trip.

2. There were eleven in this party. . . . It was the largest group that she had ever conducted, but she was determined that more and more slaves should know what freedom was like.

   Summary of details: _____

3. She had never been in Canada. The route beyond Philadelphia was strange to her. But she could not let the runaways who accompanied her know this. As they walked along she told them stories of her own first flight, she kept painting vivid word pictures of what it would be like to be free.

   Summary of details: _____

4. She lifted the gun, aimed it at the despairing slave. She said, "Go on with us or die." The husky low-pitched voice was grim.

   Summary of details: _____

5. They had come to trust her implicitly, totally. They, too, had come to believe her repeated statement, "We got to go free or die." She was leading them into freedom, and so they waited until she was ready to go on.

   Summary of details: _____

   Main idea of the selection: _____

Name _____ Date _____

from **"Harriet Tubman: Conductor on the Underground Railroad"** by Ann Petry
Literary Analysis: Narrative Essay

A **narrative essay** tells the story of real events experienced by real people in real places. Narrative essays share these features with fictional stories:

- People's traits and personalities are developed through their words, actions, and thoughts.
- The setting of the action may be an important element.

In "Harriet Tubman: Conductor on the Underground Railroad," the author tells a true story about how a former slave led other slaves to freedom in the mid-1800s. The author provides details about the setting, particular events, and interactions with others. The details help the reader understand Harriet Tubman's personality, her personal strength, and her success as a leader.

DIRECTIONS: *Answer the following questions. Your answers will help you identify the details that the author provides to develop Harriet Tubman's personality.*

1. What kinds of stories does Harriet Tubman tell to the fugitives in order to build their courage?

   _____

   _____

2. What would probably happen to Tubman if she were caught?

   _____

   _____

3. What time of day does the group travel, and what is the weather like?

   _____

   _____

4. After being refused shelter, how does Tubman react?

   _____

   _____

5. Why does Tubman admire the Quaker, Thomas Garrett?

   _____

   _____

6. What does Tubman do when she and her group make it to Canada?

   _____

   _____

Name _____ Date _____

from "**Harriet Tubman: Conductor on the Underground Railroad**" by Ann Petry
Vocabulary Builder

Word List

bleak	disheveled	dispel	fastidious
fugitives	incentive	invariably	mutinous

A. DIRECTIONS: *Look at the underlined vocabulary word in each question. Then, answer the question.*

1. Why would <u>fugitives</u> sleep during the day and travel at night?

   _____

2. What might be an <u>incentive</u> to apply for a job at a health club?

   _____

3. If someone is <u>disheveled</u>, what might he or she look like?

   _____

4. If a student is <u>mutinous</u>, what might he or she do?

   _____

5. How would you expect a <u>fastidious</u> person's house to look?

   _____

6. How might someone <u>dispel</u> a rumor?

   _____

7. Why does every class <u>invariably</u> include someone who answers every question?

   _____

8. Do you find a desert landscape <u>bleak</u>?

   _____

B. WORD STUDY The suffix *-ly* is usually used to create adverbs that describe how, when, or how often something is done. Use what you know about the suffix *-ly* and the meaning of the base word to write whether each adverb describes how, when, or how often.

1. Why doesn't anyone take teenagers <u>seriously</u>?
2. Exercising <u>daily</u> for hours on end is not a wise idea.
3. Answering questions <u>sarcastically</u> is sure to annoy Mr. Kohn.

Name _____ Date _____

from **"Harriet Tubman: Conductor on the Underground Railroad"** by Ann Petry
Enrichment: Defining by Example

Harriet Tubman could have stayed in Canada or New Jersey, living her life as a free woman. She chose, instead, to undertake dangerous journeys time and again for the sake of slaves. Thomas Garrett and the German farmers could have turned the fugitives away, but they risked their own safety to provide food, shoes, and shelter. These actions show courage in life-threatening situations.

Personal courage can take many forms. Sometimes being courageous means standing up for what you believe, even when the majority disagrees, or doing something that is difficult but not dangerous.

A. DIRECTIONS: *Fill in the following chart by describing why these ordinary actions take courage. The first one is done for you.*

Action	Why the Action Takes Courage
1. Join a club composed of students you do not know.	**1.** You must overcome the fear of not being liked or accepted.
2. Refuse to join in the teasing of a classmate.	
3. Try out for a part in the school play.	
4. Tell a classmate he or she cannot copy your homework because copying is cheating.	

B. DIRECTIONS: *On the lines provided, write about a courageous person. He or she may be someone you know personally, or a public figure from the past or present. Explain why you consider that person courageous.*

_____

_____

_____

_____

_____

Name _____ Date _____

Integrated Language Skills: Grammar

Adjectives and Articles

An **adjective** is a word that modifies, or describes, a noun or a pronoun. Adjectives make the nouns and pronouns they modify more vivid and precise. They answer questions such as *what kind? which one? how many?* and *how much?* about those nouns and pronouns. The words *a, an,* and *the* are special adjectives, called **articles.** The underlined words below are adjectives. The arrows point to the word each adjective modifies.

what kind? <u>lovely</u> sunset   **which one?** <u>this</u> dog

how many? <u>two</u> pages   **how much?** <u>enough</u> food

An adjective usually comes before the noun it modifies, as in the examples above. Sometimes adjectives come after the nouns or pronouns they modify.

Gold is <u>precious</u>.

A. PRACTICE: *Underline the adjective or adjectives in each sentence. Draw an arrow from every adjective to the noun or pronoun it modifies.*

1. We always played many games after school.
2. Sometimes we made up our own rules for the games.
3. These rules often were complex.
4. One game was a unique version of Hide and Seek.
5. In this game, we all hid in places within fifty feet of the seeker.
6. Seekers wore a big scarf over their eyes.
7. All players made soft sounds to lead the seekers toward them.
8. Games we played were long and fun.

B. Writing Application: *Make the nouns and pronouns in these sentences more vivid and precise by adding adjectives that answer the questions in parentheses. Write each adjective on the line after the question.*

1. The *(what kind?)* _____ cat jumped from the floor to the table.
2. We kicked our feet through the *(what kind?)* _____ leaves that had fallen from the trees.
3. My father brought *(how many?)* _____ CDs to listen to in the car.
4. My little cousin decided she wanted *(which one?)* _____ toy for her birthday.

50

Name _____ Date _____

from **"Harriet Tubman: Conductor on the Underground Railroad"** by Ann Petry
"Baseball" by Lionel G. García

Integrated Language Skills: Support for Writing a Biographical Sketch

A **biography** is a written account of a person's life. A **biographical "sketch"** is a much shorter piece of writing in which the author tells something important about a real person.

DIRECTIONS: *Use the graphic organizer below to help plan your biographical sketch about someone who took risks in order to achieve a worthy goal or someone who did something in a new way. Based on the details you generate about the person, come up with a main idea for your sketch.*

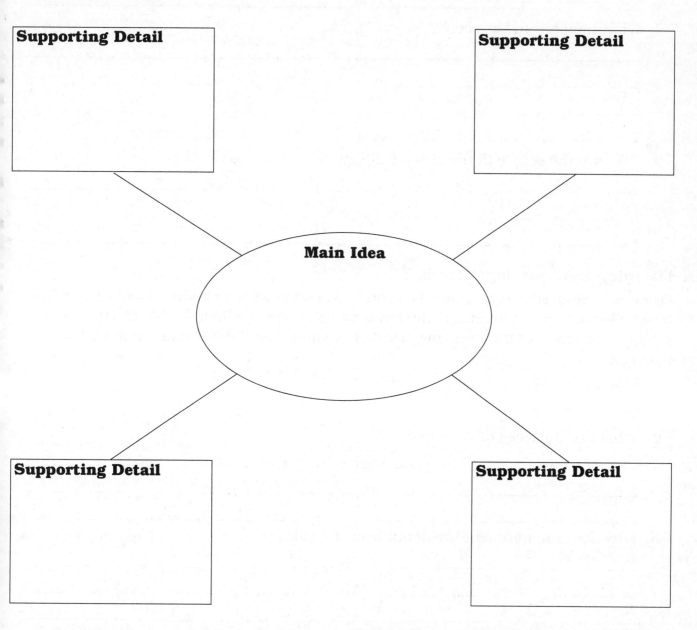

Now, revise your main idea as appropriate, write the body of the biographical sketch, and end with a strong concluding sentence that restates your main idea in different words.

Name _____ Date _____

from "Harriet Tubman: Conductor on the Underground Railroad" by Ann Petry
"Baseball" by Lionel G. García

Integrated Language Skills: Support for Extend Your Learning

Listening and Speaking: "Harriet Tubman: Conductor on the Underground Railroad"

Discuss in your small group which scenes from the essay about Harriet Tubman you will write about. On the lines below, record your group's responses to the following questions. Then, use the information to write your dialogue.

1. Who are the people in your scene?

   _____

2. What happens in the scene?

   _____
   _____
   _____
   _____

3. How are the people in the scene feeling?

   _____
   _____
   _____

Listening and Speaking: "Baseball"

Discuss in your small group the skit you will present about children who are playing baseball when an argument breaks out over rules. On the lines below, record your group's responses to the following questions. Then, use the information to write your dialogue.

1. Who are the speakers in your skit?

   _____

2. What are the rules of the game?

   _____
   _____

3. Why does an argument break out over the rules?

   _____
   _____
   _____

Name _____ Date _____

from "Harriet Tubman: Conductor on the Underground Railroad" by Ann Petry
Open-Book Test

Short Answer *Write your responses to the questions in this section on the lines provided.*

1. Harriet Tubman waited for a clear night when she could see the North Star before she began an escape. Why did she wait until she could see the North Star?

   _____

   _____

2. The network of people who helped slaves escape to the North was called the Underground Railroad. Why did it have that name?

   _____

   _____

   _____

3. Thomas Garrett was an important person in the Underground Railroad. The narrator of "Harriet Tubman" describes his appearance, his character, and his actions. What do those details reveal about Garrett? Cite two details to support your response.

   _____

   _____

   _____

   _____

4. In "Harriet Tubman," some of the fugitives became mutinous before the group reached Philadelphia. What might have happened if the fugitives had stayed mutinous? Base your answer on the meaning of *mutinous*.

   _____

   _____

   _____

   _____

5. Harriet Tubman told the fugitives stories of other slaves who had escaped to freedom. What was her purpose in telling those stories?

   _____

   _____

   _____

   _____

6. The details in this diagram are from "Harriet Tubman." Think about what they have in common. Then, complete the diagram by writing the implied main idea that the three details support. Finally, on the line below, state what the main idea says about Harriet Tubman.

Tubman had never traveled to Canada before.	Tubman took a big group of fugitives with her.	Tubman sometimes fell asleep without warning.

_____

7. When Harriet Tubman fell asleep during the trip north, the fugitives waited patiently for her to wake up. What does their waiting for her tell you about their relationship with Tubman?

_____

_____

8. One main idea in "Harriet Tubman" is that the fugitives faced harsh conditions. Cite one detail from the essay that supports this idea.

_____

_____

9. In "Harriet Tubman," we learn that Tubman returned to the South many times to lead fugitives north. What character trait of Tubman's is revealed by her taking those trips south? Explain your answer.

_____

_____

10. Harriet Tubman decided to settle in Canada. Why did she make that decision?

_____

_____

_____

Essay

Write an extended response to the question of your choice or to the question or questions your teacher assigns you.

11. The author of "Harriet Tubman" writes that the farther north Tubman traveled, the safer she felt. Still, there was danger in the North. In an essay, describe some of the difficulties the fugitives encountered, and explain why the journey remained dangerous. Cite three details from the essay to support your points.

12. Several times Harriet Tubman says, "We got to go free or die." In an essay, discuss whether that idea still motivates people today. Provide examples from the lives of friends or relatives or from the lives of people in the news.

13. Harriet Tubman felt justified in threatening to take the life of the man who wanted to turn back. In an essay, explain Tubman's motives. Give two reasons to explain why she apparently felt that way. Then, state whether you agree with those reasons. Explain your answer.

14. **Thinking About the Big Question: How much information is enough?** Harriet Tubman risked her life to lead others to freedom. Do you think that the essay "Harriet Tubman" explains why Tubman took such risks? In an essay, discuss whether you understand her motives. If you do, explain what they were. If you do not understand them, tell what additional information you would need in order to understand them.

Oral Response

15. Go back to question 7, 8, or 9 or to the question your teacher assigns you. Take a few minutes to expand your answer and prepare an oral response. Find additional details in "Harriet Tubman" that support your points. If necessary, make notes to guide your oral response.

Name _____ Date _____

Critical Reading *Identify the letter of the choice that best answers the question.*

____ 1. When did the escape reported in "Harriet Tubman" begin?
    A. early summer
    B. late summer
    C. fall or winter
    D. spring

____ 2. Why did Harriet Tubman wait to see the North Star before beginning the escape?
    A. Tubman needed light to make sure the group stayed together.
    B. The star helped the fugitives feel hopeful.
    C. Tubman needed the star to guide their way north.
    D. The group needed light to see the trail.

____ 3. How did Harriet Tubman respond when one of the runaways wanted to turn back?
    A. She threatened him with a gun.
    B. She told the story of Frederick Douglass.
    C. She sang "Go Down, Moses."
    D. She tied his hands together.

____ 4. In "Harriet Tubman," what was the runaways' final destination?
    A. Massachusetts
    B. Vermont
    C. New York
    D. Canada

____ 5. According to "Harriet Tubman," what did the Quaker named Thomas Garrett give fugitives besides shoes?
    A. jackets and pants
    B. a warm welcome
    C. advice about jobs
    D. newspapers

____ 6. Which of the following is an example of Harriet Tubman's courage?
    A. Tubman kills a bear that attacked the group of fugitives.
    B. Tubman returns to the South many times to lead fugitives north.
    C. Tubman leads the group across a flooded river.
    D. Tubman finds the fugitives jobs.

_____ 7. Which of the following was *not* a reason Harriet Tubman made her home in Canada?
   A. African American citizens could vote.
   B. African American citizens could hold office.
   C. There was public transportation.
   D. African American children went to school.

_____ 8. Which of the following is a reason to read about Tubman and the Underground Railroad?
   A. to learn about the Revolutionary War
   B. to learn the history of U.S. rail travel
   C. to learn about the struggle of slaves
   D. to learn about life on a plantation

_____ 9. What did Harriet Tubman do to encourage fugitives along the way?
   A. She told stories about her children.
   B. She told of other slaves who escaped.
   C. She talked about paid work in the North.
   D. She found extra food in farmers' gardens.

_____ 10. Which is *not* a way Harriet Tubman announced her presence on a plantation?
   A. by making a sound like a whippoorwill
   B. by singing a forbidden spiritual
   C. by making a sound like a hoot owl
   D. by shooting her gun three times

_____ 11. Which of the following details does *not* support the idea that Harriet Tubman took risks?
   A. She traveled an unfamiliar route.
   B. She took a very large group.
   C. She loved the beauty of Maryland.
   D. She might fall asleep without warning.

Vocabulary and Grammar

_____ 12. Which of the following is closest in meaning to *fugitives*?
   A. authorities
   B. runaways
   C. stand-ins
   D. detours

_____ **13.** Which sentence contains an adjective?

A. She combed her clean hair.

B. We saw an eagle flying above us.

C. The snow crunched under our boots.

D. He played his guitar.

_____ **14.** Which word is closest in meaning to *disheveled*?

A. unhappy

B. discouraged

C. messy

D. motivated

_____ **15.** Which word in the following sentence is an adjective?

We found our perfect campsite after hiking tirelessly for miles.

A. perfect

B. campsite

C. tirelessly

D. for

Essay

16. The author wrote that the farther north Harriet Tubman traveled, the safer she felt. Still, Tubman found danger in the North. In a short essay, describe how the journey became harder and remained dangerous.

17. Harriet Tubman was courageous, intelligent, determined, and unselfish. She exhibited these qualities often on her journey north with the fugitives. Write an essay in which you give examples of when Tubman acted in these ways. Be sure to explain how or why your examples are appropriate.

18. Thinking About the Big Question: How much information is enough? Harriet Tubman risked her life to lead others to freedom. Do you think that the essay "Harriet Tubman" explains why Tubman took such risks? Support your opinion in an essay that cites specific examples from the text.

from **"Harriet Tubman: Conductor on the Underground Railroad"** by Ann Petry
Selection Test B

Critical Reading *Identify the letter of the choice that best completes the statement or answers the question.*

_____ 1. Among the slaves, Harriet Tubman was known as
  A. the Great Emancipator.
  B. Moses.
  C. Spartacus.
  D. Miss Tubman.

_____ 2. Based on "Harriet Tubman," why was Saturday night a good time for slaves to escape?
  A. Slaves had more free time on Saturday.
  B. Saturdays were considered lucky.
  C. Owners could not act until Monday.
  D. Owners slept late on weekends.

_____ 3. Why did Harriet Tubman take the fugitives all the way to Canada?
  A. The Fugitive Slave Law was being enforced.
  B. There were more jobs available in Canada.
  C. The fugitives preferred Canada to Vermont.
  D. Canada had always been the last stop on the Underground Railroad.

_____ 4. The Underground Railroad, described in "Harriet Tubman," was so named because
  A. the slaves traveled on freight boxcars.
  B. the slaves dressed as train passengers.
  C. the railroad tracks ran underground.
  D. homes on the route were like stations.

_____ 5. Why did Harriet Tubman tell the fugitives stories of others who had escaped to freedom?
  A. to inspire them
  B. to shame them into going north
  C. to ease their boredom
  D. to teach them some history

_____ 6. In "Harriet Tubman," what was the main danger of letting a runaway return to a plantation?
  A. The runaway might conclude that slavery is preferable to freedom.
  B. The runaway might report details of Tubman's methods for escape.
  C. The runaway might be killed.
  D. The runaway might discourage other slaves from attempting escape.

_____ 7. Which detail in "Harriet Tubman" best supports the idea that fugitives faced harsh conditions?
  A. One runaway wanted to return to slavery.
  B. Runaways waited for Tubman to awake.
  C. The weather in Canada was cold.
  D. Strangers offered shelter.

___ 8. Why did Harriet Tubman *not* tell the fugitives that she had never gone to Canada?
  A. The information was not important.
  B. She had one of her fits of sleep.
  C. She did not want to add to their fears.
  D. She wanted to surprise them on arrival.

___ 9. How do you know that the fugitives had come to trust Harriet Tubman as their guide?
  A. They sang "Go Down, Moses" to her.
  B. They told Thomas Garrett.
  C. They waited patiently while she slept.
  D. They let her return for their friends.

___ 10. According to "Harriet Tubman," what was Thomas Garrett's role in the Underground Railroad?
  A. He was a public official in Canada.
  B. He gave fugitives shoes and shelter.
  C. He was a former plantation owner.
  D. He accompanied Tubman on her trips.

___ 11. In "Harriet Tubman," how long did it take to travel from the plantation to St. Catharines?
  A. about a week
  B. about a month
  C. three months
  D. a year

___ 12. What main idea does the following passage from "Harriet Tubman" support?
  She discovered that freedom meant more than the right to change jobs at will, more than the right to keep the money that one earned.

  A. Freedom means keeping one good job.
  B. Freedom cannot be defined.
  C. Freedom is more than material gains.
  D. Freedom means earning a salary.

___ 13. Why did Harriet Tubman decide to settle in Canada?
  A. She became used to cold weather.
  B. She wanted to help former slaves there.
  C. She liked the freedoms for African Americans there.
  D. She had many friends there.

___ 14. In "Harriet Tubman," what main idea do the details about William Still's records support?
  A. The fugitives' trip north was difficult.
  B. The escaping slaves were not able to carry much with them as they traveled north.
  C. Harriet Tubman was justified in threatening to take a slave's life.
  D. Information about escaping slaves had to be kept secret until slavery was abolished.

____ 15. What causes the author of "Harriet Tubman" to think the eleven runaways stayed with Frederick Douglass?
   A. a passage in Douglass's autobiography
   B. a letter from Tubman to Douglass
   C. a newspaper account from that era
   D. a plaque in front of Douglass's home

Vocabulary and Grammar

____ 16. Which of the following words or phrases is closest in meaning to *fastidious*?
   A. quick   C. fascinating
   B. not trustworthy   D. not easy to please

____ 17. Which of the following sentences contains an adjective?
   A. My mother sings loudly.   C. He runs marathons often.
   B. Mary's athletic friends play   D. She ate her sandwich.
      basketball.

____ 18. Which word is an adjective in the following sentence?
      Huge birds dove silently and quickly into pools of water.

   A. huge   C. quickly
   B. silently   D. of

____ 19. Which word is opposite in meaning to *mutinous*?
   A. loyal   C. ravenous
   B. rebellious   D. angry

____ 20. In which sentence is *disheveled* used correctly?
   A. He disheveled his messy   C. Jay looked disheveled after
      notebook.   camping.
   B. Susie disheveled all of her   D. Jane hoped for a disheveled gift.
      clothes.

Essay

21. Write an essay in which you discuss how Harriet Tubman's motto—"We got to go free or die"—still motivates people today. Give examples from the personal lives of friends and relatives, or discuss people you have heard about but do not personally know.

22. Harriet Tubman possessed a number of special qualities that contributed to her repeated success in leading so many fugitives to freedom. Write an essay in which you describe these qualities. Use examples from the text that illustrate the qualities you name.

23. Why do you think Harriet Tubman felt justified in threatening to take the life of the man who wanted to turn back? Explain your answer in an essay, giving specific reasons and using examples from the text.

24. **Thinking About the Big Question: How much information is enough?** Harriet Tubman risked her life to lead others to freedom. Do you think that the essay "Harriet Tubman" explains why Tubman took such risks? In an essay, discuss whether you understand her motives. If you do, explain what they were. If you do not understand them, tell what additional information you would need in order to understand them.

Vocabulary Warm-up Word Lists

Study these words from "Always To Remember: The Vision of Maya Ying Lin." Then, complete the activities.

Word List A

appropriate [uh PROH pree it] *adj.* right for a certain purpose
What do you think is an <u>appropriate</u> thing to do about gossip?

architect [AR ki tekt] *n.* a person whose job is to design buildings
An <u>architect</u> follows a building project until it is completed.

attending [uh TEND ing] *v.* being present at an event
Five thousand people were <u>attending</u> the concert in the arena.

durable [DOOR uh buhl] *adj.* staying in good condition for a long time
I like jeans because they are <u>durable</u> and comfortable.

political [puh LIT i kuhl] *adj.* relating to government actions and policies
My mom says we should not have <u>political</u> discussions during dinner.

response [ri SPAHNS] *n.* a reply to something
Aaron's <u>response</u> to my birthday party invitation was a big smile.

site [SYT] *n.* the place where something is being built
The <u>site</u> where our new high school will be built is a cornfield now.

tribute [TRIB yoot] *n.* something given, said, or done to show respect or give thanks
Our whole town turned out for the <u>tribute</u> to the police chief.

Word List B

distinguished [dis TING gwisht] *adj.* successful and respected
Can you name any of the <u>distinguished</u> people who have received the Nobel Prize?

enrolled [en ROHLD] *v.* officially joined a school or class
Many of my friends <u>enrolled</u> in the local junior college.

harmony [HAR muh nee] *n.* the combination of parts to create a pleasing whole
The color and shape of the vase was in perfect <u>harmony</u> with the flowers chosen.

horizontal [hawr i ZAHN tl] *adj.* flat; level with the ground
The bird's wings formed a <u>horizontal</u> line to the earth.

merits [MER its] *n.* good qualities of something or someone
Graham spoke to the sixth-graders about the <u>merits</u> of school clubs.

nationally [NASH uh nuhl lee] *adv.* by people throughout a whole country
The young singer from Texas became known <u>nationally</u> for her great voice.

relates [ri LAYTS] *v.* shows or proves a connection between things
The subject of my English class often <u>relates</u> to my social studies theme.

sculpture [SKUHLP chuhr] *n.* the art of carving or molding statues
<u>Sculpture</u> is a great hobby for people who like to work with their hands.

"Always to Remember: The Vision of Maya Ying Lin" by Brent Ashabranner
Vocabulary Warm-up Exercises

Exercise A *Fill in each blank in the paragraph below with an appropriate word from Word List A. Use each word only once.*

Yesterday, when we were [1] _____ the opening of our brand-new

library, we got to meet the [2] _____. I believe his design for the

building is just perfect for its [3] _____. He used natural yet

[4] _____ materials like stone and wood so that the library would remain

standing for many years. Mom and Dad said that choosing the design was a real

[5] _____ battle, though. The mayor and some other people in govern-

ment wanted a very modern building that they hoped would be [6] _____

for the computer age. The [7] _____ of one large group of people to

this idea was negative. I think the natural beauty of the chosen design is a

[8] _____ to the city's respect for our surroundings.

Exercise B *Answer each question with a complete explanation.*

1. Why aren't the daily events of towns and cities talked about on the news <u>nationally</u>?
   _____

2. What happens when one person <u>relates</u> well to another?
   _____

3. Is a skyscraper usually built following a <u>horizontal</u> design?
   _____

4. Once you are <u>enrolled</u> in a class, what should you do?
   _____

5. Does <u>sculpture</u> usually result in art that you would hang on a wall?
   _____

6. What are the <u>merits</u> of your favorite television show?
   _____

7. Which adult who you know would you describe as <u>distinguished</u>?
   _____

8. How would you describe a sofa that is in <u>harmony</u> with the room it sets in?
   _____

"Always to Remember: The Vision of Maya Ying Lin" by Brent Ashabranner
Reading Warm-up A

Read the following passage. Pay special attention to the underlined words. Then, read it again, and complete the activities. Use a separate sheet of paper for your written answers.

Maya Ying Lin, the college student and <u>architect</u> who designed the Vietnam Veterans Memorial, had a strong idea about fitting the Wall into its surroundings. Her plans found an <u>appropriate</u> way to connect this new structure to the land and to the other memorials around it. Her ideas for the <u>site</u> seemed as perfect as anyone could have hoped to see.

What Maya and others could not possibly have known was the level of <u>response</u> the memorial would stir up in visitors. The organizers of the effort hoped that the Wall would help to heal the <u>political</u> division caused by the Vietnam War. They have been thrilled with the results. Visitors often let their emotions show. Many are stunned by the impact the memorial has on them.

Visitors often bring things to leave behind at the Wall. Together, these objects are a huge <u>tribute</u> to the men and women who served our country. More than fifty thousand objects have been left at the Wall. They are collected twice daily by the National Park Service. When the weather is bad, the objects are picked up more often. This way, the less <u>durable</u> items are not damaged. Treated as precious, the items are carefully entered into the Vietnam Veterans Memorial Collection. Exceptions are living things, such as plants, and flags. The flags are given to hospitals for former soldiers and groups like the Boy Scouts or Girl Scouts. The flags also are given to people who are <u>attending</u> special events at the memorial.

The things most often left are writings such as poems or letters. Bracelets worn to remember soldiers who are still missing are plentiful, too. Rubbings of the names on the wall are often left as well. Things that soldiers owned and photographs also are among the most commonly left items.

1. Underline the words naming what Maya Ying Lin did as an <u>architect</u>. Then, explain what an *architect* does for a living.

2. Circle the words that name what was already part of the memorial's <u>site</u>. Then, explain why the best designs would be viewed as *appropriate* for a building *site*.

3. Underline words throughout the paragraph that describe the visitors' <u>response</u>. Then, describe a time when a *response* of your own surprised you.

4. Circle the words naming what caused <u>political</u> division. Then, explain the word *political*.

5. Underline the words naming the people to whom the objects are a <u>tribute</u>. Then, explain the different forms a *tribute* can take.

6. Circle the sentence that explains how less <u>durable</u> objects are protected. Make a list of some of these less *durable* objects.

7. Underline the words naming what people are <u>attending</u>. Then, explain what *attending* means.

"Always to Remember: The Vision of Maya Ying Lin" by Brent Ashabranner
Reading Warm-up B

Read the following passage. Pay special attention to the underlined words. Then, read it again, and complete the activities. Use a separate sheet of paper for your written answers.

Students who have <u>enrolled</u> at Juniata College in Pennsylvania have an unusual opportunity. By traveling just a few minutes from campus, they can see a work by <u>distinguished</u> artist Maya Ying Lin, who designed the Vietnam Veterans Memorial in Washington, D.C., and the Civil Rights Memorial in Montgomery, Alabama. Though not as well known <u>nationally</u> as these two works, the Peace Chapel at Juniata College is quite impressive.

The Peace Chapel is not a building or a monument. Instead, it is a place designed to help visitors feel complete <u>harmony</u> with nature. The materials include polished steps of granite leading up a hill. At the top of this path is a shallow well that is lined with rough granite stones, forming a 40-foot circle. This circular area is designed as a meeting place for groups.

A few hundred yards away and slightly higher is another part of the chapel. This area is designed for individuals. It <u>relates</u> to the larger area, but it is isolated and private. This individual area consists of one thing: a <u>horizontal</u>, round, polished piece of granite set in the ground amid trees. When a person stands on this stone, the view is awesome.

Visitors to the Peace Chapel believe its <u>merits</u> are found in its simplicity. Maya Lin's Chinese influences shine through in the way she works with nature. As she says: "What I choose to introduce onto the land does not try to dominate or overwhelm the existing landscape, but instead tries to work with it to produce a new experience of that place." Her creative use of stones at the Peace Chapel would seem to give <u>sculpture</u> a new face. Yet, it is somehow tied to the mysterious and ancient use of stones in certain places in Europe. The Peace Chapel truly is a place that will last through the ages.

1. Underline the name of the state in which students have <u>enrolled</u> in Juniata College. Then, explain what *enrolled* means.

2. Explain why someone <u>distinguished</u> in a field of work probably would also be known <u>nationally</u>.

3. Circle the words describing what type of <u>harmony</u> visitors to Peace Chapel might feel. Then, explain the word *harmony*.

4. Underline the words naming what the individual area of the Peace Chapel <u>relates</u> to. Then, explain what *relates* means.

5. Circle other words that describe the <u>horizontal</u> stone. Explain why the granite piece had to be *horizontal*.

6. Underline the word that tells about the <u>merits</u> of Peace Chapel. Then, describe the *merits* of a place you like to visit.

7. Why does the word <u>sculpture</u> make sense when used to describe the work done to create Peace Chapel?

Always to Remember by Brent Ashabranner
Writing About the Big Question

How much information is enough?

Big Question Vocabulary

accumulate	challenge	decision	development	discrimination
explanation	exploration	factor	global	inequality
quality	quantity	reveal	statistics	

A. *Write a word from the Big Question vocabulary list that best answers each question below.*

1. Which word describes something that happens all over the world?

_____

2. Which word describes something that is hard to do? _____

3. Which word means "make something known"? _____

B. *Follow the directions in responding to each of the items below.*

1. Write a two-sentence description of a person or event that you would like to honor in a memorial. Explain why that person or event deserves a memorial. Use at least two list words in your sentences.

_____

_____

2. What kind of memorial should the person or event have? Include one or more list words in your answer.

_____

_____

C. *Complete the sentence below. Then, write a short paragraph in which you connect this answer to the Big Question.*

Exploration of history requires _____

_____

_____

_____

"Always to Remember: The Vision of Maya Ying Lin" by Brent Ashabranner

Reading: Make Connections Between Supporting Paragraphs and the Main Idea

Main ideas are the most important points in a literary work. Writers often organize essays so that main ideas are part of a clear structure. An introduction states the main idea, and then each paragraph supports or develops it. **Make connections between supporting paragraphs and the main idea.**

• Pause to note the main idea of paragraphs or sections.
• Write notes, or complete an organizer to track main ideas and key details.
• Review the main ideas and details in each section to see how they support the essay's main idea.

Read this passage from the selection about Maya Ying Lin.

> Announcement of the competition in October, 1980, brought an astonishing response. The Vietnam Veterans Memorial Fund received over five thousand inquiries. They came from every state in the nation and from every field of design.

The details support the main idea: the astonishing support for the competition.

DIRECTIONS: *For each passage, list details that support the stated main idea.*

1. Maya Lin grew up in an environment of art and literature. She was interested in sculpture and made both small and large sculptural figures, one cast in bronze. She learned silversmithing and made jewelry. She was surrounded by books and read a great deal. . . .

   Main idea of whole section: Maya Lin's home was full of art and literature.

   Supporting details: _____

   _____

2. On the day of their visit, Maya Lin remembers, Constitution Gardens was awash with a late November sun; the park was full of light, alive with joggers and people walking beside the lake.

   Main idea of whole section: Maya's visit to the building site was memorable.

   Supporting details: _____

   _____

3. The designs were displayed without any indication of the designer's name so that they could be judged anonymously, on their design merits alone. The jury spent one week reviewing all the designs. . . . On May 1 it made its report to the Vietnam Veterans Memorial Fund; the experts declared Entry Number 1,026 the winner.

   Main idea of whole section: Designs were judged impartially.

   Supporting details: _____

   _____

"**Always to Remember: The Vision of Maya Ying Lin**" by Brent Ashabranner
Literary Analysis: Biography and Autobiography

- A **biographical essay** is a short work in which a writer tells about an important event in the life of another person.
- An **autobiographical essay** is also a true account, but it is written by the person who experienced the event himself or herself. It includes the writer's thoughts and feelings about an event.

Both types of writing look at the influence of personal experiences, such as schooling, on the later personalities and accomplishments of a person.

DIRECTIONS: *Complete the following outline by providing the details given in the biographical essay about Maya Ying Lin.*

Maya Ying Lin

I. Background and education

   A. Background

      1. _____

      2. _____

      3. _____

   B. Education

     _____

II. The Vietnam Veterans Memorial contest

   A. Steps to winning

      1. _____

      2. _____

   B. Rewards

      1. _____

      2. _____

III. The Vietnam Veterans Memorial

   A. Specifications

      1. _____

      2. _____

      3. _____

   B. Judges' reactions to winning entry

      1. _____

      2. _____

Name _____ Date _____

"Always to Remember: The Vision of Maya Ying Lin" by Brent Ashabranner
Vocabulary Builder

Word List

    anonymously   authorized   criteria   eloquent   harmonious   unanimous

A. DIRECTIONS: *Complete each of the following sentences with a vocabulary word.*

1. What _____ did the teacher use in grading the research papers?

2. The senator's speech before Congress was _____.

3. The spices created a(n) _____ blend of flavors in the stew.

4. Opinion was _____; everyone agreed to the suggestion.

5. An _____ biography is one that the subject approves.

6. Our newspaper does not print letters people send _____.

B. WORD STUDY The Greek root -*nym*- means "name." Answer each question that follows with one of these words containing the root -*nym*-: *synonym, anonymous, acronym, homonyms.*

1. What is a word formed from the first letters of a phrase?

   _____

2. What is a word that has the same or nearly the same meaning as another word?

   _____

3. What are two words that sound the same but are spelled differently?

   _____

4. What is a word that describes a work whose author is unknown?

   _____

C. DIRECTIONS: *Identify each item as synonyms, homonyms, or an acronym.*

1. their/there _____

2. NATO _____

3. buy/purchase _____

4. do/due _____

5. LOL _____

"Always to Remember: The Vision of Maya Ying Lin" by Brent Ashabranner

Enrichment: Memorial Design

Maya Ying Lin is also known for designing the Civil Rights Memorial in Montgomery, Alabama. In researching the background of the civil rights movement, she came across words by Martin Luther King, Jr., inspired by biblical verses: "We will not be satisfied until justice rolls down like waters, and righteousness like a mighty stream." King's words, in turn, inspired Lin to use water as a main design element of the monument, which would memorialize those who had been killed in the cause of marching for civil rights.

Lin's plan developed into a 12-foot disk of granite, inscribed around the perimeter with individuals' names. A black granite wall behind the disk rises nine feet and is inscribed with King's words. Water flows down the wall and across the disk, touching each name.

DIRECTIONS: *Based on what you now know about the concepts that influenced Maya Ying Lin in designing two monuments, put yourself in her shoes. Imagine that you are designing a memorial for a person, group, or cause that you admire. A memorial, keep in mind, does not have to be a physical object. Answer the following questions.*

1. What or whom would you honor, and why?

   _____

   _____

2. If you are thinking of a monument such as Lin's, what are your initial thoughts about its appearance? Describe your ideas in words on the lines below, sketch your ideas in the box, or respond in both words and visuals.

   _____

   _____

3. If you are thinking of a memorial of a different kind—for example, a painting, a song, a tree—describe what you have in mind.

   _____

   _____

4. What would you want people to feel or think when visiting or experiencing your memorial?

   _____

   _____

Name _____   Date _____

"Always to Remember: The Vision of Maya Ying Lin" by Brent Ashabranner
Open-Book Test

Short Answer *Write your responses to the questions in this section on the lines provided.*

1. A biographical essay is a short work in which a writer tells about an important event in the life of another person. An autobiographical essay is a true account written by the person who experienced the account. Which kind of essay is "Always to Remember"? How do you know?

    _____

    _____

2. According to "Always to Remember," the Vietnam Veterans Memorial was intended "to soothe passions, not stir them up." Why was that goal important?

    _____

    _____

    _____

3. "Always to Remember" describes the competition to design the Vietnam Veterans Memorial. According to the essay, the competition was intense. What detail supports this main idea?

    _____

4. In "Always to Remember," Ashabranner describes some of the criteria for the design of the Vietnam Veterans Memorial. What was the purpose of setting criteria for the competition? Base your answer on the definition of *criteria*.

    _____

    _____

    _____

5. According to "Always to Remember," the competing designs for the Vietnam Veterans Memorial were displayed without showing the names of the designers. What was the purpose of showing the designs without revealing the designers' names?

    _____

    _____

    _____

Unit 3 Resources: Types of Nonfiction
© Pearson Education, Inc. All rights reserved.
71

6. In "Always to Remember," a number of details support the idea that Maya Lin's design was the best one submitted. Carefully read the part of the essay that describes the choosing of Lin's design. Then, in this diagram, write three details that support the main idea.

Lin's design was the best one submitted.

Detail:

Detail:

Detail:

How does the idea that Lin's design was the best one connect to the idea that the design "had to soothe passions, not stir them up"?

_____

_____

7. In "Always to Remember," the judges said that Maya Lin's design was "eloquent." What about the design was eloquent? Focus on the meaning of the word to support your answer.

_____

_____

8. In "Always to Remember," Ashabranner describes Maya Lin's background. For example, he describes her parents' professions and her own interests and college experiences. What is the point of including that information?

_____

_____

9. In describing Maya Lin's background in "Always to Remember," Ashabranner reveals a number of details that may explain Lin's interest in architecture. Cite the detail that may have had the strongest influence on Maya Lin's decision to study architecture. Explain your answer.

_____

_____

_____

_____

Name _____   Date _____

10. In "Always to Remember," Ashabranner describes Maya Lin's visit to the park in Washington, D.C., where the Vietnam Veterans Memorial would be built. Why did Lin's visit to the park prove to be a good idea? Cite two reasons to support your answer.

_____

_____

_____

_____

Essay

Write an extended response to the question of your choice or to the question or questions your teacher assigns you.

11. "Always to Remember" presents biographical details about Maya Ying Lin. In a brief essay, identify two details from Lin's background that may have influenced the design she submitted for the Vietnam Veterans Memorial. Explain how her experiences influenced her design.

12. In "Always to Remember," Brent Ashabranner mentions certain details of Maya Lin's life and personality that appear to have little to do with the subject of the war memorial contest. In an essay, identify two of those extra details. Discuss why the writer of the essay might have included them. Explain what, if anything, they add to the essay.

13. "Always to Remember" identifies several reasons for the judges' choice of Maya Lin's design for the Vietnam Veterans Memorial. In an essay, describe two aspects of Lin's design that greatly impressed the judges. Cite details in the essay to support your response. Then, explain how the judges' reasons relate to Maya Lin's own remarks, toward the end of the essay, about what she hoped to accomplish with her design.

14. Thinking About the Big Question: How much information is enough? "Always to Remember" is an essay about the Vietnam Veterans Memorial. It also includes photographs of the memorial, of Maya Lin, and of another memorial she designed. In an essay, explain whether the text and pictures together give you enough information to understand why the Vietnam Veterans Memorial is considered to be such a moving monument to the soldiers who lost their lives in Vietnam. In your essay, use details from "Always to Remember" to explain why the memorial is moving, or describe what additional information might help you better understand the memorial's impact.

Oral Response

15. Go back to question 3, 5, or 8 or to the question your teacher assigns you. Take a few minutes to expand your answer and prepare an oral response. Find additional details in "Always to Remember" that will support your points. If necessary, make notes to guide your oral response.

Name _____ Date _____

"Always to Remember: The Vision of Maya Ying Lin" by Brent Ashabranner
Selection Test A

Critical Reading *Identify the letter of the choice that best answers the question.*

____ 1. According to "Always to Remember," who had the idea that Vietnam veterans deserved a memorial?
A. two lawyers
B. a Vietnam veteran, Jan Scruggs
C. Maya Ying Lin's professor at Yale
D. the author, Brent Ashabranner

____ 2. According to "Always to Remember," who was particularly interested in entering the memorial competition?
A. college students
B. war veterans
C. designers and sculptors
D. residents of Washington, D.C.

____ 3. According to "Always to Remember," who had the idea for Maya Ying Lin to submit a design to the competition?
A. her college professor
B. Maya Ying Lin herself
C. her parents
D. her friends

____ 4. Based on your reading of "Always to Remember," which word best describes the response to the design competition for a memorial?
A. enthusiastic
B. lukewarm
C. uninterested
D. angry

____ 5. "Always to Remember" tells that Maya Ying Lin visited the park where the memorial would be built before she created a design. Why was the visit a good idea?
A. She needed to take a break from her studies.
B. She was able to talk with local people about the memorial they envisioned.
C. She did historical research in a Washington, D.C., library.
D. She was able to imagine a design that fit the landscape.

_____ 6. According to "Always to Remember," what was *not* an important condition for the design of the memorial?

    A. It had to be easy to take care of.

    B. It had to fit in the park's environment.

    C. It had to be very tall.

    D. It had to have artistic merit.

_____ 7. According to "Always to Remember," why were the judges surprised by who won the design competition?

    A. The winner had an artistic background.

    B. The winner was inexperienced.

    C. The winner was not from Washington, D.C.

    D. The winner entered at the last minute.

_____ 8. According to "Always to Remember," which word best describes the home in which Maya Ying Lin grew up?

    A. wealthy

    B. artistic

    C. poor

    D. unhappy

_____ 9. According to "Always to Remember," what subject did Maya Ying Lin decide to concentrate on in college?

    A. art history

    B. ceramics

    C. literature

    D. architecture

_____ 10. According to "Always to Remember," when was the deadline for building the memorial?

    A. Veterans Day, 1982

    B. New Year's Day, 2000

    C. President's Day, 1970

    D. George Washington's Birthday, 1952

_____ 11. Whom does the Vietnam Veterans Memorial honor?

    A. those in support of U.S. action in the war

    B. those against U.S. action in the war

    C. the officers who led troups in the war

    D. U.S. military killed or missing in the war

Vocabulary and Grammar

___ 12. Which of the following phrases does *not* contain an adverb?
   A. speak angrily   C. carefully listen
   B. fancy hat   D. drive cautiously

___ 13. Which word is the closest in meaning to *eloquent*?
   A. expressive   C. boring
   B. absent   D. unjust

___ 14. What is the adverb in the following sentence?
   The children sang sweetly at their school's holiday concert.
   A. children   C. sweetly
   B. sang   D. concert

___ 15. Which word or phrase is closest in meaning to *unanimous*?
   A. justified   C. divided
   B. in agreement   D. not accurate

Essay

16. In a short essay, write about some of the reasons Maya Ying Lin's plan won the competition for designs of a Vietnam Veterans Memorial, according to "Always to Remember." Be sure to be specific in your description of her memorial design.

17. "Always to Remember" presents biographical details about Maya Ying Lin. Write a brief essay in which you identify two of her experiences that may have influenced the design she submitted in the contest for a Vietnam Veterans Memorial.

18. **Thinking About the Big Question: How much information is enough?** "Always to Remember" is an essay about the Vietnam Veterans Memorial. It also includes photographs of the memorial, of Maya Lin, and of another memorial she designed. In an essay, explain whether the text and pictures together give you enough information to understand why so many people consider the Vietnam Veterans Memorial a moving tribute to the soldiers who lost their lives in Vietnam. Support your opinion with details from the essay.

"Always to Remember: The Vision of Maya Ying Lin" by Brent Ashabranner
Selection Test B

Critical Reading *Identify the letter of the choice that best completes the statement or answers the question.*

_____ 1. According to "Always to Remember," the idea for a Vietnam veterans memorial came from
A. two lawyers.
B. a senator.
C. the President.
D. a Vietnam vet.

_____ 2. According to "Always to Remember," what was the motivation for creating the memorial?
A. to honor those who opposed the war in Vietnam
B. to honor American military personnel who had been killed or listed as missing in Vietnam
C. to impress on everyone that the war had helped maintain freedom
D. to create a means for young architects to show their talent

_____ 3. According to "Always to Remember," which of the following was *not* an important design criterion for the Vietnam Veterans Memorial?
A. harmony with surroundings
B. ease of maintenance
C. specific dimensions
D. high artistic merit

_____ 4. According to "Always to Remember," why did the memorial have "to soothe passions, not stir them up"?
A. People enjoyed relaxing in the park where it would be located.
B. People had been bitterly divided by the war.
C. The contest planners wanted to discourage crime in the area.
D. The city's park planners had not included facilities for athletic events.

_____ 5. In "Always to Remember," what was *not* cited by the judges as a merit of the winning entry?
A. its air of quietness
B. its ability to blend with other monuments
C. its impressive vertical dimensions
D. its horizontal design

_____ 6. According to "Always to Remember," the greatest surprise about the winner, Maya Ying Lin, was her
A. education.
B. inexperience.
C. ethnicity.
D. gender.

_____ 7. Based on "Always to Remember," which statement is true of Maya Ying Lin's education?
A. Lin never formally studied architecture.
B. Lin read little as a child.
C. Lin had mediocre grades in high school.
D. Lin was unsure of what to major in.

_____ 8. In "Always to Remember," how did Maya Ying Lin benefit by visiting the proposed site?
A. The long train ride allowed time to read about other memorials in America and Europe.
B. She and her classmates were able to share ideas with one another.
C. She was inspired to envision a design that would capitalize on the site itself.
D. Seeing the other monuments in Washington, D.C., filled her with patriotic spirit.

_____ 9. Why did the creators of the design contest, discussed in "Always to Remember," specify that they did not want a statue of soldiers or of a dove?
A. These designs had been used in monuments for other wars.
B. They felt that these images did not capture the sacrifice of the soldiers.
C. They did not want to build a monument to those who supported or opposed the war.
D. They needed an easy-to-maintain monument.

_____ 10. Which aspect of Maya Ying Lin's past, discussed in "Always to Remember," may have influenced the student's interest in architecture?
A. Her father was a successful ceramicist and dean of fine arts at a university.
B. Growing up, she loved to read novels that discussed good and evil.
C. She was co-valedictorian at her high school graduation.
D. Her parents had emigrated from China during the 1940s.

_____ 11. Why did Professor Burr encourage his students to enter the design contest discussed in "Always to Remember"?
A. He needed a new idea for a class project.
B. He thought it would be a good experience for his students.
C. He knew one of his students would probably win.
D. He had strong feelings about the U.S. role in the Vietnam War.

_____ 12. What design element did Jan Scruggs insist on for the memorial, according to "Always to Remember"?
A. The memorial must be made of stone.
B. Every U.S. state must be represented.
C. The memorial must suggest peace.
D. It must list everyone killed or missing.

_____ 13. According to "Always to Remember," the entries for the Vietnam Veterans Memorial were displayed without the names of the designers. Why?
A. so that the judges would not be influenced by a familiar or an unfamiliar name
B. so that the designers would not be influenced by one another's entries
C. so that more people would feel comfortable entering the contest
D. so the display area would be less crowded

___ 14. Why does the author of "Always to Remember" discuss Maya Ying Lin's background?
   A. to show that she experienced hardships
   B. to appeal to Chinese American readers
   C. to show its influence on her design
   D. to show her disinterest in architecture

Vocabulary and Grammar

___ 15. Which of the following words or phrases is closest in meaning to *harmonious*?
   A. independent
   B. correctly stated
   C. greedy
   D. pleasingly combined

___ 16. An adverb cannot modify
   A. another adverb.
   B. a verb.
   C. a noun.
   D. an adjective.

___ 17. Which of the following phrases contains an adverb?
   A. very wealthy
   B. uncertain weather
   C. the blue jacket
   D. lovely day

___ 18. In which of the sentences is *eloquent* used correctly?
   A. We all fit into my parents' eloquent car.
   B. She responded to my eloquent appeal.
   C. His success was unexpectedly eloquent.
   D. He dined at the eloquent restaurant.

___ 19. Which of the following is closest in meaning to *criteria*?
   A. standards
   B. restaurant
   C. statues
   D. agenda

Essay

20. According to "Always to Remember," Maya Ying Lin had several life experiences that affected the nature of her design for the Vietnam Veterans Memorial. Write an essay in which you explain how three of these experiences made an impact on her finished work.

21. "Always to Remember" identifies several reasons that the judges selected Maya Ying Lin's design for the Vietnam Veterans Memorial. In a brief essay, discuss three aspects of Lin's design that greatly impressed the judges.

22. The author of "Always to Remember," Brent Ashabranner, mentions certain details of Maya Ying Lin's personality and life that appear to have little to do with the subject of the war memorial contest. In an essay, identify some of these extra details, and discuss why he may have included them.

23. **Thinking About the Big Question: How much information is enough?** "Always to Remember" is an essay about the Vietnam Veterans Memorial. It also includes photographs of the memorial, of Maya Lin, and of another memorial she designed. In an essay, explain whether the text and pictures together give you enough information to understand why the Vietnam Veterans Memorial is considered to be such a moving monument to the soldiers who lost their lives in Vietnam. In your essay, use details from "Always to Remember" to explain why the memorial is moving, or describe what additional information might help you better understand the memorial's impact.

Vocabulary Warm-up Word Lists

Study these words from I Know Why the Caged Bird Sings. *Then, complete the activities.*

Word List A

accurate [AK yuhr it] *adj.* correct in every way
My answer will be <u>accurate</u> if I understand all of the facts.

assured [uh SHOORD] *v.* made certain something would happen
Getting an *A* on the test <u>assured</u> Ben's place on the honor roll.

essence [ES uhns] *n.* the most basic, important quality of something
The <u>essence</u> of summer vacation is free time.

judgment [JUHJ muhnt] *n.* the ability to make a decision or form an opinion
The referee's <u>judgment</u> during games was not to be questioned.

numerous [NOO muh ruhs] *adj.* many
As early as October, I saw <u>numerous</u> trees with bare limbs.

romantic [roh MAN tik] *adj.* having to do with feelings of love
Would you rather see a <u>romantic</u> movie or an action film?

unexpected [un ek SPEK tid] *adj.* surprising
The <u>unexpected</u> result of all my work was a feeling of satisfaction.

wiry [WY ree] *adj.* thin but strong
The <u>wiry</u> wrestler easily pinned many larger opponents.

Word List B

absolute [AB suh loot] *adj.* complete and total
I could always tell when Mom's decision on something was <u>absolute</u>.

clarity [KLAR i tee] *n.* the quality of speaking, writing, or thinking in a clear way
My voice has great <u>clarity</u> onstage; the audience hears me easily.

enchantment [en CHANT muhnt] *n.* delight
Certain children's books bring <u>enchantment</u> to readers of all ages.

exotic [eg ZAHT ik] *adj.* unusual and interesting
In the restaurant, an <u>exotic</u> smell made my mouth water.

obsession [uhb SE shuhn] *n.* intense and abnormal interest
My little brother has an <u>obsession</u> with a baseball cap that he wears night and day.

provisions [pruh VIZH uhnz] *n.* food supplies
We always have fun shopping for <u>provisions</u> before a camping trip.

staples [STAY puhlz] *n.* basic foods that are used often
Many people consider milk, salt, and flour to be <u>staples</u>.

valid [VAL id] *adj.* based on strong reasons or facts
I thought her idea for a science fair project was a <u>valid</u> one.

from **I Know Why the Caged Bird Sings** by Maya Angelou
Vocabulary Warm-up Exercises

Exercise A *Fill in each blank in the paragraph below with an appropriate word from Word List A. Use each word only once.*

Should a first date be [1] _____? My answer, which might be

[2] _____ and viewed as strange, is no. I think the [3] _____

of a first date is getting to know another person. Your [4] _____ about

whether or not you like a person will be most error-free and [5] _____ if you

learn the facts about him or her. Suppose your date is [6] _____, a look that

you find attractive. However, you find out right away that this person spends hours each

day working out and worrying about being too thin! Yes, many people will say that finding

out more about a person has [7] _____ that they have not wasted their time

on a bad match. [8] _____ reports from many of my friends support

my ideas.

Exercise B *Write a complete sentence to answer each question. For each question, use a word from Word List B to replace each underlined word or group of words without changing its meaning.*

1. What are some <u>needed foods</u> that you might collect for the homeless?

   _____

2. How is an <u>unhealthy interest</u> with something like ice skating different from a hobby
   or pastime?

   _____

3. What job do you think would strongly require <u>clear thinking</u>?

   _____

4. Why do police check to see if people's statements about crimes are <u>based on fact</u>?

   _____

5. What <u>unusual</u> animal would you want for a pet?

   _____

6. Who should have <u>complete</u> control in a courtroom?

   _____

7. If you were alone on an island for a week, what <u>food supplies</u> would you take as
   treats?

   _____

8. What moment of <u>delight</u> do you most clearly remember from childhood?

   _____

from **I Know Why the Caged Bird Sings** by Maya Angelou
Reading Warm-up A

Read the following passage. Pay special attention to the underlined words. Then, read it again, and complete the activities. Use a separate sheet of paper for your written answers.

Phillip Blake was the <u>essence</u> of high school "cool." He drove a hot car, played <u>numerous</u> sports well, and was the student body president. Phillip, with his dark curly hair, was the object of many <u>romantic</u> ideas among the girls. However, the one he called "my girl" was not found at Patrick Henry High. Her name was Ruth Lewis, and she lived alone in a fancy house on Elm Street. She was seventy years old, and she was Phillip's best buddy.

Phillip's <u>unexpected</u> friendship with Miss Ruth, as he called her, began when he was thirteen. He was looking to earn money by doing yardwork. Back then, he was a <u>wiry</u> kid. He wasn't afraid of anything or anyone. His friends would never have approached the grand old lady of Elm Street. Phillip, on the other hand, just marched up the steps and knocked on her front door. Miss Ruth, who took pride in her good <u>judgment</u> about people, looked Phillip up and down, and then asked him inside.

The two strangers worked out the details of his duties and pay as her new gardener. They also discussed what was going on in their lives. Phillip talked about his first girlfriend and wanting to earn money so he could take her to the movies. Miss Ruth talked about her club activities and her hopes that her wealth had <u>assured</u> the college education of her grandchildren. A friendship was born.

Whenever the kids at school mentioned Miss Ruth around Phillip, he made sure that what they said was <u>accurate</u>. Since no one had ever bothered to get to know her, Phillip felt it was his duty to protect her from gossip. He showed by his words and actions how to be a true friend. He also proved that friends do not have to be at all alike.

1. Underline the words in the paragraph that might define the <u>essence</u> of high school "cool." Then, write a definition of *essence*.

2. Make a list of the <u>numerous</u> sports Phillip might have played.

3. Circle the words telling who had <u>romantic</u> ideas about Phillip. Then, explain the word *romantic*.

4. Underline the words telling when the <u>unexpected</u> friendship began. Then, explain why it is called *unexpected*.

5. Circle the words in the next sentence that hint at the meaning of <u>wiry</u>. Then, define *wiry*.

6. Underline the words that describe how Miss Ruth made her <u>judgment</u> about Phillip. Explain why she would be proud of having good *judgment*.

7. Circle the words naming what Miss Ruth hoped her wealth <u>assured</u>. Then, explain the word *assured*.

8. Underline the words naming what Phillip wished to be <u>accurate</u>. Explain why you like people to say only *accurate* things about you.

Name _____ Date _____

from **I Know Why the Caged Bird Sings** by Maya Angelou
Reading Warm-up B

Read the following passage. Pay special attention to the underlined words. Then, read it again, and complete the activities. Use a separate sheet of paper for your written answers.

In the late 1800s and early 1900s, the general store was the <u>absolute</u> center of small towns across North America. There was no question about it. More than just a place to shop for <u>provisions</u> and other supplies, the general store was the communication hub.

Most stores had a front porch or another outdoor meeting place. In cold weather, a pot-bellied stove inside was the place where gossip, sharing of <u>valid</u> news, and political discussions occurred. The talks would become so exciting that some stores hired a person who made sure people did not get too close to the stove and burn themselves!

Some general stores also served as the town post office. Later, stores might have been the place to find the only telephone or gas pump in town. Whatever people wanted or needed, from <u>staples</u> to clothing to toys, the general store tried to provide it.

For a family living several miles outside of town, a trip to the store was always a fun adventure. The <u>enchantment</u> of the store was different for each person. Children, of course, delighted in the huge selection of candies. Quite a few could be bought for just one penny! Adults liked admiring <u>exotic</u> new products such as fancy fabrics and canned foods from faraway places. However, they probably enjoyed seeing their old friends even more. Folks often gained <u>clarity</u> about current events by discussing them with one another.

Today, people have a growing <u>obsession</u> with the old-fashioned general store. Many towns have opened new shops designed to look like the stores of long ago. Uneven wooden floors, bins and barrels, and products from the turn of the century all are making a comeback. No doubt, people shopping in these stores hope to develop strong feelings of connection to others in their community. Then, the old general stores would truly come back to life.

1. Underline the sentence that hints at the meaning of <u>absolute</u>. Then, explain what *absolute* means.

2. Circle the word that hints at the meaning of <u>provisions</u>. List some *provisions* people might shop for weekly.

3. Circle a word in the sentence that could be the opposite of <u>valid</u> news. Compare the meaning of this word to *valid* news.

4. Underline the word in the sentence that gives a hint to the meaning of <u>staples</u>. Then, explain what *staples* means.

5. Circle words naming the <u>enchantment</u> of general stores for children. Describe another source of *enchantment* they might find there.

6. Underline the words naming <u>exotic</u> things. Describe something *exotic* you've seen in a grocery store.

7. Explain why discussions with others can lead to <u>clarity</u> of ideas.

8. Circle the words naming a modern <u>obsession</u>. Then, explain what *obsession* means.

from **I Know Why the Caged Bird Sings** by Maya Angelou
Writing About the Big Question

How much information is enough?

Big Question Vocabulary

accumulate	challenge	decision	development	discrimination
explanation	exploration	factor	global	inequality
quality	quantity	reveal	statistics	valuable

A. *Use a word from the list above to complete each sentence.*

1. What were the _____ for our team last year?

2. Let's _____ information on stocks for our investment club.

3. Is our information of high _____?

4. Lewis and Clark made a famous journey of _____.

B. *Follow the directions in responding to each of the items below.*

1. Write a two-sentence description of a relative whom you admire. Explain why you hold that person in high esteem. Use at least two list words in your description.

   _____

   _____

   _____

2. Rate the **quality** and **quantity** of the information about your relative.

   _____

   _____

C. *Complete the sentence below. Then, write a short paragraph in which you connect this answer to the Big Question.*

   The accumulation of knowledge is _____

   _____

   _____

   _____

   _____

Name _____   Date _____

from **I Know Why the Caged Bird Sings** by Maya Angelou
Reading: Make Connections Between Supporting Paragraphs and the Main Idea

Main ideas are the most important points in a literary work. Writers often organize essays so that main ideas are part of a clear structure. An introduction states the main idea, and then each paragraph supports or develops it. **Make connections between supporting paragraphs and the main idea.**

- Pause to note the main idea of paragraphs or sections.
- Write notes, or complete an organizer to track main ideas and key details.
- Review the main ideas and details in each section to see how they support the essay's main idea.

Read this passage from the selection by Maya Angelou.

Customers could find food staples, a good variety of colored thread, mash for hogs, corn for chickens, coal oil for lamps, light bulbs for the wealthy, shoestrings, hair dressing, balloons, and flower seeds. Anything not visible had only to be ordered.

The details about the items support the section's main idea: the store fills needs.

DIRECTIONS: *For each passage, list details that support the stated main idea.*

1. Over the years it became the lay center of activities in town. On Saturdays, barbers sat their customers in the shade on the porch of the Store, and troubadours on their ceaseless crawlings through the South leaned across its benches and sang their sad songs. . . .

   Main idea of whole section: The Store is at the center of a thriving community.

   Supporting details: _____

   _____

2. I don't think I ever saw Mrs. Flowers laugh, but she smiled often. A slow widening of her thin black lips to show even, small white teeth, then the slow effortless closing. When she chose to smile on me, I always wanted to thank her. The action was so graceful and inclusively benign.

   Main idea of whole section: The author enjoys Mrs. Flowers's kindness and attention.

   Supporting details: _____

   _____

3. Her voice slid in and curved down through and over the words. She was nearly singing. I wanted to look at the pages. Were they the same that I had read? Or were these notes, music, lined on the pages, as in a hymn book? Her sounds began cascading gently.

   Main idea of whole section: Mrs. Flowers had a beautiful reading voice.

   Supporting details: _____

   _____

Name _____   Date _____

from **I Know Why the Caged Bird Sings** by Maya Angelou
Literary Analysis: Biography and Autobiography

- A **biographical essay** is a short work in which a writer tells about an important event in the life of another person.
- An **autobiographical essay** is also a true account, but it is written by the person who experienced the event himself or herself. It includes the writer's thoughts and feelings about an event.

Both types of writing look at the influence of personal experiences, such as schooling, on the later personalities and accomplishments of a person.

In her autobiographical essay, Maya Angelou describes many of her thoughts and feelings. What does the following passage reveal about the author's feeling toward her grandmother?

> Her crisp meat pies and cool lemonade, when joined to her miraculous ability to be in two places at the same time, assured her business success.

Angelou admires her grandmother's cooking, energy, and talent as a businesswoman.

DIRECTIONS: *Write two thoughts or feelings expressed by the author in each of the following passages from* I Know Why the Caged Bird Sings.

1. Alone and empty in the mornings, it looked like an unopened present from a stranger. Opening the front doors was pulling the ribbon off the unexpected gift. . . . Whenever I walked into the Store in the afternoon, I sensed that it was tired. I alone could hear the slow pulse of its job half done.

   Thoughts or feelings:

   _____

   _____

   _____

2. She pronounced my name so nicely. Or more correctly, she spoke each word with such clarity that I was certain a foreigner who didn't understand English could have understood her.

   Thoughts or feelings:

   _____

   _____

   _____

3. I was liked, and what a difference it made. I was respected not as Mrs. Henderson's grandchild or Bailey's sister but for just being Marguerite Johnson.

   Thoughts or feelings:

   _____

   _____

   _____

from **I Know Why the Caged Bird Sings** by Maya Angelou
Vocabulary Builder

Word List

benign   ceaseless   enchantment   fiscal   infuse   intolerant   valid

A. DIRECTIONS: *Revise each sentence so that the underlined vocabulary word is used logically. Be sure to keep the vocabulary word in your version.*

1. Our teacher asked us to write a <u>fiscal</u> report describing the poet's use of rhyme.

   _____

   _____

2. When the children roller-bladed over her garden, Jean responded with a <u>benign</u> look.

   _____

   _____

3. The plot was serious, so the director asked the actors to <u>infuse</u> their lines with humor.

   _____

   _____

4. The easygoing babysitter was <u>intolerant</u> of the children's loud games.

   _____

   _____

5. People used earplugs to block the <u>ceaseless</u> peace and quiet.

   _____

6. His driver's license was <u>valid</u>, so the man got a ticket.

   _____

7. The best way to get good grades is through <u>enchantment</u>.

   _____

B. WORD STUDY The Latin root *-val-* means "strong." Complete the following sentences using one of these words containing the root *-val-*: *value, valor, valedictorian.*

1. Sometimes the cheapest item is not the best _____.

2. The _____ gave a short but powerful speech at graduation.

3. Knights of old demonstrated their _____ in jousting matches.

Name _____ Date _____

from I Know Why the Caged Bird Sings by Maya Angelou
Enrichment: Mentoring

In today's language, Mrs. Bertha Flowers played the role of mentor to Marguerite. A mentor is someone who counsels and guides another person (usually a younger person) and takes an interest in the person's development. The person under the guidance of a mentor is called a protégé.

A. DIRECTIONS: *What qualities does a person need to be an effective mentor? How do these qualities help a protégé? Think of someone besides Mrs. Flowers who would be a strong mentor. Complete the chart by filling in columns for your ideal mentor. The columns for Mrs. Flowers are filled in as examples for you.*

	Qualities of Mentor	Benefits to Protégé
Mrs. Bertha Flowers	1. Speaks clearly and distinctly	1. Provides example of speaking properly and making oneself understood
	2. Well mannered and graceful	2. Helps young girl learn poise
My Ideal Mentor	1.	1.
	2.	2.

B. DIRECTIONS: *Suppose you decide to become a mentor to a younger person. Tell of one quality or skill you can teach your protégé.*

_____

_____

_____

_____

_____

_____

_____

_____

from **I Know Why the Caged Bird Sings** by Maya Angelou
"Always to Remember: The Vision of Maya Ying Lin" by Brent Ashabranner
Integrated Language Skills: Grammar

Adverbs

An **adverb** modifies, or describes, a verb, an adjective, or another adverb.

Adverbs modifying verbs:

He carefully studied the map.   She walked quietly to her seat.

Adverbs modifying adjectives:

My dog has a very loud bark.   Her hair is extremely long.

Adverbs modifying other adverbs:

She won the race so easily.   Her car accelerates more quickly than mine.

Adverbs, which make the information in a sentence more vivid, usually answer questions such as *when? where? in what way?* and *to what extent?* Note that most words ending in *-ly* are usually adverbs: for example, *carefully* and *finally*, but not *friendly*. Note also that common words *not* ending in *-ly* are adverbs: *rather, always, here, then, only, once.*

A. PRACTICE: *Underline the adverb or adverbs in each sentence, and draw an arrow from every adverb to the word it modifies.*

1. During the Civil War, Lincoln considered his political options very cautiously.

2. He viewed restoration of the Union as an exceedingly important issue.

3. That goal clearly required a victory in the war itself.

4. To that end, he worked quite tirelessly on both the political and military fronts.

5. Border states generally had remained loyal to the Union.

6. Lincoln eventually made his decision about slavery.

B. Writing Application: *Make each sentence more vivid by adding an adverb that answers the question at the end of the sentence. Write each adverb on the blank line.*

1. Rhea is having a party _____. (*when?*)

2. Many people are _____ anxious about getting an invitation. (*to what extent?*)

3. Rhea _____ plans on inviting everyone. (*in what manner?*)

from **I Know Why the Caged Bird Sings** by Maya Angelou
"Always to Remember: The Vision of Maya Ying Lin" by Brent Ashabranner
Integrated Language Skills: Support for Writing
a Reflective Essay

Think about a piece of artwork or music that you particularly admire. What makes it linger in your mind? What new ideas does it inspire? Use the chart to organize your thoughts for your composition. First, list some memorable details about the piece of music or the artwork. For each detail, describe briefly why it made an impression on you or what you learned from it.

Memorable Detail From an Artwork or Music	What I Learned/Why It Impressed Me

Now, use your notes to generate main ideas, which you will support with details for your draft.

from **I Know Why the Caged Bird Sings** by Maya Angelou
"Always to Remember: The Vision of Maya Ying Lin" by Brent Ashabranner
Integrated Language Skills: Support for Extend Your Learning

Research and Technology: *from* **I Know Why the Caged Bird Sings**

To prepare for your group's proposal for a multimedia presentation about the Great Depression, gather some basic information about that period. You might assign each group member to a particular source to search for ways to represent life during the Great Depression. Use the following lines to record your findings.

1. When did the Great Depression occur?

   _____

2. How did the Great Depression affect the lives of ordinary Americans?

   _____

   _____

   _____

3. What were some of the causes of the Great Depression?

   _____

   _____

   _____

Research and Technology: "Always to Remember: The Vision of Maya Ying Lin"

To prepare for your group's proposal for a multimedia presentation about the U.S. involvement in Vietnam, gather some basic information about that period. You might assign each group member to a particular source to search for ways to represent the impact of the war on people's attitudes at the time. Use the following lines to record your findings.

1. When did America's involvement in the Vietnam War occur?

   _____

2. What were some objections to American involvement?

   _____

   _____

   _____

3. What effects did the Vietnam War have on people's lives?

   _____

   _____

   _____

Name _____   Date _____

from I Know Why the Caged Bird Sings by Maya Angelou
Open-Book Test

Short Answer *Write your responses to the questions in this section on the lines provided.*

1. A biographical essay is a short work in which a writer tells about an important event in the life of another person. An autobiographical essay is a true account written by the person who experienced the event. Which kind of essay is the excerpt from *I Know Why the Caged Bird Sings*? How do you know?

   _____

   _____

2. In *I Know Why the Caged Bird Sings*, Maya Angelou refers to "troubadours on their ceaseless crawlings through the South." What does she mean by "ceaseless crawlings"? Base your answer on the meaning of *ceaseless*.

   _____

   _____

3. In *I Know Why the Caged Bird Sings*, Maya Angelou names the items that were sold in the Store. Among them were "light bulbs for the wealthy." What do these words tell you about the people who shopped at the Store?

   _____

   _____

4. In *I Know Why the Caged Bird Sings*, Angelou describes the Store as looking "like an unopened present from a stranger." What main idea about the Store does this detail support?

   _____

   _____

5. In *I Know Why the Caged Bird Sings*, Maya Angelou says that Mrs. Flowers "threw me my first lifeline." What does she mean by this?

   _____

   _____

6. In *I Know Why the Caged Bird Sings*, Mrs. Flowers says, "Words mean more than what is set down on paper." What does she mean by this?

   _____

   _____

7. In *I Know Why the Caged Bird Sings*, Mrs. Flowers tells Maya Angelou to be "understanding of illiteracy." What does she mean by this?

   _____

   _____

8. In *I Know Why the Caged Bird Sings*, Maya Angelou describes Mrs. Flowers's reading voice. Those descriptions support a main idea of the excerpt. What is that idea?

_____

_____

9. In the excerpt from *I Know Why the Caged Bird Sings,* Maya Angelou mentions her grandmother; her brother, Bailey; and Mrs. Flowers. Although she does not say much here about her grandmother and her brother, it is possible to figure out how she feels about them. There is a great deal of evidence for how she feels about Mrs. Flowers. Complete this chart by writing a word that describes Angelou's feelings for each of these people. Then, on the line below, describe what Angelou's feelings for the other people in her life tell you about Angelou herself.

Person	Feeling
Grandmother	
Bailey	
Mrs. Flowers	

_____

_____

10. In this excerpt from *I Know Why the Caged Bird Sings*, Maya Angelou learns a lot from Mrs. Flowers. What is the most important lesson she learns?

_____

_____

Essay

Write an extended response to the question of your choice or to the question or questions your teacher assigns you.

11. Maya Angelou has many memories of her grandmother's store. In an essay, describe the Store. Include details about the products sold, the Store's importance to the community, and Angelou's feelings about the Store.

12. The excerpt from *I Know Why the Caged Bird Sings* is divided into two sections. In an essay, write a brief summary of each part. Then, give each part of the essay a title that reflects its main idea.

13. In *I Know Why the Caged Bird Sings*, Mrs. Flowers has a significant influence on Maya Angelou. In an essay, describe Angelou's thoughts and feelings during her visit with Mrs. Flowers. Cite two details from the essay to support your points. Then, explain what you think Angelou learned from the older woman.

14. **Thinking About the Big Question: How much information is enough?** After reading the excerpt from *I Know Why the Caged Bird Sings*, did you feel that you had enough information about Maya Angelou to understand why she went on to become a successful poet? In an essay, explain your answer. If you felt you had enough information, cite details from the essay to support your response. If you felt you did not have enough information, explain what additional information would help you understand Angelou more fully.

Oral Response

15. Go back to question 5, 7, or 8 or to the question your teacher assigns you. Take a few minutes to expand your answer and prepare an oral response. Find additional details in the excerpt from *I Know Why the Caged Bird Sings* that support your points. If necessary, make notes to guide your oral response.

Name _____ Date _____

from I Know Why the Caged Bird Sings by Maya Angelou
Selection Test A

Critical Reading *Identify the letter of the choice that best answers the question.*

____ 1. Who is the *I* in the autobiography titled *I Know Why the Caged Bird Sings*?
A. Momma
B. Mrs. Flowers
C. Bailey
D. Maya Angelou

____ 2. Which word or phrase does *not* apply to Momma in *I Know Why the Caged Bird Sings*?
A. a good businesswoman
B. a good cook
C. impatient
D. energetic

____ 3. What food does the author of *I Know Why the Caged Bird Sings* especially like?
A. pineapples
B. sugar cookies
C. licorice candy
D. meat pies

____ 4. How does the author of *I Know Why the Caged Bird Sings* feel about working in the Store?
A. She would rather have been reading.
B. She finds it enjoyable.
C. She would rather have been cooking.
D. She finds it dull.

____ 5. In *I Know Why the Caged Bird Sings*, who is Bailey?
A. the author's brother
B. the author's dog
C. Momma's brother
D. Mrs. Flowers's son

____ 6. How does the author of *I Know Why the Caged Bird Sings* describe Mrs. Flowers?
A. the richest white woman in town
B. proud and self-centered
C. the aristocrat of Black Stamps
D. an avid gardener

_____ 7. What problem does Mrs. Flowers bring up with the author of *I Know Why the Caged Bird Sings*?
   A. The author cheats customers in the store.
   B. Teachers say the author does not speak.
   C. The author is not doing well in school.
   D. Momma is thinking of moving the Store.

_____ 8. In *I Know Why the Caged Bird Sings*, what main idea is supported by the paragraphs about Mrs. Flowers's reading voice?
   A. Mrs. Flowers reads quickly.
   B. Mrs. Flowers reads without expression.
   C. Mrs. Flowers's voice is musical.
   D. Mrs. Flowers reads slowly.

_____ 9. Of the following statements, which is an example of Mrs. Flowers's "lessons in living" in *I Know Why the Caged Bird Sings*?
   A. Appreciate wisdom gained over years of living.
   B. Keep a house clean and ready for visitors.
   C. Give generously to good causes.
   D. Volunteer to help schoolchildren.

_____ 10. Which character in *I Know Why the Caged Bird Sings* is the author describing in the following sentence?
   Her voice slid in and curved down through and over the words.
   A. Momma
   B. a troubadour
   C. Marguerite
   D. Mrs. Flowers

_____ 11. What does the author of *I Know Why the Caged Bird Sings* learn from Mrs. Flowers?
   A. She learns to have confidence in herself.
   B. She learns to make tea cookies.
   C. She learns to read.
   D. She learns how to start a business.

Vocabulary and Grammar

____ **12.** Which word best completes the following sentence?

The words of Mrs. Flowers _____ the author with hope.

   A. fiscal

   B. benign

   C. infuse

   D. intolerant

____ **13.** Which word in the following sentence is an adverb?

The small girl jumped quickly onto the swing.

   A. small

   B. girl

   C. jumped

   D. quickly

____ **14.** Which word or phrase is closest in meaning to *intolerant*?

   A. indecisive

   B. not willing to accept

   C. not able to accomplish

   D. flexible

____ **15.** Which of the sentences contains an adverb?

   A. Tom went to football practice.

   B. The team ran steadily for half an hour.

   C. Tom found the practices challenging.

   D. He hoped the team would win.

Essay

16. Write a brief essay in which you explain why the author admires Mrs. Flowers. Consider thoughts the author has about Mrs. Flowers both before and during her visit to the woman's home. What things does the author observe? What, in particular, does the author admire? Be sure to use specific examples in your answer.

17. Maya Angelou has many memories of her grandmother's store. In an essay, describe the Store. Include details about products the store offered, how the Store was important to the town, and how the author felt about the Store.

18. **Thinking About the Big Question: How much information is enough?** After reading the excerpt from *I Know Why the Caged Bird Sings,* did you feel that you had enough information about Maya Angelou to understand why she became a successful poet? Explain your answer in a brief essay supported by details from the essay.

Name _____ Date _____

from **I Know Why the Caged Bird Sings** by Maya Angelou
Selection Test B

Critical Reading *Identify the letter of the choice that best completes the statement or answers the question.*

_____ 1. In *I Know Why the Caged Bird Sings*, what work did Momma do before she built the Store?
A. She managed the barber shop.
B. She baked for the town restaurant.
C. She sold lunches to local workmen.
D. She was a chef.

_____ 2. What can you conclude from the following list of items found at the Store in *I Know Why the Caged Bird Sings*?
. . . mash for hogs, corn for chickens, coal oil for lamps, light bulbs for the wealthy . . .
A. Supplies could be costly.
B. Hogs preferred a certain brand of food.
C. Not everyone had electricity.
D. Most people shopped only once a month.

_____ 3. Why does the author of *I Know Why the Caged Bird Sings* enjoy estimating the weight of a sack of flour before weighing it?
A. The customers are amazed at her ability.
B. She avoids using messy equipment.
C. She likes the texture of the grain.
D. Her grandmother is impressed.

_____ 4. What is "the fine" when the author of *I Know Why the Caged Bird Sings* estimates weights inaccurately?
A. a cut in her salary
B. washing the dinner dishes
C. no chocolate drops
D. a quarter

_____ 5. What feeling for her grandmother does the author of *I Know Why the Caged Bird Sings* convey in her descriptions?
A. impatience
B. respect
C. dislike
D. protectiveness

_____ 6. What main idea about the Store does this quotation from *I Know Why the Caged Bird Sings* support?
. . . it looked like an unopened present from a stranger.
A. The author's family enjoyed holidays.
B. The Store welcomed travelers.
C. The author found the Store exciting.
D. The Store was exceptionally orderly.

____ 7. What main idea of *I Know Why the Caged Bird Sings* is supported by the following quotation?

> I wanted to gobble up the room entire and take it to Bailey, who would help me analyze and enjoy it.

A. The author brags about her adventures.
B. The author cannot think for herself.
C. The author is jealous of Bailey.
D. The author is close to Bailey.

____ 8. Why does Mrs. Flowers tell Maya Angelou to be "understanding of illiteracy"?
A. Mrs. Flowers is illiterate.
B. The author has trouble reading.
C. Some people who cannot read are smart.
D. She is teaching the author new words.

____ 9. Why does Mrs. Flowers encourage the author of *I Know Why the Caged Bird Sings* to listen to "mother wit"?
A. Mrs. Flowers thinks that wisdom can be passed down through generations.
B. Mrs. Flowers thinks that a sense of humor is important in life.
C. Mrs. Flowers thinks the author spends too much time alone reading.
D. Mrs. Flowers thinks the author should be more obedient at home.

____ 10. In *I Know Why the Caged Bird Sings*, how does the author react when Mrs. Flowers reads a passage from *A Tale of Two Cities*?
A. She barely recognizes the familiar lines.
B. Mrs. Flowers's voice frightens her.
C. She asks Mrs. Flowers to read more.
D. She knows she will become a writer.

____ 11. In *I Know Why the Caged Bird Sings*, explain Mrs. Flowers's statement: "Words mean more than what is set down on paper."
A. A word cannot have an exact meaning.
B. Speech brings additional life to words.
C. One cannot read without a dictionary.
D. There are many languages in the world.

____ 12. Why does Mrs. Flowers give the author of *I Know Why the Caged Bird Sings* a book of poems?
A. Mrs. Flowers had already read the book
B. Mrs. Flowers expects the author to recite a poem on her next visit.
C. Mrs. Flowers suggests that the author write a poem.
D. Mrs. Flowers wants the author to read aloud to her grandmother.

____ 13. Which detail about Mrs. Flowers seems most important to the author of *I Know Why the Caged Bird Sings*?
A. her calm and gentle nature
B. her fine dresses and hats
C. her kindness and encouragement
D. her loyalty to the author's grandmother

_____ 14. How does the author of *I Know Why the Caged Bird Sings* feel after her visit with Mrs. Flowers?
A. liked
B. embarrassed
C. uneducated
D. hungry

_____ 15. What does Maya Angelou mean when she says that Mrs. Flowers "threw me my first lifeline"?
A. Mrs. Flowers gave her a reason to live.
B. Mrs. Flowers helped her learn to swim.
C. Mrs. Flowers told her fortune.
D. Mrs. Flowers became a close friend.

Vocabulary and Grammar

_____ 16. Which word or phrase is closest in meaning to *infuse*?
A. put into   B. reject   C. light   D. ask

_____ 17. An adverb can modify a
A. noun.   B. verb.   C. preposition.   D. pronoun.

_____ 18. Which word in the following sentence is an adverb?
Our car swerved dangerously close to the cliff on the narrow road.
A. swerved   B. dangerously   C. cliff   D. narrow

_____ 19. Which word is closest in meaning to *fiscal*?
A. rational   B. mobile   C. financial   D. miraculous

Essay

20. You have read two excerpts from *I Know Why the Caged Bird Sings*. The first excerpt is the author's memories of her family's store. The second excerpt is her memory of an experience with one person. In a brief essay, summarize each excerpt. Be sure to include examples in your summaries. Then, propose a title for each excerpt.

21. In *I Know Why the Caged Bird Sings*, the Store plays such an important part in the life of the town that the author says it is at the center of activities. In a brief essay, describe ways in which the Store contributes to the well-being of the townspeople. Use examples from the selection to support your answer.

22. In *I Know Why the Caged Bird Sings*, Mrs. Flowers has a significant effect on the author. Write an essay in which you describe the author's thoughts and feelings during her visit with Mrs. Flowers. Then, explain what you think the author learns from the older woman.

23. **Thinking About the Big Question: How much information is enough?** After reading the excerpt from *I Know Why the Caged Bird Sings*, did you feel that you had enough information about Maya Angelou to understand why she went on to become a successful poet? In an essay, explain your answer. If you felt you had enough information, cite details from the essay to support your response. If you felt you did not have enough information, explain what additional information would help you understand Angelou more fully.

"**Forest Fire**" by Anaïs Nin
"**Why Leaves Turn Color in the Fall**" by Diane Ackerman
"**The Season's Curmudgeon Sees the Light**" by Mary C. Curtis
Vocabulary Warm-up Word Lists

Study these words from the selections. Then, complete the activities.

Word List A

alarmingly [uh LAHRM ing lee] *adv.* frighteningly
   The water in the dam rose <u>alarmingly</u> close to the top.

humid [HYOO mid] *adj.* (of weather) feeling warm and wet
   A hot, <u>humid</u> day makes many people uncomfortable.

maneuver [muh NOO ver] *n.* a skillful movement
   The cab driver performed a tight <u>maneuver</u> in heavy traffic.

mortar [MAWR ter] *n.* a mixture that holds bricks or stones together
   The damp leaves filled the sidewalk cracks like <u>mortar</u>.

reminder [ri MYND er] *n.* something that makes you remember
   The brisk wind is a <u>reminder</u> that winter is on its way.

sizzling [SIZ ling] *adj.* causing strong feelings or excitement
   The <u>sizzling</u> leaf colors made the trees appear to be on fire.

unruly [un ROO lee] *adj.* messy or hard to control
   The woman depended on her hairdresser to take care of her <u>unruly</u> hair

venture [VEN chuhr] *v.* to go somewhere when it could be risky
   If you <u>venture</u> out into the snow, please stop at the store.

Word List B

abundance [uh BUN duhns] *n.* a large amount
   There is an <u>abundance</u> of reading material in the doctor's office.

compelled [kuhm PELD] *adj.* forced to do something
   Out of curiosity, I felt <u>compelled</u> to stare at the accident scene.

dizzyingly [DI zee ing lee] *adv.* makes one feel off balance
   The roller coaster ride was <u>dizzyingly</u> exciting.

foliage [FOH lee ij] *n.* plant leaves
   <u>Foliage</u> from tall maples shaded the house from May to October.

fragile [FRAJ il] *adj.* easy to break or damage
   The <u>fragile</u> glassware got broken in shipment.

pungent [PUHN juhnt] *adj.* strong-smelling or strong-tasting
   The air was <u>pungent</u> with the smell of barbecue sauce.

spectacular [spek TAK yuh luhr] *adj.* amazing or impressive
   We attended a <u>spectacular</u> display of fireworks on July Fourth.

splotches [SPLAHCH ez] *n.* spots or stains with random shapes
   The car seat was covered with <u>splotches</u> of spilled ketchup.

"**Forest Fire**" by Anaïs Nin
"**Why Leaves Turn Color in the Fall**" by Diane Ackerman
"**The Season's Curmudgeon Sees the Light**" by Mary C. Curtis
Vocabulary Warm-up Exercises

Exercise A *Fill in each blank in the paragraph below with an appropriate word from Word List A. Use each word only once.*

The [1] _____ colors of swimsuits and umbrellas in the shop windows

were a [2] _____ that summer was just around the corner. In fact, the

hot, [3] _____ weather we'd been experiencing made summer seem too

[4] _____ close for my taste. On those long, hot days to come, I knew I

wouldn't [5] _____ outdoors if I could help it. And then, I would attempt

my famous [6] _____ from house to car to mall without losing the

air conditioning. I disliked sweating and how the damp air turned my hair into an

[7] _____ mess. I preferred the cool bricks and [8] _____

of the library's interior walls. That's when I first thought I should have lived my life in

the Arctic.

Exercise B *Answer each question with a complete explanation.*

1. In the Northeast, during what seasons would you expect to find an <u>abundance</u> of green <u>foliage</u> on the trees?

   _____

2. Why might you feel <u>compelled</u> to find out what the <u>pungent</u> odor of cooking is?

   _____

3. How would you wrap something <u>fragile</u> when you're moving?

   _____

4. What might a painting with <u>spectacular</u> <u>splotches</u> of color look like?

   _____

5. What kind of sport might be <u>dizzyingly</u> delightful?

   _____

Name _____ Date _____

"**Forest Fire**" by Anaïs Nin
"**Why Leaves Turn Color in the Fall**" by Diane Ackerman
"**The Season's Curmudgeon Sees the Light**" by Mary C. Curtis
Reading Warm-up A

Read the following passage. Pay special attention to the underlined words. Then, read it again, and complete the activities. Use a separate sheet of paper for your written answers.

The large house and the sprawling land around it were a <u>reminder</u> of what the neighborhood was like years ago. Developers were building modern homes made of bricks and <u>mortar</u>. Now, the beautiful old house was about to fall, as were its <u>unruly</u> plantings: elm trees, oak trees, and rose bushes, standing proudly in the garden in no order whatsoever.

One <u>humid</u> afternoon during our spring vacation, Jane and I decided to <u>venture</u> out into the neighborhood, despite the risk of thunderstorms. It would be our last look at the old mansion.

We recalled the <u>sizzling</u> colors of the trees in fall and the carpet of fallen red and yellow leaves. We also mourned the loss of the spring and summer flowers that cheered us with their bright red, pink, and white petals.

The next day, under clear skies, Jane and I decided to go watch the demolition. We figured that first the trees would go and then the house, but we were wrong. A giant wrecking ball had already begun to eat away at the house. Some of the workers were standing <u>alarmingly</u> close to it. Jane wanted to rush up and warn them. I stopped her, insisting they knew enough to stand out of harm's way.

Following one expert <u>maneuver</u> after another, what had probably taken months to build was gone in a few hours. After its last movement, the wrecking ball came to rest. A huge bulldozer hurled itself through the gate to clean up.

It took longer than we had expected to clear the land. Too late, Jane thought of asking for a log as a souvenir. We learned later that builders would be putting up a strip mall on the land. Now, whenever I pass those stores, I still picture the old towering house, the even taller trees, and a hundred years of history.

1. Underline the words that give you a clue that <u>reminder</u> has to do with memory. Then, write a sentence for *reminder*.

2. Circle the word that gives you a clue to the meaning of <u>mortar</u>. Then, use *mortar* in a sentence.

3. Circle the words that give a clue to the meaning of <u>unruly</u>. Use *unruly* in a sentence.

4. Underline the word in the paragraph that gives a clue to the meaning of <u>humid</u>. Write your own sentence for *humid*.

5. Circle the word in the next sentence that gives a clue to the meaning of <u>venture</u>. Use *venture* in a sentence.

6. Give a synonym for <u>sizzling</u>. Then, use *sizzling* in a sentence.

7. Circle the word in the next sentence that explains <u>alarmingly</u>. Then, write a sentence using *alarmingly*.

8. Underline the word in the paragraph that is a synonym for <u>maneuver</u>. Then, use *maneuver* in a sentence.

Unit 3 Resources: Types of Nonfiction

Name _____ Date _____

"Forest Fire" by Anaïs Nin
"Why Leaves Turn Color in the Fall" by Diane Ackerman
"The Season's Curmudgeon Sees the Light" by Mary C. Curtis
Reading Warm-up B

Read the following passage. Pay special attention to the underlined words. Then, read it again, and complete the activities. Use a separate sheet of paper for your written answers.

Philadelphia: November 22, 1963. We heard the news while we were playing touch football at gym. It was odd, because the game was a Kennedy family favorite. My first thought was that now, with John dead, the family needed a new player.

School officials let us out early. Although some of autumn's colorful <u>foliage</u> was still hanging on the trees, the landscape seemed as dreary as the cloudy sky. <u>Splotches</u> of fall colors suddenly became bloodstains in my eyes. A brown leaf fell from a tree in front of the school, a reminder of how <u>fragile</u> life is, as if we needed one.

The damp air was <u>pungent</u> with the smell of burning leaves, strange because I thought the city had outlawed burning. What did that matter now, such a small offense compared to the one our nation had seen that afternoon.

I was strangely <u>compelled</u> to walk to the bus instead of taking the subway as usual. It was as if something were pulling me there. As I reached the intersection where Old York Road split off from Broad Street, I was suddenly struck with a sight no less than <u>spectacular</u>. It was a row of birch trees that still seemed to be holding on to all their leafy <u>abundance</u>, in sharp contrast to the gray sky.

The <u>dizzyingly</u> colorful display was definitely a sign that nature did not echo human emotions. My head almost spinning from gazing at the patterns of golden leaves against black-and-white trunks, I grasped the tree's message. Don't despair.

By the time I got back to school, rain and wind had stripped the trees of all but their last few leaves, which had become a golden a soggy carpet on the grass. Several weeks later, I painted those trees from memory. I titled the picture "The Assassination of John F. Kennedy: A Memorial."

1. Underline the words that tell where the <u>foliage</u> was. Then, use *foliage* in a sentence.

2. Circle the word that describes <u>splotches</u>. Then, use *splotches* in a sentence.

3. Underline the words that give an example of something <u>fragile</u>. Then, write a sentence for *fragile*.

4. Underline the words that tell what was <u>pungent</u>. Then, use *pungent* in a sentence.

5. Underline the sentence that explains <u>compelled</u>. Then, describe something you have felt *compelled* to do.

6. Circle the words that provide a clue to <u>spectacular</u>. Then, use *spectacular* in a sentence.

7. Circle the words that help you figure out the meaning of <u>abundance</u>. Use *abundance* in a sentence of your own.

8. Underline the words that explain <u>dizzyingly</u>. Then, use *dizzyingly* in your own sentence.

"Forest Fire" by Anaïs Nin
"Why Leaves Turn Color in the Fall" by Diane Ackerman
"The Season's Curmudgeon Sees the Light" by Mary C. Curtis
Writing About the Big Question

How much information is enough?

Big Question Vocabulary

accumulate	challenge	decision	development	discrimination
explanation	exploration	factor	global	inequality
quality	quantity	reveal	statistics	valuable

A. *Use a word from the list above to complete each sentence.*

1. During the fall, leaves _____ their underlying colors.

2. One _____ in the forest fire was dry conditions.

3. What is your _____ for preferring summer to spring?

4. Through _____ you can discover a lot about nature.

B. *Follow the directions in responding to each of the items below.*

1. Write a two-sentence description of your favorite season. Use at least two list words in your sentences.

   _____

   _____

2. Which season do you like least? Use at least two list words in your explanation.

   _____

   _____

C. *These essays highlight different ways of appreciating nature. Complete the sentence below. Then, write a short paragraph in which you connect this sentence to the Big Question.*

The part of nature that I value the most is _____ because _____

   _____

   _____

   _____

"Forest Fire" by Anaïs Nin
"Why Leaves Turn Color in the Fall" by Diane Ackerman
"The Season's Curmudgeon Sees the Light" by Mary C. Curtis
Literary Analysis: Comparing Types of Organization

Types of Organization

To present information in the most useful way possible, writers can choose among several **types of organization.** Here are three of the most common organizational plans.

- **Chronological order** relates events in the order in which they occurred.
- **Cause-and-effect order** examines the relationship between an event and its result or results.
- **Comparison and contrast** shows similarities and differences.

DIRECTIONS: *Answer the following questions about the organization of the essays.*

1. List six of the main events in "Forest Fire" in the order that they occur.

   Event 1 _____   Event 4 _____

   Event 2 _____   Event 5 _____

   Event 3 _____   Event 6 _____

2. Why is chronological order the best type of organization for "Forest Fire"?

   _____

   _____

3. Based on "Why Leaves Turn Color in the Fall," explain the causes and effects that make leaves colorful in the fall.

   _____

   _____

   _____

   _____

4. Why is cause-and-effect order the best type of organization for "Why Leaves Turn Color in the Fall"?

   _____

   _____

5. How do the author's feelings change in "The Season's Curmudgeon Sees the Light"?

   _____

   _____

6. Why is comparison and contrast the best type of organization for "The Season's Curmudgeon Sees the Light"?

   _____

   _____

Name _____ Date _____

"**Forest Fire**" by Anaïs Nin
"**Why Leaves Turn Color in the Fall**" by Diane Ackerman
"**The Season's Curmudgeon Sees the Light**" by Mary C. Curtis
Vocabulary Builder

A. DIRECTIONS: *Revise each sentence so that it uses the underlined vocabulary word logically. Be sure to keep the vocabulary word in your revision.*

1. The principal is <u>consoling</u> the student by disciplining him.

   _____

   _____

2. The children are <u>predisposed</u> to illness; they never get sick.

   _____

   _____

3. I call Lillian <u>capricious</u> because she does not like changing anything.

   _____

   _____

4. The <u>evacuees</u> left the movie theater laughing and discussing the funny movie.

   _____

   _____

5. The stage set was <u>macabre</u> and cheerful.

   _____

   _____

6. Scott has a <u>tenacious</u> personality, so he readily compromises.

   _____

   _____

B. DIRECTIONS: *Circle the letter of the word that is most nearly* opposite *in meaning to the word in CAPITAL LETTERS.*

1. CONSOLING
   A. scheming
   B. cheering
   C. blending
   D. agitating

2. PREDISPOSED
   A. able
   B. unwilling
   C. ready
   D. upgraded

3. TENACIOUS
   A. relaxed
   B. sturdy
   C. pressure
   D. stretched

4. CAPRICIOUS
   A. inconstant
   B. lighthearted
   C. steadfast
   D. unrealistic

Name _____ Date _____

"**Forest Fire**" by Anaïs Nin
"**Why Leaves Turn Color in the Fall**" by Diane Ackerman
"**The Season's Curmudgeon Sees the Light**" by Mary C. Curtis

Support for Writing to Compare Essay Organization

Before you write your essay about the organization of two of the essays, use the graphic organizer below to list ideas about all three essays.

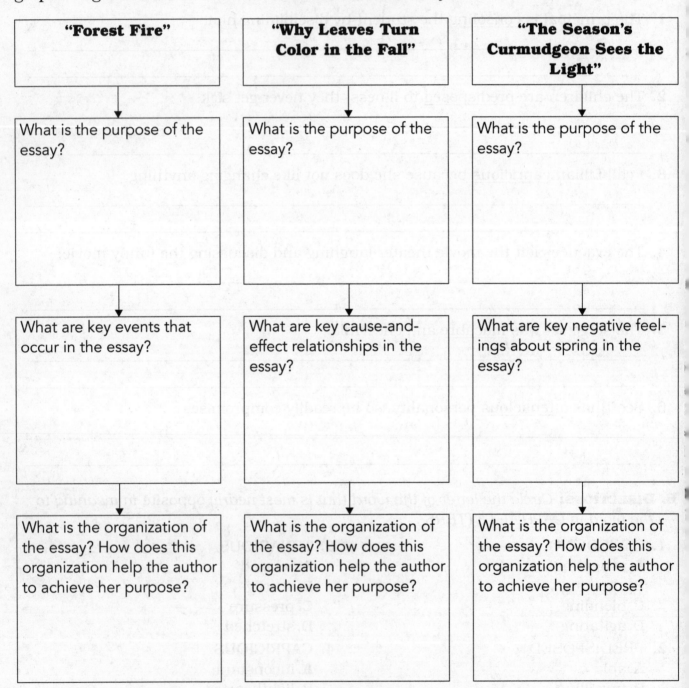

"Forest Fire"	"Why Leaves Turn Color in the Fall"	"The Season's Curmudgeon Sees the Light"
What is the purpose of the essay?	What is the purpose of the essay?	What is the purpose of the essay?
What are key events that occur in the essay?	What are key cause-and-effect relationships in the essay?	What are key negative feelings about spring in the essay?
What is the organization of the essay? How does this organization help the author to achieve her purpose?	What is the organization of the essay? How does this organization help the author to achieve her purpose?	What is the organization of the essay? How does this organization help the author to achieve her purpose?

Now, choose two of the three essays, and explain how the organization of each matches or supports the writer's topic and purpose.

Name _____ Date _____

"Forest Fire" by Anaïs Nin
"Why Leaves Turn Color in the Fall" by Diane Ackerman
"The Season's Curmudgeon Sees the Light" by Mary C. Curtis
Open-Book Test

Short Answer *Write your responses to the questions in this section on the lines provided.*

1. In "Forest Fire," the animals that have escaped from the forest run back into the fire. Why do they do that?

   _____

   _____

2. In "Forest Fire," Anaïs Nin prepares to leave her home. What is the only thing she plans to save, and why does she make that choice?

   _____

   _____

   _____

3. In "Forest Fire," Nin is prepared to become an evacuee. Why does she not become one? Base your answer on the definition of *evacuees.*

   _____

   _____

4. In "Forest Fire," Nin describes a fire and mentions a mudslide. One event has led to the other. How are they connected?

   _____

   _____

   _____

5. In the first paragraph of "Why Leaves Turn Color in the Fall," Diane Ackerman compares people with leopards. What point is she making with that comparison?

   _____

   _____

   _____

6. According to the fourth paragraph of "Why Leaves Turn Color in the Fall," fall foliage is brighter in the northeastern United States than in Europe. What is the reason for that difference?

   _____

   _____

   _____

7. Ackerman's main purpose in writing "Why Leaves Turn Color in the Fall" is to show why the leaves in fall turn from green to red, yellow, and orange. In presenting that information, what type of organization does she use? Explain your answer.

_____

_____

8. Mary C. Curtis begins "The Season's Curmudgeon Sees the Light" by describing her dislike of spring. What are her feelings about the season by the end of the essay? Explain your answer.

_____

_____

9. In "The Season's Curmudgeon Sees the Light," Mary Curtis describes her feelings about two seasons of the year. How does the organization of the essay help Curtis make her point?

_____

_____

10. "Forest Fire," "Why Leaves Turn Color in the Fall," and "The Season's Curmudgeon Sees the Light" use different types of organization to present information. In this chart, write the organizational technique that the author of each essay uses. Then, tell what information each author presents in her essay.

Essay	Organizational Technique	Information Presented
"Forest Fire"		
"Why Leaves Turn Color"		
"The Season's Curmudgeon"		

Essay

Write an extended response to the question of your choice or to the question or questions your teacher assigns you.

11. The authors of the essays in this section—"Forest Fire," "Why Leaves Turn Color in the Fall," and "The Season's Curmudgeon Sees the Light"—present information clearly. The authors also use one type of organization more than any other. In a brief essay, describe the type of organization used in two of the essays. Consider these questions as you prepare to write: What is the topic of each essay? How is each essay organized? How does the organization of each essay help the author achieve her purpose for writing?

12. An author always has at least one purpose for writing, yet some authors are more successful than others at achieving their purpose. In an essay, compare the success of the authors of "Why Leaves Turn Color in the Fall" and "The Season's Curmudgeon Sees the Light." First, explain why each author writes her essay. Then, evaluate each author's success in achieving her main purpose. Be sure to include details from the essays to support your points.

13. The three essays in this section—"Forest Fire," "Why Leaves Turn Color in the Fall," and "The Season's Curmudgeon Sees the Light"—hint at lessons about life that can be learned by observing nature. In an essay of your own, discusses the lessons taught in the three essays. In your essay, consider these questions: What did the authors experience in nature? What do the authors want readers to learn about nature? What lesson did you find most valuable, and why? Use details from the essays to support your points.

14. **Thinking About the Big Question: How much information is enough?** Both "Forest Fire" and "Why Leaves Turn Color in the Fall" present factual information. Write an essay of your own about one of those essays. In your essay, tell whether the author provided enough information for you to understand the topic fully. Then, discuss how the method of organization of the essay you are writing about affected your understanding of the topic. If you think additional information would have helped you understand the topic better, describe the information that is lacking and explain how it could have helped you.

Oral Response

15. Go back to question 2, 7, or 9 or to the question your teacher assigns you. Take a few minutes to expand your answer and prepare an oral response. Find additional details in "Forest Fire," "Why Leaves Turn Color in the Fall," and "The Season's Curmudgeon Sees the Light" that support your points. If necessary, make notes to guide your oral response.

"Forest Fire" by Anaïs Nin
"Why Leaves Turn Color in the Fall" by Diane Ackerman
"The Season's Curmudgeon Sees the Light" by Mary C. Curtis
Selection Test A

Critical Reading *Identify the letter of the choice that best answers the question.*

____ 1. Whom does the narrator of "Forest Fire" assist when the fire is forcing people to pack their cars?
   A. her neighbor's children
   B. her elderly neighbors
   C. her parents
   D. her close friends

____ 2. How did the narrator of "Forest Fire" probably react when a reporter criticized her for saving books, not items of more obvious "human interest," from the fire?
   A. The narrator probably wondered if the reporter was right.
   B. The narrator probably wanted to cry about all she was losing.
   C. The narrator probably continued to believe in the value of her diaries.
   D. The narrator probably wanted to force the reporter to read her diaries.

____ 3. What word might the author of "Forest Fire" use to describe the fire burning around her home?
   A. irritating
   B. slight
   C. bothersome
   D. destructive

____ 4. For what reason does the author of "Forest Fire" describe the mudslides that occur in January?
   A. She wants to boast about a second natural disaster she lived through.
   B. She wants to explain how she got to know the forest rangers.
   C. She wants to impress readers with her skill in photography.
   D. She wants to describe the bad results the fire had on the environment.

____ 5. According to "Why Leaves Turn Color in the Fall," why do trees stop sending nutrients to their leaves in late summer?
   A. The trees run out of nutrients.
   B. Tree trunks and branches need the nutrients during cold weather.
   C. The trees need to prepare for new leaves in spring.
   D. Scientists do not know the answer.

____ 6. What natural force helps leaves fall from trees in "Why Leaves Turn Color in the Fall"?

    A. wind

    B. rain

    C. snow

    D. people

____ 7. For what purpose does the author of "Why Leaves Turn Color in the Fall" organize the essay according to cause and effect?

    A. She wants to describe how cold weather affects nature.

    B. She wants to explain the process by which the color green disappears from leaves.

    C. She wants to explain the scientific process called photosynthesis.

    D. She wants to describe how the fall colors affect her.

____ 8. What is the author's main purpose in "Why Leaves Turn Color in the Fall"?

    A. She wants to persuade readers to stop pollution.

    B. She wants to inform readers of scientific facts about autumn leaves.

    C. She wants to explain the origin of macabre fall holidays.

    D. She wants to entertain readers with an imaginative fable about leaves.

____ 9. In "The Season's Curmudgeon Sees the Light," which season is the author's favorite, according to the beginning of the essay?

    A. spring

    B. summer

    C. fall

    D. winter

____ 10. According to the final statement in "The Season's Curmudgeon Sees the Light," what is the author's thought about the season she originally disliked?

    A. Spring gives us a fresh start.

    B. Spring rains are fun for splashing in.

    C. Fall fashions are sophisticated.

    D. Winter activities are wholesome.

____ 11. What kind of organization is used in "The Season's Curmudgeon Sees the Light"?

    A. chronological order

    B. cause-and-effect order

    C. comparison and contrast

    D. narrative

____ **12.** Which kind of organization describes events in the order in which they occurred?

    A. chronological order

    B. cause-and-effect order

    C. comparison and contrast

    D. all of the above

Vocabulary and Grammar

____ **13.** What are *evacuees* usually trying to avoid when they leave a place?

    A. noisy crowds

    B. chores and responsibilities

    C. excessive heat or cold

    D. life-threatening dangers

____ **14.** Firefighting is difficult work; handling the water hoses requires a
_____ grip.

    A. pungent   **B.** consoling   **C.** tenacious   **D.** macabre

____ **15.** Which word is most similar in meaning to *macabre*?

    A. reckless   **B.** silly   **C.** horrible   **D.** lovely

Essay

16. Each of the essays "Forest Fire," "Why Leaves Turn Color in the Fall," and "The Season's Curmudgeon Sees the Light" has a clear organization. In an essay, compare and contrast the organization of any two of the essays. The following questions will help you prepare to write your essay: What is the topic of each of the two essays? How is each of the essays organized? How does the ogranization of each help its author achieve her purpose for writing?

17. Both "Forest Fire" and "Why Leaves Turn Color in the Fall" present lessons about nature. Write an essay explaining what each author is saying about nature. What did each author experience in nature? How does each author use details from nature to teach her lesson?

18. **Thinking About the Big Question: How much information is enough?** Both "Forest Fire" and "Why Leaves Turn Color in the Fall" present a variety of facts to the reader. Choose one of these selections, and write an essay in which you explain whether or not the author provided enough information for you to understand the topic fully. Support your answer with details from the selection you have chosen.

"**Forest Fire**" by Anaïs Nin
"**Why Leaves Turn Color in the Fall**" by Diane Ackerman
"**The Season's Curmudgeon Sees the Light**" by Mary C. Curtis
Selection Test B

Critical Reading *Identify the letter of the choice that best completes the statement or answers the question.*

_____ 1. In "Forest Fire," why do the animals from the forest run back into the fire?
   A. The animals are afraid of the water from firefighters' hoses.
   B. The animals are not concerned about the fire.
   C. The animals are frightened by the lights from the reporters' cameras.
   D. The animals are more afraid of the crowds of people than of the fire.

_____ 2. In "Forest Fire," why does the narrator plan to save a stack of diaries if she must evacuate?
   A. She is too scared to think of anything else.
   B. The diaries are important to her.
   C. The furniture in her house is too heavy.
   D. The newspaper photographer wants to take a picture of her with the diaries.

_____ 3. What is the connection between the forest fire and the mudslide in "Forest Fire"?
   A. The mudslide prevents firefighters from reaching the fire.
   B. The mudslide is due to heavy rains.
   C. The mudslide is due to rains and lack of trees to hold the wet earth on the mountain.
   D. The mudslide occurs because of the stampede by animals trying to escape the fire.

_____ 4. Why might the author have chosen to organize "Forest Fire" in chronological order?
   A. She wanted to create the same suspense for readers as she felt at the time.
   B. She wanted readers to understand the causes of the fire.
   C. She was afraid that she would leave out some details if she did not organize it this way.
   D. She wanted readers to be able to compare and contrast the fire and the mudslide.

_____ 5. "Forest Fire" is a good essay to read if your purpose is to find out how
   A. a forest fire looks, sounds, smells, and feels.
   B. people can prevent forest fires.
   C. to prepare an evacuation plan.
   D. to become a newspaper photographer.

_____ 6. In "Why Leaves Turn Color," the author compares people and leopards in order to stress
   A. that leopards are endangered.
   B. that leopards hide.
   C. how powerful people are.
   D. how carefully we must observe nature.

____ 7. Which sentence is a main idea of "Why Leaves Turn Color in the Fall"?
    A. Leaves stop making chlorophyll as summer ends.
    B. Leaves reflect the colors of corn, pumpkins, and cranberries in the fall.
    C. Photosynthesis begins in the fall.
    D. Longer days and shorter nights cause leaves to turn color.

____ 8. According to "Why Leaves Turn Color," why is fall foliage brighter in the northeast United States than in Europe?
    A. Europe has too much air pollution.
    B. The United States has many varieties of maple trees, but Europe does not.
    C. The United States has colder nights and drier, sunnier days in fall than Europe does.
    D. The leaves fall too early in Europe.

____ 9. According to "Why Leaves Turn Color in the Fall," what is the adaptive reason that leaves turn color?
    A. The change in colors helps trees survive the winds and rains of fall.
    B. There does not seem to be any adaptive reason for the colors.
    C. The leaves change color to signal to the world that cold weather is on the way.
    D. Each tree variety turns color for different reasons.

____ 10. What purpose might have inspired this final sentence of "Why Leaves Turn Color in the Fall"?
    Sometimes one finds in fossil stones the imprint of a leaf, long since disintegrated, whose outlines remind us how detailed, vibrant, and alive are the things of this earth that perish.
    A. to make readers angry about the idea of death in nature
    B. to provide readers with a sense of wonder about nature
    C. to make readers laugh
    D. to explain how fossils are formed

____ 11. "Why Leaves Turn Color in the Fall" is presented in cause-and-effect order because the author wants to explain
    A. the effects of rainwater on trees.
    B. the effects of hot weather on trees.
    C. what causes leaves to change colors and fall.
    D. how to keep leaves on trees longer.

____ 12. In "The Season's Curmudgeon Sees the Light," what do the blossoms of spring trigger?
    A. sneezes
    B. love
    C. energy
    D. misery

____ 13. In the second half of "The Season's Curmudgeon Sees the Light," there is a change in the author's attitude toward
    A. books
    B. her house
    C. autumn
    D. spring

____ 14. Why does the author organize "The Season's Curmudgeon Sees the Light" as she does?
   A. to contrast fall weddings and song with spring weddings and song
   B. to contrast reading with gardening
   C. to show how her feelings about spring have changed
   D. to compare what she likes about fall and spring

Vocabulary

____ 15. *Evacuees* usually leave a place so that they can avoid
   A. unruly crowds.
   B. life-threatening dangers.
   C. chores and responsibilities.
   D. excessive heat or cold.

____ 16. Which word is most *opposite* in meaning to *tenacious*?
   A. strong
   B. plentiful
   C. weak
   D. scarce

____ 17. What is an example of something that could be considered *consoling*?
   A. a sudden, loud noise
   B. a frigid, winter storm
   C. a dark, hidden passageway
   D. a soft, soothing song

____ 18. Which vocabulary word best completes this sentence?
   A person becomes a teacher because he or she is _____ to helping young people.
   A. tenacious
   B. macabre
   C. predisposed
   D. capricious

____ 19. What kind of costumes at a party might frighten young children?
   A. tenacious
   B. macabre
   C. consoling
   D. predisposed

Essay

20. Some authors are more successful than others at achieving their purposes. In an essay, compare the success of the authors of "Why Leaves Turn Color in the Fall" and "The Season's Curmudgeon Sees the Light." First, explain why each author writes her essay. Then, evaluate how successfully each author achieves her purpose(s). Be sure to include examples from the essays to prove your points.

21. Both "Forest Fire" and "Why Leaves Turn Color in the Fall" hint at lessons about life that can be learned by observing nature. Write an essay that discusses the lessons taught in both essays. What did the authors experience in nature? What do the authors want readers to learn about nature? Which lesson did you more appreciate learning? Explain.

22. **Thinking About the Big Question: How much information is enough?** Both "Forest Fire" and "Why Leaves Turn Color in the Fall" present factual information. Write an essay of your own about one of those essays. In your essay, tell whether the author provided enough information for you to understand the topic fully. Then, discuss how the method of organization of the essay you are writing about affected your understanding of the topic. If you think additional information would have helped you understand the topic better, describe the information that is lacking and explain how it could have helped you.

Name _____   Date _____

Exposition: How-to Essay

Prewriting: Gathering Details

Use the timeline below to help organize the sequence of steps your explanation will describe.

Step 1	Step 2	Step 3	Step 4	Step 5	Step 6	Step 7

Drafting: Providing Elaboration

After writing each paragraph, stop and think. Is there a detail that needs elaboration? Answer the questions that will add to the detail and give readers more precise explanations of terms and materials that may be unfamiliar.

Which detail?	What kind?	How much?	How long?	To what degree?
First Paragraph:				
Second Paragraph:				
Third Paragraph:				
Fourth Paragraph:				

Writing Workshop—Unit 3, Part 1
How-to Essay: Integrating Grammar Skills

Comparative and Superlative Forms

The **comparative form** is used to compare two items. The **superlative form** is used to compare three or more items. The most common way to form these degrees is by adding -er or -est to words with one or two syllables. *More, most, less,* and *least* are used with longer modifiers and most adverbs ending in -ly.

Positive	Comparative	Superlative
high	higher	highest
heavy	heavier	heaviest
truly	more truly	most truly
nutritious	less nutritious	least nutritious

The patterns of irregular adjectives and adverbs must be memorized.

Positive	Comparative	Superlative
bad or badly	worse	worst
good or well	better	best
many or much	more	most
far (distance)	farther	farthest
far (extent)	further	furthest

A. DIRECTIONS: *Underline the correct word for each set of choices in the sentences.*

1. Of my three sisters, Ginny is *(close, closer, closest)* to me in age.

2. Jason is a *(good, better, best)* friend than Paul.

3. Toby writes well, but Mickey writes *(well, better, best)*.

4. My two-year-old brother speaks *(clearer, more clearly, most clearly)* than this child.

B. DIRECTIONS: *On the lines provided, rewrite these sentences using the correct comparative or superlative form.*

1. Fries and a soda make one of the less nutritious lunches of all.

   _____

2. For a healthiest lunch than fries and a soda, try a salad.

   _____

3. Of all these desserts, carrot cake has the more calories.

   _____

4. To lose weight, you must exercise most seriously than you now do.

   _____

Unit 3: Types of Nonfiction
Benchmark Test 5

MULTIPLE CHOICE

Reading Skill: Main Idea *Read the selection. Then, answer the questions that follow.*

Stuart had at least an hour before his report was due. After six weeks of work, he was finally finished. Stuart had already printed it out and checked it for errors. All he had left to do was to attach a cover and deliver it. He was filled with relief. Stuart was proud that he had completed what at first he thought was an impossible task. By finishing his report, Stuart now knows that he can do anything that he sets his mind to.

1. Which of the following is the best statement of the main idea?
   A. Stuart finished his report an hour before it was due.
   B. Stuart completed the challenging task of writing his report.
   C. Stuart worked on his report for six weeks.
   D. Stuart feels relieved after completing his paper.

2. Which of the following details best supports the main idea?
   A. Stuart printed out the paper and checked it for errors.
   B. Stuart needed to attach a cover.
   C. Stuart worked for six weeks on his report.
   D. Stuart was proud of himself.

3. Which of the following is the implied main idea of the passage?
   A. Stuart was relieved that he did well on his report.
   B. Stuart was barely able to finish his report.
   C. Writing the report was an unsettling experience.
   D. Writing the report was a rewarding challenge for Stuart.

4. Which detail best supports the implied main idea?
   A. By finishing the report, Stuart now believes in himself.
   B. Stuart did everything but check the paper for errors.
   C. Stuart was filled with relief about finishing his paper on time.
   D. Stuart had only an hour to turn in his paper.

Read the selection. Then, answer the questions that follow.

As early as 1744, a popular book describes playing a game called base ball. A pitcher throws a ball to a batter, who attempts to hit the ball with a bat that has a flat end. A catcher stands behind the batter. If the batter hits the ball, he runs to a base and back again to score a point. The bases are marked with posts, rather than the modern-day bags, and the pitcher throws the ball underhand.

In 1828, another book describes a game called rounders. It was very much like modern baseball, with a diamond-shaped infield and a base on each corner. A batter was out after three strikes. If he hit a pitch, he could run. A fielder who caught the ball could throw out the runner by throwing the ball and hitting him with it.

5. Which of the following best states the main idea of each of these two paragraphs?
   A. Early baseball was played with a flat bat, and was unlike baseball today; the game of rounders was similar to modern baseball.
   B. The game of baseball has been played since 1744; rounders was a game similar to baseball.
   C. A game called base ball was played in 1744; a game called rounders, similar to modern baseball, was played in 1828.
   D. Baseball was started in 1744 using flat bats; another game called rounders was played with bats and bases.

6. Which of the following might be the main idea of an essay containing these two paragraphs?
   A. Games similar to modern baseball have been played for over 200 years.
   B. There are many different types of baseball.
   C. Modern baseball has been around for several hundred years.
   D. The game of baseball has gone through many changes.

7. Which of the following is a key detail that supports the main idea of the first paragraph?
   A. A popular book describes a game called base ball.
   B. Bases were marked with posts rather than bags.
   C. A batter attempts to hit the ball thrown to him.
   D. Batters can score a point if they hit the ball.

Reading Skill: Analyze Treatment, Scope, and Organization of Ideas

CHANGE

It was a cold, icy day in January of 1848. James Marshall, a carpenter from New Jersey, was building a sawmill for John Sutter, an immigrant from Switzerland who had bought a large tract of land in California in the hopes of establishing an agricultural empire there. Digging a trench by the American River, whose waters were to power the sawmill, Marshall and his crew unexpectedly found a few nuggets of what looked like gold. Marshall brought the nuggets to Sutter, who performed a simple test with nitric acid that showed the nuggets were pure gold. Though the two men tried to keep the discovery secret, word of it spread. Soon the hills above the American River were dotted with tents and cabins where the first of thousands of prospectors came looking for gold. By 1849 there were over 40,000 people mining for gold in the region, and thousands of others were there to feed, clothe, and house them. They trampled Sutter's crops, stole his livestock, and generally made life so difficult that he and his family were forced to give up their land and resettle in Pennsylvania. Though many struck it rich in California, John Sutter died in near poverty.

8. Which of the following would be most similar in its presentation of this information?
   A. an article in a science magazine about how to identify gold
   B. an encyclopedia entry about the history of Spanish California
   C. a history textbook chapter about the California Gold Rush
   D. a biography of a miner who went west to search for gold

9. Which of the following would be the best source to use to confirm the accuracy of most of the information in the selection?
   A. a California newspaper written in 1850
   B. a novel about the California Gold Rush
   C. a speech given by a California politician in 1847
   D. a collection of charts showing changes in the American River

10. How is the information in the selection presented?
    A. It is organized according to geographic locations.
    B. It is told from several different points of view.
    C. It is dramatized using eyewitness quotations.
    D. It is related in chronological order.

Literary Analysis: Biography and Autobiography *Read the selection, and then answer the four questions that follow.*

Emily Dickinson is considered one of America's greatest poets, but few of her poems were published in her lifetime. Born in 1830, Dickinson grew up in Amherst, Massachusetts, and attended school there and in nearby Holyoke. She was no doubt familiar with other popular New England writers of her day, especially Ralph Waldo Emerson. Dickinson had a fairly normal social life until she reached her mid-twenties, after which she rarely left the home she inherited from her parents. Instead, she seems to have been able to understand the world better by viewing it from a distance. With a sharp eye and keen intellect, she pondered nature, friendship, love, and death in poems of powerful simplicity. Only about seven were published during her lifetime, all without her consent. When she died in 1886, relatives found over 1500 more of Dickinson's poems, many of them written on napkins and slips of paper neatly tied up with ribbons.

11. What does this biographical essay emphasize?
    A. Emily Dickinson's childhood and adolescence
    B. Emily Dickinson's love of nature
    C. Emily Dickinson's family love and other personal relationships
    D. Emily Dickinson's odd habits and writing career

12. Which statement best explains why this selection is biographical, not autobiographical?
    A. It tells about important events in the subject's life.
    B. It tells about the writer's contacts with the subject, Emily Dickinson.
    C. It is one person's account of events in the life of another person.
    D. It gives the years of birth and death for Emily Dickinson.

13. Based on this selection, what can you conclude about Emily Dickinson?
    A. She was talented but retiring.
    B. She was a lifelong snob.
    C. She was clever but mean.
    D. She was warm and outgoing.

Name _____ Date _____

Literary Analysis: Types of Organization

14. Which type of organization is used in this selection?
    A. cause-and-effect
    B. chronological
    C. comparison and contrast
    D. problem and solution

15. What type of organization might you use to describe what happens when a hurricane strikes a city or town?
    A. chronological
    B. cause-and-effect
    C. order of importance
    D. comparison and contrast

16. On which of the following topics would you use comparison and contrast?
    A. tornadoes
    B. the seasons of the year
    C. dolphins
    D. a football game

Vocabulary: Roots and Suffixes

17. What is the meaning of *invariably* in the following sentence?
    Doing things with Chuck is frustrating because he is invariably late.
    A. never
    B. infrequently
    C. always
    D. understandably

18. What is the definition of *ignorance* in the following sentence?
    Our ignorance of the real danger we faced helped keep us calm.
    A. ideas that are not real or true
    B. lack of knowledge or awareness
    C. indifference to
    D. concern about

19. Which of the following words has the same root as *valid*?
    A. valuable
    B. valley
    C. valise
    D. vaporize

20. A word with the suffix *-ly* is usually what part of speech?
    A. a noun
    B. a verb
    C. an adjective
    D. an adverb

21. Which word has the same suffix as *tolerance*?
    A. alliance
    B. insistence
    C. tolerate
    D. outdance

22. What is the meaning of *evaluation* in the following sentence?

    Miranda was pleased with the wonderful evaluation she received from her boss.

    A. an offer of employment
    B. a decision to end someone's job
    C. something that lowers the worth or value of a person or thing
    D. something that determines the worth or value of a person or thing

Grammar: Adjectives and Articles

23. Which of these sentences contains an article?
    A. Tall trees sway in windy skies.
    B. Those girls were very late to class.
    C. Dr. James prescribed some medicine.
    D. Andrew was the last to arrive.

24. In the following sentence, which question does the adjective answer?

    After school, Jerry ordered two pieces of pizza.

    A. what kind?   C. how many?
    B. which one?   D. whose?

25. In the following sentence, identify the adjective that is not an article. What word does the adjective modify?

    The hungry man quickly looked around the park for a place where he could eat lunch.

    A. he   C. park
    B. looked   D. man

Grammar: Adverbs

26. Which word in the following sentence is an adverb?

    Wild animals are very cautious when they sense the presence of human beings.

    A. wild   C. cautious
    B. very   D. presence

27. What question does the adverb in this sentence answer?

    Mrs. Lorenzo sang joyfully in the choir.

    A. when?   C. in what manner?
    B. where?   D. to what extent?

28. How many adverbs does this sentence contain?

    Yesterday the main dish was so spicy that Maria barely tasted the rest of the meal.

    A. one   C. three
    B. two   D. four

Grammar: Comparative and Superlative Forms

29. Which of the following statements is true of the comparative form?
    A. Only adjectives have comparative forms.
    B. Its forms usually end in -ly.
    C. It uses *most* with two-syllable adverbs.
    D. It is used to compare two items.

30. Which word in the following sentence is the superlative form of an adjective?

    Even though the flashlight helped us see the path more clearly, it did little good in the darkest part of the forest.

    A. more   C. little
    B. clearly   D. darkest

31. Which of these sentences uses comparative and superlative forms correctly?
    A. I can walk farther in those shoes than in these.
    B. The original version is more good than the remake.
    C. Of the two top runners, who is fastest?
    D. That is the worstest song I ever heard.

ESSAY

32. Think of some activity that you enjoy, such as playing a particular sport, planting a flower, cooking or baking a particular dish, or some other activity. Then, imagine that you are going to explain the activity to someone who has never seen it. Write a brief essay explaining each step in the process.

33. Think of someone who did something that you admire, either a historical figure, an acquaintance such as a teacher or a friend, or a family member. Write a brief essay describing the event in that person's life that makes you admire him or her. Make sure your essay clearly states why you admire the person's action.

34. Write a brief reflective essay about something that has recently made an impression upon you. It might be a story in the news, a movie, a book or poem, or an article in a magazine. Think about why this story or article has impressed you. What did you think about when you first heard or read it? When you write your essay, be sure to state how this story or article relates to your life and why you think it is important.

Name _____

Starting Date _____　Ending Date _____

Unit 3: Types of Nonfiction Skills Concept Map—2
How much information is enough?

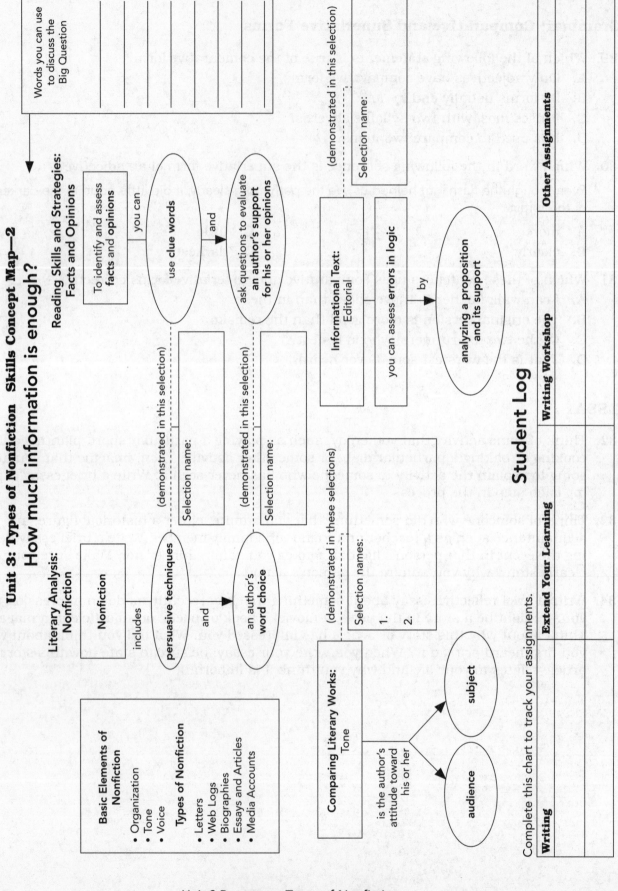

Words you can use to discuss the Big Question

Reading Skills and Strategies:
Facts and Opinions

To identify and assess facts and opinions → you can → use clue words → and → ask questions to evaluate an author's support for his or her opinions

(demonstrated in this selection)

Selection name: _____

Literary Analysis:
Nonfiction

Nonfiction → includes → persuasive techniques → and → an author's word choice

(demonstrated in this selection)

Selection name: _____

(demonstrated in this selection)

Selection name: _____

Informational Text:
Editorial

you can assess errors in logic → by → analyzing a proposition and its support

(demonstrated in this selection)

Selection name: _____

Basic Elements of Nonfiction

- Organization
- Tone
- Voice

Types of Nonfiction

- Letters
- Web Logs
- Biographies
- Essays and Articles
- Media Accounts

Comparing Literary Works:
Tone

is the author's attitude toward his or her → subject / audience

(demonstrated in these selections)

Selection names:
1.
2.

Student Log

Complete this chart to track your assignments.

Writing	Extend Your Learning	Writing Workshop	Other Assignments

Vocabulary Warm-up Word Lists

Study these words from "The Trouble With Television." Then, complete the activities.

Word List A

calculate [KAL kyuh layt] *v.* to figure out by using math
   How do you <u>calculate</u> the area of a rectangle?

crisis [KRY sis] *n.* time when a situation is bad or dangerous
   The quarrel between the two countries reached a <u>crisis</u>.

cultivate [KUHL tuh vayt] *v.* to develop; to encourage
   Dagmar tried to <u>cultivate</u> a love of poetry, but she just couldn't.

fare [FAIR] *n.* something given for use or enjoyment
   The top-forty radio station plays familiar <u>fare</u> day in, day out.

perceived [puhr SEEVD] *n.* understood or noticed
   His request was not <u>perceived</u> as being important.

precision [pri SIZH uhn] *n.* exactness
   Halley used a band saw to cut the board with great <u>precision</u>.

prime [PRYM] *adj.* main; most important
   The <u>prime</u> reason kids get into mischief is boredom.

verbal [VUHR buhl] *adj.* relating to words; spoken
   Dan had excellent <u>verbal</u> skills, which made him a great debater.

Word List B

assumptions [uh SUHMP shuhnz] *n.* things one believes to be true
   Adults sometimes make false <u>assumptions</u> about teenagers.

humanity [hyoo MAN i tee] *n.* all people
   A cure for cancer would be a great gift to <u>humanity</u>.

imperative [im PER uh tiv] *n.* something that must be done
   Cleaning the house is an <u>imperative</u> before Mom gets home.

perpetual [per PECH oo uhl] *adj.* continuous; going on a long time
   During the holidays, the mall plays a <u>perpetual</u> tape of carols.

skeptically [SKEP ti kuhl ee] *adv.* with doubt
   We tried the veggie burger <u>skeptically</u>, but found it tasty.

substitute [SUHB sti toot] *n.* replacement; something different
   Cramming for a test is no <u>substitute</u> for studying a bit each night.

tolerance [TAHL er uhns] *n.* ability to put up with something
   Teens have more <u>tolerance</u> to loud music than the elderly do.

virtually [VUHR choo uh lee] *adv.* almost all; nearly
   There is a television in <u>virtually</u> every home in the country.

"The Trouble With Television" by Robert MacNeil
Vocabulary Warm-up Exercises

Exercise A *Fill in each blank in the paragraph below with an appropriate word from Word List A. Use each word only once.*

Going to school in early America was quite different from today. The
[1] _____ reason for teaching most children was so they could learn
to read the Bible. Due to the shortage of writing materials, teachers often used
[2] _____ instruction. Some children also learned to
[3] _____ number problems with great [4] _____. This
was a useful skill to [5] _____ if planning to run a business. This sim-
plest of educational [6] _____ might be [7] _____ today
as laughable, but it served its population well. These days, students learn much more
than children of long ago. However, the news always reports an educational
[8] _____. We seem to be in danger of not preparing our students for the
world of tomorrow.

Exercise B *Write a complete sentence to answer each question. For each answer, use a word from Word List B to replace each underlined word without changing its meaning.*

1. Why is developing <u>an ability to put up with</u> different kinds of personalities <u>something that must be done</u>?
   _____

2. Do you know anyone who is in a <u>continuous</u> good mood?
   _____

3. What kind of communication has become <u>nearly</u> a <u>replacement</u> for letter writing?
   _____

4. What was one of <u>the things believed</u> by <u>all people</u> about the Earth's shape before it was proved to be round like a ball?
   _____

5. Why is it important to watch weight-loss commercials <u>with doubt</u>?
   _____

"The Trouble With Television" by Robert MacNeil
Reading Warm-up A

Read the following passage. Pay special attention to the underlined words. Then, read it again, and complete the activities. Use a separate sheet of paper for your written answers.

Hunter was having a <u>crisis</u>. He should have seen the danger coming, but he often liked to ignore what he did not want to face.

Hunter had worked at the television network for ten years. He could <u>calculate</u> with <u>precision</u> the number of viewers watching each of the network's programs. He could rattle off the list of advertisers for each half hour. He could create pie charts on the computer and give convincing presentations at important meetings.

So what was Hunter's problem? No matter how hard he tried, he could no longer <u>cultivate</u> a taste for a single one of the network's shows. He had to admit that he simply hated what the programming department put on the air.

It wasn't that Hunter had a taste for unusual television <u>fare</u>. The menu of programs during his first year at the network had included three or four shows he genuinely liked. Now, he barely managed to sit in the screening room before the beginning of the season. Luckily, no one asked for his opinions because he was <u>perceived</u> by others as just "that numbers guy." He did have opinions, though. Secretly, he hoped that some day bad manners would overcome him and he would blurt them out.

Hunter's dislike of the programs was not limited to <u>prime</u> time. Hunter couldn't stand the soap operas, the game shows, and the talk shows that filled the daytime slots. The news people were worst of all. It wasn't that they didn't have strong <u>verbal</u> skills. They spoke quite well, in fact. It was the oral presentation of news that bothered him. There was nothing written—nothing to review so a person could grasp the greater meaning.

He finally faced the inevitable. It was time to look for a new job.

1. Underline a word in the paragraph that hints at the meaning of <u>crisis</u>. Then, tell about a *crisis* you faced.

2. Circle the words that help you understand "<u>calculate</u> with <u>precision</u>." Then, rewrite the sentence using synonyms for *calculate* and *precision*.

3. Underline the words that tell what the writer could not <u>cultivate</u>. Then, write something you tried to *cultivate*.

4. Circle the words in the next sentence that suggest the meaning of <u>fare</u>. What is your favorite television *fare*?

5. Underline the word that tells by whom the narrator was <u>perceived</u>. Then, write a sentence for *perceived*.

6. Circle the word that tells what was <u>prime</u>. What hours do you think make up *prime* time?

7. Circle the word in the next sentence that hints at the meaning of <u>verbal</u>. Then, explain whether you prefer *verbal* or written news.

"The Trouble With Television" by Robert MacNeil
Reading Warm-up B

Read the following passage. Pay special attention to the underlined words. Then, read it again, and complete the activities. Use a separate sheet of paper for your written answers.

Critics of television often point out what's wrong with television without saying what's right with it. They make <u>assumptions</u> that are not true of all television viewers. They often think that people are hypnotized by television and fail to make a choice. They believe that viewers use television as a replacement for reading and a <u>substitute</u> for "real life."

So what *is* right about television? Because of its reach all around the world, it allows people to share experiences with the rest of <u>humanity</u>. Political and cultural events in faraway places are as close as the click of the remote control. Becoming familiar with the lives of people quite different from themselves allows television viewers to develop more <u>tolerance</u> for the customs and beliefs of others.

What about the exercise of choice? Flipping the dial is in itself an exercise of choice. <u>Virtually</u> every subject appears on television. People can share the lives of real and fictional people. They can see movies made long before they were born.

What about watching television as a substitute for reading or doing something in the "real world"? It is an <u>imperative</u> that people do not turn to television for all their information or entertainment. Television does not exercise the brain the way reading does. A movie adapted from a book, however, can lead a person into reading, and so can a show on an interesting subject. It is another important point that television is no substitute for participating in sports or dancing. It cannot exercise the muscles.

Critics sometimes say the average television viewer sits in a <u>perpetual</u> haze, always staring blankly into the screen. They may <u>skeptically</u> grant that some viewers are lively and intelligent. They obviously cannot see what it going on in living rooms across the country, but you are prepared to prove them wrong, aren't you?

1. Underline the words that help you figure out the meaning of <u>assumptions</u>. Then, write a sentence about an *assumption* you once made but no longer do.

2. Circle the word that is a synonym for <u>substitute</u>. Write your own definition of *substitute*.

3. Underline a synonym for <u>humanity</u>. Write about something that benefits *humanity*.

4. Circle the words that indicate how one builds <u>tolerance</u> for someone. Explain why *tolerance* is important.

5. Circle the word that <u>virtually</u> modifies, or changes. Tell how it changes the meaning of that word.

6. Underline the words that mean the same as <u>imperative</u>. Describe an *imperative* in your life.

7. Underline the word that is a synonym for <u>perpetual</u>. Write what you think *perpetual* motion means and tell if you think it can exist.

8. Circle the word that <u>skeptically</u> modifies. Rewrite the sentence, substituting a synonym for *skeptically*.

Name _____ Date _____

"The Trouble With Television" by Robert MacNeil
Writing About the Big Question

How much information is enough?

Big Question Vocabulary

accumulate	challenge	decision	development	discrimination
explanation	exploration	factor	global	inequality
quality	quantity	reveal	statistics	valuable

A. *Use a word from the list above to complete each sentence.*

1. Let me _____ some information about television.

2. The _____ of television changed people's lives forever.

3. What is the _____ for why some people watch hours of television a day?

B. *Follow the directions in responding to each of the items below.*

1. How would you rate the quality of television programming? What factors entered into your decision?

   _____

   _____

2. Write two sentences speculating about how your life would change if you stopped watching television. Use at least two Big Question words in your sentences.

   _____

   _____

   _____

   _____

C. *Complete the sentence below. Then, write a short paragraph in which you connect this answer to the Big Question.*

The exploration of ideas on TV news shows is usually _____ and

   _____

   _____

   _____

   _____

   _____

"The Trouble With Television" by Robert MacNeil

Reading: Use Clue Words to Distinguish Fact From Opinion

A **fact** is information that can be proved based on evidence. An **opinion** may be supported by factual evidence, but it cannot be proved. A **generalization** is a conclusion based on facts. Like an opinion, a generalization can be supported by facts. However, an author may sometimes use an **overgeneralization,** a conclusion stated in a more extreme way than can be supported by facts.

Statements may be a combination of opinions and generalizations, or they may be opinions written to sound like facts. As you read, **use clue words** to determine when a statement should be read carefully and evaluated to determine whether it is an opinion, a fact, a generalization, or an overgeneralization.

- Words that communicate judgment, such as *best* and *worst,* or specific words that suggest the writer's good or bad feelings about the topic usually indicate an opinion. Sometimes, opinions are signaled directly with words such as *I believe* or *I think.*
- Words that indicate connections, such as *therefore, so,* and *because,* may signal generalizations or opinions that should be supported by facts. Extreme statements that include words such as *always, everything, anything, nothing, never,* and *only* may be overgeneralizations.

As you read nonfiction, distinguish facts and supported generalizations from opinions and overgeneralizations to evaluate the strengths and weaknesses of a writer's argument. In "The Trouble With Television," Robert MacNeil makes a strong argument for limiting the time many people spend watching television. He uses a combination of all of these devices to convince his readers. His essay leads to a logical conclusion based on long observation and careful thought.

DIRECTIONS: *Read the passages from the selection, and then answer the questions.*

1. "Yet its dominating communications instrument, its principal form of national linkage, is one that sells neat resolutions to human problems that usually have no neat resolutions."
   On what fact is this generalization based?

   _____

2. "One study estimates that some 30 million adult Americans are 'functionally illiterate' and cannot read or write well enough to answer a want ad or understand the instructions on a medicine bottle."
   How could you prove that this statement is a fact?

   _____

3. "But it has come to be regarded as a given, . . . as though General Sarnoff, or one of the other august pioneers of video, had bequeathed to us tablets of stone commanding that nothing in television shall ever require more than a few moments' concentration."
   Why might this statement be considered an overgeneralization?

   _____

"The Trouble With Television" by Robert MacNeil
Literary Analysis: Persuasive Techniques

Persuasive techniques are the methods that a writer uses to convince an audience to think or act a certain way.

- **Repetition** is an effective way to drive home a point.
- **Rhetorical questions** (questions with obvious answers) make readers more likely to agree with later, more controversial points.

In "The Trouble With Television," Robert MacNeil uses both repetition and rhetorical questioning to drive home a point to his audience. Here is an example of the latter.

> Who can quarrel with a medium that so brilliantly packages escapist entertainment as a mass-marketing tool?

This rhetorical question forces readers to acknowledge the obvious answer: It is hard to argue against such a successful combination of entertainment and marketing.

DIRECTIONS: *Decide whether you find each of the following passages from the selection convincing, and then answer the questions.*

1. "It has become fashionable to think that, like fast food, fast ideas are the way to get to a fast-moving, impatient public."

   A. MacNeil use the word *fast* three times. What three things is he describing?

   _____

   B. How does the repetition in the preceding sentence convey the author's negative attitude toward television?

   _____

2. "When before in human history has so much humanity collectively surrendered so much of its leisure to one toy, one mass diversion?"

   A. How would you answer the rhetorical question?

   _____

   B. Does answering the question help persuade you to support the author's argument? Explain.

   _____

3. "When before in human history has so much humanity collectively surrendered so much of its leisure to one toy, one mass diversion? When before has virtually an entire nation surrendered itself wholesale to a medium for selling?"

   A. Why might MacNeil have repeated the word *surrendered*?

   _____

   B. Do you find the repetition effective? Explain.

   _____

"The Trouble With Television" by Robert MacNeil
Vocabulary Builder

Word List

constructive   diverts   passively   pervading   skeptically   trivial

A. DIRECTIONS: *Circle* T *if the statement is true or* F *if the statement is false. Then, explain your answer.*

1. When you need to concentrate on finishing a complicated project, you should find something that *diverts* your attention.

   T / F _____

2. If a problem with a car is *trivial,* you don't need to repair it immediately.

   T / F _____

3. If a burning smell were *pervading* the room, you would expect it to disappear immediately.

   T / F _____

4. If you respond to a speech *skeptically,* you are likely to trust the speaker.

   T / F _____

5. *Constructive* criticism can help actors improve their performances.

   T / F _____

6. The crowd protested *passively* by lying down in the street.

   T / F _____

B. WORD STUDY The Latin root *-vad-* means "to go." Words with *-vad-* include *pervade,* "go into every part of"; *invade,* "enter for conquest"; and *evade,* "slip away." Use the meaning of the root to help you answer the following questions.

1. What might a home *invader* be doing?

   _____

2. Why might someone *evade* responsibility for a mistake?

   _____

3. What kind of smell might *pervade* an enormous auditorium?

   _____

Name _____ Date _____

"The Trouble With Television" by Robert MacNeil
Enrichment: Television and Society

Television may or may not reflect American society. Take this opportunity to defend or criticize television as a mirror of the society you live in.

A. DIRECTIONS: *Explain why television does or does not reflect realistically each of the following aspects of our society. Consider all types of television programming— documentaries, news reports, television movies, situation comedies, and so on.*

1. teenagers

   _____
   _____
   _____

2. school

   _____
   _____
   _____

3. family

   _____
   _____
   _____

B. DIRECTIONS: *Imagine that you have been hired to develop a new weekly television show that will reflect American society as you experience it. Describe the show you will present.*

_____
_____
_____
_____
_____
_____
_____
_____
_____
_____

Name _____ Date _____

"The Trouble With Television" by Robert MacNeil
Open-Book Test

Short Answer *Write your responses to the questions in this section on the lines provided.*

1. At the beginning of "The Trouble With Television," Robert MacNeil says that after childhood, Americans spend 10,000 hours a decade watching television. What does he think we should do with that time instead?

   _____

   _____

   _____

2. MacNeil writes in the third paragraph of "The Trouble With Television" that television "diverts us only to divert." What does he mean by that statement? Base your answer on the two meanings of *divert*.

   _____

   _____

   _____

3. In "The Trouble With Television," MacNeil claims that the values of television are pervading the nation and its life. How are they doing that? Focus on the meaning of *pervading* in your response.

   _____

   _____

   _____

4. Midway through "The Trouble With Television," MacNeil says that "like fast food, fast ideas are the way to get to a fast-moving, impatient public." What persuasive technique is MacNeil using in this statement? Explain your answer.

   _____

   _____

   _____

5. Robert MacNeil voices an opinion about television news midway through "The Trouble With Television." What does he think about it?

   _____

   _____

6. In "The Trouble With Television," MacNeil says that much of television news is "machine gunning with scraps." What does he mean by this remark?

   _____

   _____

   _____

7. In "The Trouble With Television," MacNeil writes about the effect of television on literacy. What relationship does he see between television and literacy?

_____

_____

_____

8. Toward the end of "The Trouble With Television," MacNeil asks, "When before has virtually an entire nation surrendered so much of its leisure to one toy?" That question is rhetorical; its answer is obvious. What effect does this rhetorical question have on the reader?

_____

_____

_____

9. In "The Trouble With Television," Robert MacNeil uses facts and opinions to support his ideas. In the chart below, write two facts and two opinions from the essay. Then, choose one of the facts or opinions you included in the chart, and on the line below explain why it is a fact or an opinion.

Facts	Opinions

_____

10. "The Trouble With Television" is a persuasive essay. That is, Robert MacNeil is trying to persuade his readers to do something. What is he trying to persuade them to do?

_____

_____

Essay

Write an extended response to the question of your choice or to the question or questions your teacher assigns you.

11. In "The Trouble With Television," Robert MacNeil voices a strong opinion about television. In an essay, explain his opinion. Then, tell whether you agree or disagree with him. Support your view with at least two pieces of evidence from MacNeil's essay or from your own reading or experience.

12. In "The Trouble With Television," Robert MacNeil asks, "Who can quarrel with a medium that so brilliantly packages escapist entertainment as a mass-marketing tool?" That quotation is an example of a persuasive technique. In an essay, describe the technique. Then, evaluate its effectiveness at this point in MacNeil's essay.

13. It is well known that the Declaration of Independence refers to "certain unalienable rights." In "The Trouble With Television," Robert MacNeil refers to the Declaration when he says, "Literacy may not be an inalienable human right, but it is one that the highly literate Founding Fathers might not have found unreasonable or even unattainable." In an essay, describe the persuasive technique MacNeil uses by referring to the Declaration of Independence. Then, tell what message he is attempting to send in this section of his essay.

14. **Thinking About the Big Question: How much information is enough?** In "The Trouble With Television," Robert MacNeil provides several facts to support his opinion about television. In an essay, describe the kinds of facts he uses. Then, explain whether you think they provide you with enough information to conclude that his opinion is convincing. If the facts are not persuasive enough, describe the kind of information that might persuade you to change your mind.

Oral Response

15. Go back to question 5, 6, or 10 or to the question your teacher assigns you. Take a few minutes to expand your answer and prepare an oral response. Find additional details in "The Trouble With Television" that support your points. If necessary, make notes to guide your oral response.

"The Trouble With Television" by Robert MacNeil
Selection Test A

Critical Reading *Identify the letter of the choice that best answers the question.*

_____ 1. What does the author of "The Trouble With Television" say you could do in 5,000 hours?
A. earn a college degree
B. learn to read
C. become a news writer
D. learn to ski

_____ 2. What does Robert MacNeil believe about television?
A. It has improved Americans' way of life.
B. It helps people concentrate more.
C. It discourages hard work by viewers.
D. It is as good as taking a travel tour.

_____ 3. Which opinion about television is one that MacNeil expresses?
A. Television is too romantic.
B. Television presents information too slowly.
C. Commercials make life look hard.
D. Television may contribute to illiteracy.

_____ 4. What is Robert MacNeil's main point in "The Trouble With Television"?
A. News should not be shown on television.
B. Commercials are modern art forms.
C. People should watch less television.
D. There should be more long television shows.

_____ 5. What does MacNeil believe about television news?
A. People should read newspapers instead.
B. The stories are too short and too quick.
C. It needs more high-tech equipment.
D. It includes too much war coverage.

_____ 6. What fact does MacNeil use in his essay?
A. Every U.S. home has at least one television.
B. More children than adults watch television.
C. Commercials take too much time.
D. Thirty-million American adults are illiterate.

_____ 7. According to MacNeil, how do television programs hold people's attention?

A. They keep things brief.

B. They include a lot of violence.

C. The characters are funny.

D. They are realistic.

_____ 8. What persuasive technique does MacNeil use in the following statement?

It has become fashionable to think that, like fast food, fast ideas are the way to get to a fast-moving, impatient public.

A. rhetorical question

B. humor

C. repetition

D. overgeneralization

_____ 9. According to MacNeil, what do most television programmers fear?

A. increasing costs

B. actors leaving popular shows

C. equipment breaking down

D. losing viewers' attention

_____ 10. Which statement is an opinion?

A. Most television programs are boring.

B. Many Americans can't read or write.

C. Commercials are a marketing tool.

D. MacNeil is a broadcast journalist.

Vocabulary and Grammar

_____ 11. Which phrase does *not* contain a preposition?

A. under the bed

B. into the water

C. to the store

D. watching the sky

_____ 12. Which word is closest in meaning to *trivial*?

A. jovial

B. insignificant

C. meaningful

D. round

____ 13. In which sentence is *diverts* used correctly?

A. It diverts us to hear bad news.

B. He counted the diverts in the story.

C. Changing the topic, she diverts me.

D. Sports are a diverts from school work.

____ 14. Which sentence contains a preposition?

A. The rabbit jumped into the hat.

B. The cow ate greedily.

C. The crow flew south.

D. The lion roared loudly.

Essay

15. Write a short essay in which you explain the opinion Robert MacNeil holds in "The Trouble With Television." Then, explain two reasons the writer gives to support his view.

16. Write a short essay in which you agree or disagree with MacNeil's opinion of television. Support your view with at least two examples.

17. **Thinking About the Big Question: How much information is enough?** In "The Trouble With Television," Robert MacNeil provides several facts to support his opinion about television. In an essay, describe the kinds of facts he uses. Then, explain whether you think the facts he uses help him to make a convincing case.

Name _____   Date _____

"The Trouble With Television" by Robert MacNeil
Selection Test B

Critical Reading *Identify the letter of the choice that best completes the statement or answers the question.*

____ 1. What is Robert MacNeil trying to persuade people to do in "The Trouble With Television"?
  A. avoid certain violent shows
  B. boycott products by certain television sponsors
  C. watch less television
  D. watch more shows on public television

____ 2. What issue in the United States does MacNeil say is linked to television viewing?
  A. illiteracy
  B. reading more
  C. mental illness
  D. unemployment

____ 3. Which statement contradicts MacNeil's own stance in "The Trouble With Television?"
  A. Television creates short attention spans.
  B. Television viewers are wasting their time.
  C. Fast ideas are the best ideas.
  D. Television discourages concentration.

____ 4. Which reason does MacNeil use in his argument about television?
  A. Television gives instant gratification with no effort by the viewer.
  B. Television encourages violent behavior.
  C. Television has too many comedy shows.
  D. Television encourages children to beg for too many toys.

____ 5. When MacNeil says that much of television news is "machine gunning with scraps," he means that
  A. television news covers too much violent crime.
  B. television news stories are too short and fast.
  C. television news covers war too much.
  D. television news lacks high-tech equipment.

____ 6. What is the main point MacNeil is making in "The Trouble With Television"?
  A. Television makes people less able to focus on anything worthwhile.
  B. Escapist entertainment helps relieve the stress of modern life.
  C. Television is primarily a tool for advertising.
  D. News should not be shown on television.

____ 7. "The Trouble With Television" can best be described as
  A. a short story.
  B. a descriptive essay.
  C. a persuasive essay.
  D. an autobiography.

___ 8. Which of the following is an overgeneralization?
   A. Television has been known to divert us.
   B. Television is a profitable advertising vehicle.
   C. Television is a major factor in American lives.
   D. Television has absolutely no positive qualities.

___ 9. Which of the following is a fact?
   A. The best things in life require effort.
   B. Television is boring.
   C. MacNeil thinks of television in mostly negative terms.
   D. MacNeil writes well.

___ 10. What does MacNeil call one of the most precious human gifts?
   A. the ability to focus your attention yourself
   B. the gift of sight
   C. the ability to read and write
   D. generosity

___ 11. According to MacNeil, how do programmers primarily avoid losing viewers' attention?
   A. They use popular musical sound tracks.
   B. They concentrate on comedy shows.
   C. They include a lot of violence.
   D. They keep things brief.

___ 12. MacNeil asks,

   When before in human history has so much humanity collectively surrendered so much of its leisure to one toy, one mass diversion?

   What is this persuasive technique called?
   A. repetition
   B. a generalization
   C. a rhetorical question
   D. a controversial question

Vocabulary and Grammar

___ 13. Which word is closest in meaning to *pervading*?
   A. invading
   B. spreading
   C. looking
   D. arguing

___ 14. Something that is *trivial* is
   A. insightful.
   B. important.
   C. unusual.
   D. insignificant.

_____ 15. Which sentence includes two prepositions?
   A. Where is the up escalator?
   B. How deep is the snow?
   C. The snow won't stop until midnight.
   D. I am in love with my neighbor.

_____ 16. Which sentence does *not* contain a preposition?
   A. The bird flew around the world.
   B. My cat sleeps under the bed every day.
   C. Matt enjoys singing and playing guitar.
   D. The girls ran to the beach one day.

_____ 17. Which word has a meaning similar to that of *diverts*?
   A. distracts
   B. recommends
   C. saves
   D. holds

Essay

18. "The Trouble With Television" includes the following rhetorical question:

   Who can quarrel with a medium that so brilliantly packages escapist entertainment as a mass-marketing tool?

   In a brief essay, evaluate the effectiveness of that rhetorical question in this essay.

19. Robert MacNeil refers to the Declaration of Independence when he says:

   Literacy may not be an inalienable human right, but it is one that the highly literate Founding Fathers might not have found unreasonable or even unattainable.

   Write a short essay in which you explain how MacNeil uses this reference to support his argument against watching too much television.

20. **Thinking About the Big Question: How much information is enough?** In "The Trouble With Television," Robert MacNeil provides several facts to support his opinion about television. In an essay, describe the kinds of facts he uses. Then, explain whether you think they provide you with enough information to conclude that his opinion is convincing. If the facts are not persuasive enough, describe the kind of information that might persuade you to change your mind.

"On Woman's Right to Suffrage" by Susan B. Anthony
Vocabulary Warm-up Word Lists

Study these words from "On Woman's Right to Suffrage." Then, complete the activities.

Word List A

constitution [kahn sti TOO shuhn] *n.* a country's written laws
   After winning its freedom, the new nation wrote a <u>constitution</u>.

downright [DOWN ryt] *adj.* total; complete
   Sticking your tongue out at somebody is a <u>downright</u> insult.

endured [en DOORD] *v.* put up with; tolerated
   This awful heat cannot be <u>endured</u> one minute longer.

federal [FED uh ruhl] *adj.* relating to the central government
   It is important for the <u>federal</u> and state governments to cooperate.

promote [pruh MOHT] *v.* to help something develop or be successful
   The city officials <u>promote</u> the development of a new museum.

rebellion [ri BEL yuhn] *n.* a struggle against people in power
   The students were in <u>rebellion</u> against a longer school day.

supreme [soo PREEM] *adj.* having the highest position of power
   At home, the <u>supreme</u> law is whatever my parents say.

welfare [WEL fair] *n.* health and happiness; well-being
   Our neighbors are concerned about the <u>welfare</u> of stray cats.

Word List B

discrimination [dis krim uh NAY shuhn] *n.* unfair treatment of a group of people
   Sadly, many groups have experienced <u>discrimination</u> in our country.

domestic [duh MES tik] *adj.* happening within one country
   <u>Domestic</u> trade among the states is important to our country's economy.

entitled [en TYE tld] *adj.* having a right to do or have something
   Because his slice of cake was small, Jake feels <u>entitled</u> to another.

guaranteed [gar uhn TEED] *v.* promised
   We used a credit card, so our room reservation is <u>guaranteed</u>.

immunities [i MYOO ni teez] *n.* protections from laws or punishment
   The murder trial witness was given <u>immunities</u> because he cooperated with the police.

opponents [uh POH nuhnts] *n.* people who disagree with an idea, plan, and so on
   <u>Opponents</u> of a fair election tried to stop some people from voting.

suffrage [SUHF rij] *n.* the right to vote
   In 1971, the voting age was lowered, giving <u>suffrage</u> to eighteen-year-olds.

void [VOYD] *adj.* no longer legal
   Because she broke the terms of agreement, the contract is now <u>void</u>.

Name _____ Date _____

"On Woman's Right to Suffrage" by Susan B. Anthony
Vocabulary Warm-up Exercises

Exercise A *Fill in each blank in the paragraph below with an appropriate word from Word List A. Use each word only once.*

The small African country was in [1] _____ against its rulers. While the ruling country profited from its colony's mines, it paid no attention to the miners' needs and [2] _____. [3] _____ terrible conditions in the mines had to be [4] _____ for the sake of keeping a job. After the country declared independence, its first task was to draft a [5] _____ [6] _____ to protect all its citizens. Then, it got to work trying to [7] _____ a healthy lifestyle for the miners. Its [8] _____ efforts went into improving working conditions, raising the wage, and providing health care. In its first ten years of independence, the country's government met with great success.

Exercise B *Answer each question with a complete explanation.*

1. What do <u>opponents</u> of <u>discrimination</u> seek?
   _____

2. Do the rulers of countries usually hope for <u>domestic</u> peace?
   _____

3. Would you want to sign an agreement that is <u>void</u>?
   _____

4. If you worked really hard on an essay, would you be <u>entitled</u> to receive an *A*? Should any grade be <u>guaranteed</u>?
   _____

5. Is <u>suffrage</u> the right of fourteen-year-olds?
   _____

6. Is a law that grants <u>immunities</u> against unfair searches a good thing?
   _____

"On Woman's Right to Suffrage" by Susan B. Anthony
Reading Warm-up A

Read the following passage. Pay special attention to the underlined words. Then, read it again, and complete the activities. Use a separate sheet of paper for your written answers.

Today, many U.S. citizens seem to take for granted their right to vote. Nearly half the eligible population does not even vote in national elections. If everyone realized how long and hard their ancestors struggled for the right to vote, they would treasure it.

In 1775, the thirteen colonies' <u>rebellion</u> against Britain became a war for freedom. Even before the first battle, the colonies realized they had to work together to reach their goals. The war ended in 1781, but it took another six years for a <u>constitution</u> to be written.

It took a lot of work for the new country to succeed. Each former colony, which became a state, had to give up some of its own laws and power to the new <u>federal</u> government. Only then could any written document become the <u>supreme</u> law of the land.

The Founding Fathers believed in a government that would <u>promote</u> the <u>welfare</u> of its people. They wanted to improve the well-being of its citizens and make sure their concerns were heard. Curiously, though, they let the states decide who had a say in running that government. Over the years, laws that kept people from voting were <u>endured</u> by the poor, Catholics and non-Christians, Indians, African Americans, and women.

Wyoming allowed women to vote while it was still a territory. Other territories and states let women vote in local elections. Finally, one by one, states started to let women take part in elections. Women even began to hold elected office. Still, it was not until 1920 that they could vote everywhere in the United States.

It took many years and various changes in our laws to give all adult citizens the right to vote. We should all have a <u>downright</u> feeling of pride that we can vote. That right gives us the ability to direct the course of our own lives and that of our country's history.

1. Underline the words that give a clue to the meaning of <u>rebellion</u>. Then, tell what a *rebellion* is.

2. Underline the word or words that give a hint to the meaning of <u>constitution</u>. Tell why a *constitution* is important.

3. Circle the word that <u>federal</u> describes. Then, write a sentence for *federal*.

4. Circle the word that tells what is <u>supreme</u>. Write about something of *supreme* importance.

5. Circle the word in the next sentence that hints at the meaning of <u>promote</u>. Then, write about a cause you would *promote*.

6. Circle the synonym in the next sentence for <u>welfare</u>. Explain the things that are part of a person's *welfare*.

7. Underline the words that tell what was <u>endured</u>. Then, use *endured* in a sentence.

8. Circle the words that tell what gives a <u>downright</u> sense of pride. Tell about a time you had a *downright* sense of pride.

Name _____   Date _____

Read the following passage. Pay special attention to the underlined words. Then, read it again, and complete the activities. Use a separate sheet of paper for your written answers.

The Founding Fathers had left voting rights up to the states. None of the states allowed women to vote. If a woman tried to vote, her action was considered <u>void</u>. With no vote, women had little power over their own lives. The men who made the laws also did not allow women to own property, go to college, or enter the professions.

In the mid–1800s, some women became involved in the movement to end slavery worldwide. But during an antislavery meeting in Great Britain, Lucretia Mott, an American, was refused a seat because she was a woman. She and a friend, Elizabeth Cady Stanton, decided that if legal <u>discrimination</u> against them were going to end, they would have to help bring it about.

So Mott and Stanton organized a convention on women's rights. In July 1848, a group of two hundred women and forty men gathered in Seneca Falls in upstate New York. One of the men who attended was the antislavery leader Frederick Douglass. The biggest issue at Seneca Falls was <u>suffrage</u>. Mott, Stanton, and their followers felt that women, as citizens, were <u>entitled</u> to vote. They believed that the arguments of their <u>opponents</u> on the issue were weak.

Mott and Stanton also spoke up on other <u>domestic</u> issues involving women's rights. They pointed out that the laws and practices of the country kept women in inferior positions to men. Even in matters of marriage, women had none of the <u>immunities</u> that men did. Women needed the certainty of the protections that were <u>guaranteed</u> by law in order to direct their own lives.

Unfortunately, the women's movement lost ground because slavery became the number-one issue of the day. It would take more than seventy years until the government passed a law that granted women across the country the right to vote.

1. Underline the words in the next sentence that help to understand <u>void</u>. Then, write a sentence for *void*.

2. Underline the sentences in the first paragraph that explain <u>discrimination</u>. Explain why *discrimination* has no place in our country.

3. Circle the word in the next sentence that helps define <u>suffrage</u>. Then, explain why *suffrage* for all is important.

4. Circle the words that tell what Stanton and others thought women were <u>entitled</u> to do. Tell about something you feel *entitled* to.

5. Underline the words in the first paragraph that identify <u>opponents</u> of women's rights. Describe some *opponents* you had.

6. Underline the words in the next sentence that explain <u>domestic</u>. Name a *domestic* issue today.

7. Circle the synonym in the next sentence for <u>immunities</u>. Then, write a sentence for *immunities*.

8. Explain something that was *guaranteed* to you.

"On Woman's Right to Suffrage" by Susan B. Anthony
Writing About the Big Question

How much information is enough?

Big Question Vocabulary

accumulate	challenge	decision	development	discrimination
explanation	exploration	factor	global	inequality
quality	quantity	reveal	statistics	valuable

A. *Use a word from the list above to answer each question.*

1. Which word is an antonym of local? _____

2. When information piles up, what does it do? _____

3. Many people use this word to describe dealing with lots of information.

    _____

B. *Follow the directions in responding to each of the items below.*

1. In two complete sentences, describe Susan B. Anthony's lifelong goal. Use at least two list words in your sentences.

    _____

    _____

    _____

2. How successful was Anthony? Why? Write a two-sentence answer that includes at least one list word.

    _____

    _____

    _____

C. *Complete the sentence below. Consider the source from which Susan B. Anthony drew her ideas about gender discrimination. Then, write a short paragraph in which you connect your answer to the Big Question.*

    Discrimination based on gender is _____

    _____

    _____

    _____

    _____

Name _____   Date _____

"**On Woman's Right to Suffrage**" by Susan B. Anthony
Reading: Use Clue Words to Distinguish Fact From Opinion

A **fact** is information that can be proved based on evidence. An **opinion** may be supported by factual evidence, but it cannot be proved. A **generalization** is a conclusion based on facts. Like an opinion, a generalization can be supported by facts. However, an author may sometimes use an **overgeneralization,** a conclusion stated in a more extreme way than can be supported by facts.

Statements may be a combination of opinions and generalizations, or they may be opinions written to sound like facts. As you read, **use clue words** to determine when a statement should be read carefully and evaluated to determine whether it is an opinion, a fact, a generalization, or an overgeneralization.

- Words that communicate judgment, such as *best* and *worst,* or specific words that suggest the writer's good or bad feelings about the topic usually indicate an opinion. Sometimes, opinions are signaled directly with words such as *I believe* or *I think.*
- Words that indicate connections, such as *therefore, so,* and *because,* may signal generalizations or opinions that should be supported by facts. Extreme statements that include words such as *always, everything, anything, nothing, never,* and *only* may be overgeneralizations.

As you read nonfiction, distinguish facts and supported generalizations from opinions and overgeneralizations to evaluate the strengths and weaknesses of a writer's argument.

In "On Woman's Right to Suffrage," Susan B. Anthony makes a strong argument for women's constitutional right to vote. Her speech leads to a logical conclusion based on the language of America's Constitution.

DIRECTIONS: *Read the passages from the selection, and then answer the questions.*

1. "Hence, every discrimination against women in the constitutions and laws of the several States is to-day null and void, precisely as in every one against negroes." On what fact is this generalization based?

   _____

2. "Webster, Worcester and Bouvier all define a citizen to be a person in the United States, entitled to vote and hold office." How could you prove this fact?

   _____

3. "And it is a downright mockery to talk to women of their enjoyment of the blessings of liberty while they are denied the use of the only means of securing them. . . ." What makes this statement an opinion?

   _____

4. ". . . this oligarchy of sex . . . carries dissension, discord and rebellion into every home in the nation." Why might this statement be considered an overgeneralization?

   _____

"On Woman's Right to Suffrage" by Susan B. Anthony
Literary Analysis: Persuasive Techniques

Persuasive techniques are the methods that a writer uses to convince an audience to think or act a certain way.

- **Repetition** is an effective way to drive home a point.
- **Rhetorical questions** (questions with obvious answers) make readers more likely to agree with later, more controversial points.

In "On Woman's Right to Suffrage," Susan B. Anthony uses both repetition and rhetorical questioning to emphasize her arguments and drive home a point to her audience. These persuasive techniques are especially effective when spoken aloud.

In this passage from the selection, note the repetition of the word *we.*

> It was we, the people; not we, the white male citizens; nor yet we, the male citizens; but we, the whole people, who formed the Union.

By repeating the word *we,* the author emphasizes her point that it was everyone, both males and females, who helped develop our country.

DIRECTIONS: *In each of these passages, Susan B. Anthony uses repetition or a rhetorical question as a persuasive technique. Decide whether you find each passage convincing, and then answer the questions.*

1. "And we formed it, not to give the blessings of liberty, but to secure them; not to the half of ourselves and the half of our posterity, but to the whole people—women as well as men."

    A. Why might the author have repeated the word *half,* followed by the word *whole*?

    _____

    B. Do you find the repetition effective? Why?

    _____

2. "The only question left to be settled now is: Are women persons?"

    A. How would you answer the rhetorical question?

    _____

    B. Does answering the question help persuade you to support the author's argument? Why?

    _____

3. "It is an odious aristocracy; a hateful oligarchy of sex; the most hateful aristocracy ever established on the face of the globe; an oligarchy of wealth, where the rich govern the poor."

    A. What three words are repeated in this sentence?

    _____

    B. What impression of America's leadership do you have, based on this repetition?

    _____

"On Woman's Right to Suffrage" by Susan B. Anthony
Vocabulary Builder

Word List

derived   dissension   immunities   posterity   rebellion   violation

A. DIRECTIONS: *Write the letter of the word or phrase that best defines each word in CAPITAL LETTERS.*

____ 1. DISSENSION
    A. agreement   C. argument
    B. negotiation   D. imperfect

____ 2. IMMUNITIES
    A. protections   C. contagions
    B. insurances   D. silences

____ 3. POSTERITY
    A. stinginess   C. future generations
    B. forgotten memories   D. peacefulness

____ 4. DERIVED
    A. overturned   C. motored
    B. received   D. framed

____ 5. VIOLATION
    A. rule breaking   C. physical force
    B. misunderstanding   D. nightmare

____ 6. REBELLION
    A. retraining   C. remarking
    B. revision   D. resistance

B. WORD STUDY: The Latin root *-bellum-* means "war." Use the meaning of *-bellum-* to help you answer the questions that follow.

1. Would a *belligerent* person be more likely to fight or cooperate?

_____

2. Would contented people or unhappy people be more likely to favor *rebellion*?

_____

"On Woman's Right to Suffrage" by Susan B. Anthony

Enrichment: Community Action

Susan B. Anthony saw an injustice in society and made efforts to eliminate it. Any change—small or large—in the way a community operates almost always requires an organized effort by those who want the change.

Imagine that you are helping your school ecology club make a positive change in your neighborhood—say, establishing a community composting project by recycling leaves. How would you go about launching and completing this recycling project? If you prefer, suggest your own ecology project.

DIRECTIONS: *Use the following chart to plan a community ecology project. Complete each section of the chart.*

Ecology Project to Recycle Leaves

Goal Statement

1. _____

Tasks to Reach Goal

2. _____

3. _____

4. _____

5. _____

People Who Can Assist

6. _____

7. _____

8. _____

How to Evaluate Progress

9. _____

10. _____

"**On Woman's Right to Suffrage**" by Susan B. Anthony
"**The Trouble With Television**" by Robert MacNeil
Integrated Language Skills: Grammar

Conjunctions

Conjunctions are words that connect sentence parts. A **coordinating conjunction** connects words or groups of words of the same kind.

> The boy <u>and</u> his dog went everywhere together.

COORDINATING CONJUNCTIONS:

and	but	or	nor	for	yet	so

Correlative conjunction connect pairs of equal importance. Correlative conjunction come in pairs.

> In order to be healthy, you must both eat right and exercise regularly.

Correlative Conjunctions
both/and   either/or   neither/nor

A **subordinating conjunction** connects two ideas by making one dependent on the other.

> I bought a stereo system <u>after</u> I had earned enough money.

COMMON SUBORDINATING CONJUNCTIONS:

after	as though	since	until
although	because	so that	when
as	before	than	whenever
as if	even though	though	where
as long as	if	till	wherever
as soon as	in order that	unless	while

A. PRACTICE: *Underline the conjunctions in the following sentences.*

1. My twin brothers and my sister are in elementary school.
2. The twins were cute babies, but they cried a lot.
3. I ran outside whenever they began crying.
4. Neither Kyle nor Kevin slept much at first.

B. Writing Application: *Write a short paragraph in which you use at least five conjunctions. Underline the conjunctions.*

_____

_____

_____

_____

"On Woman's Right to Suffrage" by Susan B. Anthony
"The Trouble With Television" by Robert MacNeil

Integrated Language Skills: Support for Writing an Evaluation

An **evaluation** of a writer's arguments should identify specific supporting points that the author uses to defend his or her position. An evaluation should also determine whether each supporting point is effective.

DIRECTIONS: *Fill in the chart with Robert MacNeil's points supporting his negative view of watching television or Susan B. Anthony's points supporting women's right to vote, the persuasive techniques the person uses, and an assessment of whether the overall argument is effective and sound.*

Supporting Points	
Persuasive Techniques	
Assessment	

Now, use your notes in the chart to write your evaluation.

Name _____ Date _____

"On Woman's Right to Suffrage" by Susan B. Anthony
"The Trouble With Television" by Robert MacNeil

Integrated Language Skills: Support for Extend Your Learning

Research and Technology: "On Woman's Right to Suffrage"

Use this chart to record and organize the information you gather for your statistical snapshot of American women. When the chart is complete, ask: What, if anything, changed for women during this time span?

Category	Year	Statistics	Survey Responses

Research and Technology: "The Trouble With Television"

Use this chart to record and organize the information you gather for your statistical snapshot of television-viewing habits. When the chart is complete, ask yourself the following questions: How are viewing habits similar and different for the two groups of viewers? How do their attitudes toward television compare?

Category	Student Hours/ Week	Adult Hours/ Week	Comments
Sports			
News			
Movies			
Comedy			
Drama			
Music			
Educational/ Informational			

Name _____ Date _____

"On Woman's Right to Suffrage" by Susan B. Anthony
Open-Book Test

Short Answer *Write your responses to the questions in this section on the lines provided.*

1. At the beginning of "On Woman's Right to Suffrage," Susan B. Anthony quotes the preamble of the Constitution. The quotation begins with a reference to "the people of the United States." Anthony then discusses that term. How does she define it?

   _____

   _____

2. At the beginning of "On Woman's Right to Suffrage," after quoting the preamble of the Constitution, Anthony talks about "we, the people." In this section of her speech, she uses that phrase a number of times, each time with a different variation. What persuasive technique is she using, and what effect does it have?

   _____

   _____

   _____

3. Midway through "On Woman's Right to Suffrage," Anthony refers to "female posterity." Whom is she referring to when she uses that term? Base your answer on the meaning of *posterity*.

   _____

   _____

4. Midway through "On Woman's Right to Suffrage," Anthony talks about laws that make sex a qualification for the right to vote. She says that any such law is a violation of the Constitution. How would such a law violate the Constitution? Base your answer on the definition of *violation*.

   _____

   _____

   _____

5. Midway through "On Woman's Right to Suffrage," Anthony states that the U.S. government is "the most hateful aristocracy ever established on the face of the globe." Is Anthony's statement a fact or an opinion? How do you know?

   _____

   _____

6. In the last paragraph of "On Woman's Right to Suffrage," Anthony asks, "Are women persons?" What persuasive technique is she using by asking this question? How do you know?

   _____

   _____

Unit 3 Resources: Types of Nonfiction

7. In the last paragraph of "On Woman's Right to Suffrage," Anthony makes the point that discrimination against women is illegal. What appeal to reason does she make to try to convince her audience of her point?

_____

_____

_____

8. In the last sentence of "On Woman's Right to Suffrage," Anthony says that "every discrimination against women . . . is today null and void." On what does she base this conclusion?

_____

_____

_____

9. Anthony uses both facts and opinions to support her point in "On Woman's Right to Suffrage." Facts are statements that can be proved with evidence. Opinions cannot be proved. In this chart, write two facts and two opinions from Anthony's speech. Then, choose one of the facts or opinions you included in the chart, and on the line below explain why it is a fact or an opinion.

Facts	Opinions

_____

10. In "On Woman's Right to Suffrage," Anthony wishes to persuade her audience of a particular point. What is the main point of Anthony's speech?

_____

_____

Essay

Write an extended response to the question of your choice or to the question or questions your teacher assigns you.

11. In an essay, describe the crime that Susan B. Anthony was accused of committing, according to "On Woman's Right to Suffrage." Explain how Anthony defended herself, and include at least two reasons she used to support her claims.

12. In "On Woman's Right to Suffrage," Susan B. Anthony says she does not believe that the United States is a true democracy. In an essay, explain her reason for making that statement. In preparing your answer, consider the characteristics of a democracy. Include examples from her speech to support your response.

13. Look back at the paragraph in "On Woman's Right to Suffrage" that begins "It was we, the people." Some words and sentence structures (for example, "we," "formed," "not to . . . but to," "half," and "whole") occur more than once in that paragraph. In an essay, discuss the effect of the repetition. Does it strengthen Anthony's argument? Explain your answer.

14. **Thinking About the Big Question: How much information is enough?** Imagine that you were in the audience more than one hundred years ago when Susan B. Anthony gave the speech "On Woman's Right to Suffrage." In an essay, explain whether Anthony provided enough information to convince you of her point. If you believe she did, explain what information was most persuasive. If she did not, explain what information was lacking.

Oral Response

15. Go back to question 4, 5, or 6 or to the question your teacher assigns you. Take a few minutes to expand your answer and prepare an oral response. Find additional details in "On a Woman's Right to Suffrage" that support your points. If necessary, make notes to guide your oral response.

"On Woman's Right to Suffrage" by Susan B. Anthony
Selection Test A

Critical Reading *Identify the letter of the choice that best answers the question.*

_____ 1. To whom did Susan B. Anthony make her speech, "On Woman's Right to Suffrage"?
   A. local people
   B. a parole board
   C. an oligarchy
   D. Webster, Worcester, and Bouvier

_____ 2. What does the word *suffrage* in the title of Susan B. Anthony's speech mean?
   A. employment laws
   B. voting
   C. free speech
   D. civil rights

_____ 3. What does Susan B. Anthony insist on in the opening of "On Woman's Right to Suffrage"?
   A. She says the election results are wrong.
   B. She says the Constitution needs changes.
   C. She says she has the right to free speech.
   D. She says her voting is not a crime.

_____ 4. In quoting from the Preamble to the Constitution, what is Anthony using to support her argument in "On Woman's Right to Suffrage"?
   A. a fact
   B. an opinion
   C. a generalization
   D. an overgeneralization

_____ 5. According to Anthony in "On Woman's Right to Suffrage," what does a ballot to vote ensure?
   A. an election
   B. a say in who governs the people
   C. a polling place
   D. the right to a fair trial

____ 6. In "On Woman's Right to Suffrage," Anthony points out that the Union was formed by
   A. politicians.
   B. males.
   C. all people.
   D. a few rebels.

____ 7. In "On Woman's Right to Suffrage," what does Anthony call the United States government?
   A. an oligarchy of sex
   B. a democracy
   C. a monarchy based on England's government
   D. a playground for the privileged

____ 8. According to Anthony in "On Woman's Right to Suffrage," how do dictionaries define *citizen*?
   A. voter
   B. lawmaker
   C. person
   D. man

____ 9. In "On Woman's Right to Suffrage," to what other group does Anthony compare the plight of women?
   A. African Americans
   B. children
   C. the elderly
   D. families

____ 10. What reasoning does the author of "On Woman's Right to Suffrage" use to persuade her audience that discrimination against women is illegal?
   A. Discrimination was ruled illegal in court.
   B. Women work as hard as men, so they deserve the same rights.
   C. Women had a part in writing the Constitution.
   D. Women are persons, so they have full rights as citizens.

____ 11. What is Anthony's main point in "On Woman's Right to Suffrage"?
   A. She supports the founders of the Union.
   B. Women have a legal right to vote.
   C. She wants to run for office.
   D. Women should earn as much as men.

Vocabulary and Grammar

____ 12. Which word is closest in meaning to *posterity*?
   A. ancestors   C. relatives
   B. descendants   D. grandparents

____ 13. In which sentence is a conjunction used correctly?
   A. Bob but Joel are on the debate team.
   B. Do I want my potato mashed nor baked?
   C. It was raining, for we went inside.
   D. Natalie and her teammates cheered the winning goal.

____ 14. Which choice is closest in meaning to *dissension*?
   A. compromise   C. difference of opinion
   B. disgust   D. decision

Essay

15. Write a short essay in which you name the crime Susan B. Anthony was accused of committing. How did she defend herself? Include at least two reasons the author uses to support her claims.

16. Imagine that you are in the audience listening to Susan B. Anthony's speech, more than one hundred years ago. Write a short essay in which you explain whether you find her speech convincing. Include at least one of the author's arguments as an example.

17. **Thinking About the Big Question: How much information is enough?** Imagine that you were in the audience more than one hundred years ago when Susan B. Anthony gave the speech "On Woman's Right to Suffrage." In an essay, explain whether Anthony provided enough information to convince you of her opinion that women deserve the right to vote.

Name _____ Date _____

"On Woman's Right to Suffrage" by Susan B. Anthony
Selection Test B

Critical Reading *Identify the letter of the choice that best completes the statement or answers the question.*

_____ 1. From what does Susan B. Anthony quote at the beginning of "On Woman's Right to Suffrage"?
A. the Declaration of Independence
B. a letter to the editor of the local paper
C. the Preamble of the Constitution
D. a law textbook

_____ 2. Of what crime was the author of "On Woman's Right to Suffrage" accused?
A. voting unlawfully
B. speaking against the President
C. attempting to escape from prison
D. staging a demonstration

_____ 3. How does Anthony address the audience in "On Woman's Right to Suffrage"?
A. Senators and Representatives
B. Friends and fellow citizens
C. Mr. Mayor
D. Mr. President

_____ 4. How does Susan B. Anthony define *the people of the United States*?
A. all but women and children
B. only women
C. politicians and legal authorities
D. all people

_____ 5. Susan B. Anthony calls the plight of women "a downright mockery." This is an example of
A. a fact.
B. an opinion.
C. a generalization.
D. an overgeneralization.

_____ 6. Any American citizen, Susan B. Anthony says, is entitled to
A. attend meetings of the Senate.
B. be elected President.
C. vote and hold political office.
D. give public speeches.

_____ 7. Anthony reasons that to discriminate by sex or race is a violation of
A. one's dignity.
B. basic human rights.
C. the supreme law of the land.
D. her own personal code of ethics.

_____ 8. By referring to "female posterity," Anthony shows concern for
   A. future generations of women.
   B. her immediate family.
   C. women's right to hold public office.
   D. quality child care.

_____ 9. Anthony thinks that an "oligarchy of sex" is worse than one of race because
   A. there are more women than men.
   B. it affects family dynamics.
   C. it affects women's jobs.
   D. it excludes future politicians.

_____ 10. Anthony cites Webster, Worcester, and Bouvier as sources saying *citizens* are "people." What are these sources?
   A. representatives
   B. police officers
   C. dictionaries
   D. female supporters

_____ 11. In Susan B. Anthony's speech, "Are women persons?" is an example of
   A. a factual question.
   B. a rhetorical question.
   C. a question based on opinion.
   D. a general question.

_____ 12. When did Anthony give the speech "On Woman's Right to Suffrage"?
   A. at the Constitutional Convention
   B. during the Civil War
   C. over 100 years ago
   D. over 200 years ago

_____ 13. Anthony generalizes that all discrimination against women is "null and void." On what does she base this conclusion?
   A. Women are persons, so they also are full citizens.
   B. Women work equally as hard as men.
   C. Discrimination was ruled illegal during the Civil War.
   D. Women outnumber men in most states.

Vocabulary and Grammar

_____ 14. Which sentence contains a conjunction?
   A. My friend and I went to a poetry slam.
   B. Her sister planned to recite new poems.
   C. The poets came from several schools.
   D. They read for two full hours.

____ **15.** Which choice is closest in meaning to *oligarchy*?
  A. a nonprofit agency
  B. a partnership
  C. a small, elite group
  D. a democracy

____ **16.** If there is *dissension* in a group, what might you expect to hear?
  A. laughing
  B. arguing
  C. talking
  D. singing

____ **17.** Which word means the opposite of *posterity*?
  A. grandchildren
  B. in-laws
  C. ancestors
  D. royalty

Essay

18. Susan B. Anthony says she does not believe that she lives in a true democracy. In a brief essay, explain her reason for saying this. As you prepare your answer, consider the characteristics of a democracy. Use a specific example from the text of her speech to support your answer.

19. "On Woman's Right to Suffrage" includes this passage:

> It was we, the people; not we, the white male citizens; nor yet we, the male citizens; but we, the whole people, who formed the Union. And we formed it, not to give the blessings of liberty, but to secure them; not to the half of ourselves and the half of our posterity, but to the whole people—women as well as men.

Some words or structures—*we; formed; not to . . . but to;* and *half*—occur more than one time. In a brief essay, discuss the effect of the repetition of those items.

20. **Thinking About the Big Question: How much information is enough?** Imagine that you were in the audience more than one hundred years ago when Susan B. Anthony gave the speech "On Woman's Right to Suffrage." In an essay, explain whether Anthony provided enough information to convince you of her point. If you believe she did, explain what information was most persuasive. If she did not, explain what information was lacking.

from **"Sharing in the American Dream"** by Colin Powell
Vocabulary Warm-up Word Lists

Study these words from "Sharing in the American Dream". *Then, complete the activities that follow.*

Word List A

achieve [uh CHEEV] *v.* to succeed in doing something you want
   To <u>achieve</u> your big dreams, do small things well along the way.

denied [di NYD] *v.* stopped from having or doing something
   American women were <u>denied</u> the right to vote until 1920.

inhabit [in HAB it] *v.* to live in a particular place
   Some day I plan to <u>inhabit</u> a tree house in the middle of a rain forest.

sags [SAGZ] *v.* hangs down, especially because of the heavy weight
   Look at how the top branch of that tree <u>sags</u> under the snow!

secure [si KYOOR] *v.* to get or bring about something important
   Did you <u>secure</u> your parents' permission to spend the night?

syrupy [SEER uh pee] *adj.* thick, sticky, and sweet
   I hate how the <u>syrupy</u> sauce on this cinnamon roll makes my fingers sticky.

task [TASK] *n.* a job to be done, especially a difficult or annoying one
   A nightly <u>task</u> I must remember is to set my alarm clock.

union [YOON yuhn] *n.* separate groups joining for a purpose
   Our basketball team is a <u>union</u> of seventh-graders and eighth-graders.

Word List B

alliance [uh LYE uhns] *n.* close connection among groups of people
   Many states have an <u>alliance</u> of mayors who share ideas about city government.

commit [kuh MIT] *v.* to say that you will definitely do or support something
   My friends and I <u>commit</u> ourselves each Earth Day to picking up litter.

despite [di SPYT] *prep.* without being stopped by something
   Our team won the game <u>despite</u> the injury of our star player.

moral [MAWR uhl] *adj.* having to do with right and wrong
   I have a <u>moral</u> duty never to cheat on tests.

pledge [PLEJ] *v.* to promise, often publicly
   Didn't Catherine <u>pledge</u> to be club secretary this year?

pursuit [puhr SOOT] *n.* the act of trying to do something
   Our chess team is in <u>pursuit</u> of our first city championship.

virtue [VER choo] *n.* goodness; a worthwhile quality in someone
   I do not believe there is any <u>virtue</u> in being bossy.

vulnerable [VUHL ner uh buhl] *adj.* easily hurt or harmed
   The most <u>vulnerable</u> houses seem to be the ones hit hardest by storms.

from **"Sharing in the American Dream"** by Colin Powell
Vocabulary Warm-up Exercises

Exercise A *Fill in each blank in the paragraph below with an appropriate word from Word List A. Use each word only once.*

Our club decided to make a special Saturday lunch for people who

[1] _____ a homeless shelter during the winter months. We were able to

[2] _____ the school kitchen, where we are cooking today. However, our

request for a bus and driver was [3] _____. Luckily, our parents have

offered to drive, helping us to [4] _____ our goal. As we work side by side

among friends, a feeling of goodness surrounds our [5] _____. Every

[6] _____ seems like fun as we prepare a feast of ham-and-cheese sand-

wiches, [7] _____ peaches oozing sweetness, and a tossed salad. Each

lunch box we pack [8] _____ in the middle from the weight of the

bounty—including a brownie for dessert!

Exercise B *Decide whether each statement below is true or false. Circle T or F. Then, explain your answer.*

1. The runt, or smallest baby born to an animal, is the least <u>vulnerable</u>.
   T / F _____

2. People getting married <u>pledge</u> certain things to each other during their vows.
   T / F _____

3. When you <u>commit</u> to doing something, you should not view it as a real promise.
   T / F _____

4. Your <u>moral</u> sense sends out alarm signals to you if you are about to do something
   wrong.
   T / F _____

5. When you are in <u>pursuit</u> of a goal, you are thinking about what you might want
   to do.
   T / F _____

6. It is hard to see the <u>virtue</u> behind kind acts.
   T / F _____

7. <u>Despite</u> each group's goal of remaining independent, an <u>alliance</u> can be successfully formed.
   T / F _____

from **"Sharing in the American Dream"** by Colin Powell
Reading Warm-up A

Read the following passage. Pay special attention to the underlined words. Then, read it again, and complete the activities. Use a separate sheet of paper for your written answers.

Today will be tough for me. I have been given the <u>task</u> of speaking to a group of students about their bad behavior. These students have been in trouble at school three or more times during the last month. When I became a teacher, I never thought I would also <u>secure</u> the job of speechmaker! After all, I am the person whose requests to appear on the college television station were always <u>denied</u>. I figured that was because of the way my right eyebrow <u>sags</u>. Someone must have thought that a droopy brow wouldn't look very good on the screen.

Anyway, what I am supposed to <u>achieve</u> with my speech today is to get students fired up about being good. I can still remember the speeches I heard on this topic in my youth. Those speeches basically fell into two categories. One type used <u>syrupy</u> words and lots of "touchy-feely" remarks. I think you were supposed to feel guilty after hearing one of these speeches so you would be inspired to become a better person. The other type of speech was based on fear. We were told about the really bad kids who are sent to jail cells, which they will <u>inhabit</u> for many years. Filled with dread, we were supposed to become well behaved.

Obviously, I do not want to give either type of speech today. Instead, I want to figure out how to talk to these students in a way that respects who they are. I think that if they have a sense of <u>union</u> with the adults at our school, they might change for the better. After all, don't we all want to do things that the people we like will appreciate?

I wish you could sit beside me right now and tell me what to say. I know you would have just the right words.

1. Underline the words naming the <u>task</u> the speaker has been given. Then, explain why a *task* is different from an extracurricular activity.

2. Circle the word naming the other job the teacher would <u>secure</u>. Then, explain *secure*.

3. Underline the words naming what was <u>denied</u> to the writer in college. Then, tell about a time you were *denied* something you wanted.

4. Circle the word in the next sentence that hints at the meaning of <u>sags.</u> Then, name a common object that *sags*.

5. Underline the words telling what the speech should <u>achieve</u>. Then, explain the word *achieve*.

6. Circle the words that explain "<u>syrupy</u> words." Then, write an example of *syrupy* words.

7. Underline the words naming the place bad kids will <u>inhabit</u>. Then, describe a place that would be awful to *inhabit*.

8. Circle the two groups of people that would form a <u>union</u>. Then, explain what *union* means.

Name _____   Date _____

from **"Sharing in the American Dream"** by Colin Powell
Reading Warm-up B

Read the following passage. Pay special attention to the underlined words. Then, read it again, and complete the activities. Use a separate sheet of paper for your written answers.

Anyone who feels a <u>moral</u> duty to help those less fortunate will be drawn to the ideas of Make a Difference Day. This national day of helping others is run each October by *USA Weekend Magazine*. The magazine has an <u>alliance</u> with the Points of Light Foundation and the actor Paul Newman, among others. It holds the event to encourage people to <u>commit</u> to a specific project that will help others.

Paul Newman and his nonprofit company <u>pledge</u> $100,000 each year to the program. The money that has been promised will be divided among ten participants whose good deeds are chosen as the best of the year. More times than not, the winners pass on the cash they have received to the very people they helped on Make a Difference Day. The <u>virtue</u> of these acts is impressive. Such good deeds surely encourage others to join the program.

Over the years, millions of people have taken part in Make a Difference Day. The effort might be one person spending a couple of hours reading to others. It might involve a whole town joining together to collect and deliver food to the needy. Truly, every deed is remarkable. <u>Despite</u> our busy lives, surely we all can get behind the simple idea of the event. "Put your own cares on hold for one day to care for someone else." Before next October rolls around, get involved in your own <u>pursuit</u> of a solution to a problem in your neighborhood.

Make a Difference Day is held on the last Saturday of the month. Make plans early to spend a few hours that day on the project of your choice. The sick, the poor, and other <u>vulnerable</u> members of society will appreciate your help.

1. Underline the words describing the <u>moral</u> duty. Then, describe a *moral* duty you have.

2. Circle the names of those in the <u>alliance</u>. Then, explain what *alliance* means.

3. Underline the words naming what the magazine hopes people will <u>commit</u> to. Then, explain *commit*.

4. Circle the word in the next sentence that hints at the meaning of <u>pledge</u>. To what would you *pledge* money?

5. Underline the words in the next sentence that help to understand <u>virtue</u>. Then, explain *virtue*.

6. Reword the phrase "<u>Despite</u> our busy lives" so that it has the same meaning without the word *despite*.

7. Circle the words describing something the writer would like you to be in <u>pursuit</u> of. Then, explain what your *pursuit* might be.

8. Underline two words that might describe <u>vulnerable</u> people. Then, explain *vulnerable*.

Name _____   Date _____

from **"Sharing in the American Dream"** by Colin Powell
Writing About the Big Question

How much information is enough?

Big Question Vocabulary

accumulate	challenge	decision	development	discrimination
explanation	exploration	factor	global	inequality
quality	quantity	reveal	statistics	valuable

A. *Use a word from list above to complete each sentence.*

1. What might help you figure out whether racial discrimination still exists?

   _____

2. Which word might you use to describe tutoring a fidgety kindergarten student?

   _____

3. Which word describes something that is more important than the amount of time a person volunteers? _____

B. *Follow the directions in responding to each of the items below.*

1. Write a two-sentence explanation of how volunteerism can help overcome racial discrimination. Use at least two list words in your explanation.

   _____

   _____

   _____

2. How can volunteering benefit the volunteer? Use at least two list words in your answer.

   _____

   _____

   _____

C. *Complete the sentence below. Then, write a short paragraph in which you connect this answer to the Big Question.*

When there is inequity in society, we should _____

and _____

   _____

   _____

   _____

   _____

Name _____ Date _____

from **"Sharing in the American Dream"** by Colin Powell
Reading: Use Support for Fact and Opinion

A **fact** is information that can be proved. An **opinion** is a person's judgment or belief. As you read nonfiction, ask questions to evaluate an author's support for his or her opinions.

- A *valid opinion* can be supported by facts or by expert authority.
- A *faulty opinion* cannot be supported by facts. Instead, it is supported by other opinions and often ignores major facts that contradict it. Faulty opinions often show *bias*, an unfair preference or dislike for something.

In this selection from "Sharing in the American Dream," Colin Powell draws on facts and opinions to inspire his audience to step up and volunteer in their communities. His feelings about past and present Americans reflect both pride and hope.

The following statement from Powell's speech about America's founders is a fact because it can be proved.

They pledged their lives, their fortune and their sacred honor to secure inalienable rights. . . .

The following statement is an opinion because it is a judgment or belief.

Yet, despite all we have done, this is still an imperfect world.

Powell supports his opinion with the fact that some Americans, many of whom are children, are in need and at risk.

DIRECTIONS: *Read the following statements of opinion from the selection. Complete the chart with Powell's statements of support for each opinion. Then, decide whether you think the opinion is adequately supported, or valid.*

Opinion	Support	Adequately Supported?
1. "In terms of numbers, the task [of helping children] may seem staggering."		
2. "But if we look at the simple needs that these children have, then the truth is manageable, the goal is achievable."		
3. "There is a spirit of Philadelphia that will leave Philadelphia tomorrow afternoon and spread across this whole nation. . . ."		

Name _____ Date _____

from **"Sharing in the American Dream"** by Colin Powell
Literary Analysis: Use Word Choice to Convey Ideas

An author's **word choice** can help him or her convey a certain idea or feeling. An author might choose words that are formal or informal, simple or complex. Factors that influence an author's word choice include the following:

- the author's intended audience and purpose
- the **denotations** of words—their literal or specific meanings
- the **connotations** of words—the negative or positive ideas associated with them

In this passage from his speech to encourage volunteerism, Colin Powell chooses words that he hopes will appeal to his listeners and inspire them to act.

That is why we are here, my friends. We gather here to pledge that those of us who are more fortunate will not forsake those who are less fortunate.

By calling his listeners *my friends* and using the phrase *those of us*, the speaker creates a feeling of closeness. By using the word *pledge*, he identifies a common goal.

DIRECTIONS: *Read the following passages from the selection. Decide whether the underlined words create a formal feeling or an informal feeling. Then, explain the effect of each passage on listeners and readers.*

1. "We will reach down, we will reach back, we will reach across to help <u>our brothers and sisters</u> who are in need."

   _____

   _____

   _____

2. "These are basic needs that we <u>commit</u> ourselves to today, we <u>promise</u> today."

   _____

   _____

   _____

3. "You heard the governors and the mayors, and you'll hear more in a little minute that says the real answer is . . . <u>for each and every one of us to reach out and touch someone in need</u>."

   _____

   _____

   _____

Name _____ Date _____

from "Sharing in the American Dream" by Colin Powell
Vocabulary Builder

Word List

alliance   aspirations   compassionate   deferred   virtue   vulnerable

A. DIRECTIONS: *Use a thesaurus to find a synonym for each Word List word. Then, use each synonym in a sentence that makes the meaning of the synonym clear.*

1. *aspirations*; synonym: _____

_____

2. *deferred*; synonym: _____

_____

3. *compassionate*; synonym: _____

_____

4. *alliance*; synonym: _____

_____

5. *vulnerable*; synonym: _____

_____

6. *virtue*; synonym: _____

_____

B. WORD STUDY The Latin root *-pass-* means "to suffer" or "to endure." Words with *-pass-* include *compassion*, "sympathy for another's hardship"; *impassioned*, "showing intense feeling"; and *dispassionate*, "not influenced by strong feeling." Use the meaning of the root to revise the following sentences so that they make sense.

1. One child had so much *compassion* that she refused to donate a single present.

_____

2. After she saw the movie, she became so *impassioned* that she fell asleep immediately.

_____

3. A *dispassionate* teacher can never grade opinion essays fairly.

_____

Name _____   Date _____

from **"Sharing in the American Dream"** by Colin Powell
Enrichment: Community Service Opportunities

Colin Powell's speech is a plea for more Americans to make a regular commitment to volunteer. He suggests that people can put aside up to an hour a week to help others. Many people in every community across America are already giving time to volunteer efforts. Some people tutor students in schools; some deliver books and magazines to hospital patients; some take care of animals in shelters; some make audio recordings of books for people who can't read on their own; and some prepare and serve meals for the homeless. Former President Jimmy Carter has given countless hours of his time to volunteer activities; one of his most well-known activities is helping to build houses for the Habitat for Humanity organization.

Use the form below to survey friends, neighbors, and local community leaders about their own volunteer experiences. In addition, ask them to suggest areas where they think help is needed. You might use the information you gather to inform students at your school about volunteer opportunities in your community.

Survey

1. Do you, or does anyone you know, volunteer in our community?

_____

_____

_____

2. If so, what kind of volunteering do you or others do?

_____

_____

_____

3. If not, what kind of volunteer activity might you consider doing?

_____

_____

_____

4. What need in our community might volunteers fill?

_____

_____

_____

Unit 3 Resources: Types of Nonfiction
174

Name _____ Date _____

from "**Sharing in the American Dream**" by Colin Powell
Open-Book Test

Short Answer *Write your responses to the questions in this section on the lines provided.*

1. In the first sentence of this excerpt from "Sharing in the American Dream," Colin Powell refers to "a group of volunteers." He says that they gathered over 200 years ago "to found a new nation." Whom does he mean, and what did they volunteer to do?

   _____

   _____

   _____

   _____

2. In the third paragraph of this excerpt from "Sharing in the American Dream," Powell speaks of a "dream deferred." What is the dream, and why has it been deferred? Refer to the definition of *deferred* in answering this question.

   _____

   _____

   _____

   _____

3. In the fourth paragraph of this excerpt from "Sharing in the American Dream," Powell addresses his audience as "my friends" and refers to the needy as "our brothers and sisters." What feeling does he want to inspire with those phrases? Explain your answer.

   _____

   _____

   _____

4. In order to evaluate an author's opinion, readers must analyze the evidence the author uses to support it. In the second paragraph of this excerpt from "Sharing in the American Dream," Powell states that our world is still imperfect. Complete this diagram by writing a fact from the speech that supports that opinion. Then, on the line below, state the conclusion Colin Powell wants his audience to draw from this argument.

Fact:	→	"This is still an imperfect world."

   _____

   _____

5. Powell includes facts and opinions in "Sharing in the American Dream." He states, for example, that "up to 15 million young Americans today are at risk." Is that statement a fact or an opinion? How can you tell?

   _____

   _____

6. In "Sharing in the American Dream," Powell uses the word *we* a number of times. He says, for example, "we pledge to reach out," "if we look at the simple needs," "We know," and "We are making America's promise." What effect is he trying to convey with the use of the word *we*?

   _____

   _____

   _____

7. In "Sharing in the American Dream," Colin Powell speaks of forming a "grand alliance." Whom does he want to be part of this alliance? Focus on the meaning of *alliance* in answering this question.

   _____

   _____

   _____

8. In the next-to-last paragraph of this excerpt from "Sharing in the American Dream," Powell repeats several words, especially the noun *spirit* and the verb *will*. What is the effect of Powell's word choice in this paragraph?

   _____

   _____

   _____

9. Powell is using his speech "Sharing in the American Dream" to ask people to do something. What does he want them to do?

   _____

   _____

   _____

10. A writer always has a purpose for writing a work of literature. What was Colin Powell's purpose in writing the speech "Sharing in the American Dream"? How can you tell?

   _____

   _____

   _____

Essay

Write an extended response to the question of your choice or to the question or questions your teacher assigns you.

11. In "Sharing in the American Dream," Powell lists several benefits children will receive if his plan is successful. In an essay, explain Powell's plan. Then, describe at least two of these benefits, telling how they will help children achieve the American Dream.

12. Colin Powell states that in terms of the American Dream, America is "an imperfect society." In an essay, explain what you think Powell means by "the American Dream." Then, describe the way in which American society is imperfect, in Powell's view.

13. In "Sharing in the American Dream," Powell quotes from Langston Hughes's poem "Harlem: A Dream Deferred." Look again at the poem, which Powell quotes in full. In an essay, explain what the poet might have meant when he spoke of "a dream deferred." Then, describe the possibilities that the poet offers as a response to a dream deferred. Finally, explain the connection between Langston Hughes's poem and the rest of Powell's speech.

14. **Thinking About the Big Question: How much information is enough?** In an essay, explain what Powell is calling for in "Sharing in the American Dream." Then, explain whether Powell's speech contains enough information for you to form an opinion of his plan. If it does, state your opinion, and explain the reasons for it. Cite two details from the speech that support your opinion. If the speech does not contain enough information for you to form an opinion of Powell's plan, explain what you would like to know.

Oral Response

15. Go back to question 1, 3, or 5 or to the question your teacher assigns you. Take a few minutes to expand your answer and prepare an oral response. Find additional details in "Sharing in the American Dream" that support your points. If necessary, make notes to guide your oral response.

Name _____ Date _____

from "**Sharing in the American Dream**" by Colin Powell
Selection Test A

Critical Reading *Identify the letter of the choice that best answers the question.*

_____ 1. In "Sharing in the American Dream," what does Powell call the people who founded America?
   A. leaders
   B. volunteers
   C. politicians
   D. revolutionaries

_____ 2. What is the source of the phrase "a dream deferred," which Powell quotes to support the introduction to his speech?
   A. a poem
   B. another speech
   C. a popular song
   D. his autobiography

_____ 3. In "Sharing in the American Dream," what generalization does Powell state?
   A. No one has time to spare.
   B. No one likes to be alone.
   C. All of us can spare thirty minutes a week.
   D. All of us come from other places.

_____ 4. Powell states that "up to 15 million young Americans today are at risk. . . ." What kind of statement is this?
   A. an opinion
   B. a fact
   C. a generalization
   D. a criticism

_____ 5. In "Sharing in the American Dream," why does Powell focus on children?
   A. Children appreciate help more than adults.
   B. Children have simple, manageable needs.
   C. Children are pleasant to be around.
   D. Children are centrally located in schools.

_____ 6. What concern may listeners to "Sharing in the American Dream" raise, according to Powell?

    A. Corporate American cannot be trusted.

    B. Not enough people become teachers.

    C. Congress will not support his plan.

    D. The task of helping children is too great.

_____ 7. What feelings might Powell's words "we . . . pledge" and "we promise" call up in people listening to "Sharing in the American Dream"?

    A. pride, enthusiasm

    B. suspicion, dread

    C. boredom, dislike

    D. humor, anxiety

_____ 8. What cause is Powell supporting in "Sharing in the American Dream"?

    A. voter registration

    B. nationally subsidized day care

    C. better pay for teachers

    D. volunteerism

_____ 9. According to Powell, who already supports the goals he expresses in his speech?

    A. some governors and mayors

    B. some parents

    C. some teachers

    D. some children

_____ 10. What feelings does Powell create in listeners by mentioning the people who founded America?

    A. hope for the future

    B. guilt

    C. admiration and inspiration

    D. worry about current problems

_____ 11. What does Powell hope his listeners will do when they go back to their communities?

    A. adopt a child

    B. persuade businesses to produce more

    C. spread the word about volunteering

    D. spend more time with their families

Vocabulary and Grammar

____ 12. Which word is the best definition of *deferred*?

A. restricted   C. postponed

B. removed   D. defined

____ 13. Which of the following is *not* a prepositional phrase?

A. under the bed   C. into the water

B. watching the sunrise   D. to the store

____ 14. Which sentence contains a prepositional phrase?

A. The rabbit jumped into the hat.

B. The cow ate greedily.

C. The crow flew south.

D. The lion roared loudly.

____ 15. In which sentence is *compassionate* used correctly?

A. Jay's compassionate nature made him unpopular.

B. Compassionate people tend to be self-centered.

C. It was love at first sight; they immediately felt compassionate about each other.

D. Judy is compassionate where lost or stray animals are concerned.

Essay

16. Colin Powell is very specific about what he is asking Americans to do. In a short essay, describe Powell's idea. Then, explain whether you think his plan is possible. Use one specific example from the speech to support your opinion.

17. In his speech, Powell lists several benefits children will receive if his plan is success-ful. Write an organized essay in which you describe at least two of these benefits. Be sure to begin your essay with a clear topic sentence.

18. **Thinking About the Big Question: How much information is enough?** In "Shar-ing in the American Dream," Colin Powell calls on people to do more volunteering. In an essay, explain whether Powell's speech contains enough information for you to form an opinion of his plan. Support your response with relevant details from the selection.

from "**Sharing in the American Dream**" by Colin Powell
Selection Test B

Critical Reading *Identify the letter of the choice that best completes the statement or answers the question.*

____ 1. To whom is Colin Powell referring in this first sentence of his speech?

Over 200 years ago, a group of volunteers gathered on this sacred spot to found a new nation.

A. citizens of Philadelphia
B. the founding fathers of the United States
C. his ancestors
D. Native Americans from another area

____ 2. What problem in our country does Powell describe in "Sharing in the American Dream"?
A. No one dreams of greatness anymore.
B. Some don't share in the American dream.
C. Public schools are failing.
D. The recycling program is substandard.

____ 3. Which poet does Powell quote near the beginning of his speech?
A. Robert Frost
B. Emily Dickinson
C. Langston Hughes
D. Billy Collins

____ 4. Where did Powell present his speech?
A. Washington, D.C.
B. New York City
C. San Francisco
D. Philadelphia

____ 5. What fact does Powell use in his speech to support his ideas?
A. Up to 15 million children are at risk.
B. Thirty-nine states do not recycle.
C. Forty percent of adults are illiterate.
D. Too many people lack health insurance.

____ 6. What does Powell see as a long-term benefit of serving children?
A. Children will end up going to college.
B. Children are our future leaders.
C. Children will grow up to help others.
D. Children will know more history.

___ 7. In this sentence from "Sharing in the American Dream," what connotation does *crusade* have, and why?

    And so let us all join in this great crusade.

    A. negative connotation because crusades can be bloody
    B. positive connotation because crusades involve comradeship
    C. negative connotation because it suggests too large a sacrifice
    D. positive connotation because crusades remind us of history

___ 8. What factual information does Powell provide about his supporters?
    A. They include people from both parties.
    B. They come from over forty states.
    C. They include governors and mayors.
    D. They are all registered voters.

___ 9. What word best describes the feeling Powell creates with the words *pledge* and *promise*?
    A. commitment
    B. authority
    C. honesty
    D. desperation

___ 10. In what way does Powell anticipate that the spirit of his idea will spread across the country?
    A. in newspapers
    B. through individual people
    C. in television ads
    D. in peaceful demonstrations

___ 11. Which phrase best describes the feeling Powell wants to inspire by addressing the audience as "my friends" and referring to the needy as "brothers and sisters"?
    A. friendly gatherings
    B. casual dinners
    C. close partnership
    D. family affection

___ 12. What is Powell's purpose in giving this speech?
    A. He wants to encourage voters to elect him to office.
    B. He wants to inspire Americans to start an environmental initiative.
    C. He is appealing to Americans to start faith-based organizations.
    D. He is appealing to Americans to help those in need.

Vocabulary and Grammar

___ 13. Which word correctly completes the following sentence?

    Many fans were disappointed when the singer _____ her concert date until next month.

    A. deferred   C. distracted
    B. destroyed   D. desolated

____ 14. Which word or phrase is the best definition of *alliance*?
   A. a threatening partnership   C. reliance
   B. a united group   D. a feeling of well-being

____ 15. Identify the prepositional phrase in the following sentence.
   Mike enjoys running in the fall because that is when the leaves change color.
   A. because that   C. when the leaves change color
   B. enjoys running   D. in the fall

____ 16. Which sentence does *not* contain a prepositional phrase?
   A. The bird flew around the world.
   B. My cat sleeps under the bed every day.
   C. Matt enjoys singing and playing guitar.
   D. The girls ran to the lighthouse today.

____ 17. Which word is *not* a synonym for *aspirations*?
   A. hopes   B. breaths   C. ambitions   D. desires

Essay

18. In a topic sentence, tell what Powell was calling for, and give your reaction to his idea. Did Powell inspire you or turn you off? Then, give at least two reasons that explain why you had the reaction you did. The reasons can come from the speech itself or from your personal experience.

19. Colin Powell states that in terms of the American Dream, America is an "imperfect society." Write an essay in which you first explain what you think Powell means by *the American Dream*. Then, give at least two examples of problems that Powell thinks should be addressed.

20. **Thinking About the Big Question: How much information is enough?** In an essay, explain what Powell is calling for in "Sharing in the American Dream." Then, explain whether Powell's speech contains enough information for you to form an opinion of his plan. If it does, state your opinion, and explain the reasons for it. Cite two details from the speech that support your opinion. If the speech does not contain enough information for you to form an opinion of Powell's plan, explain what you would like to know.

Study these words from "Science and the Sense of Wonder." Then, complete the activities.

Word List A

exhaling [eks HAYL ing] *v.* breathing out
After holding his breath for ten seconds, Carlos is now <u>exhaling</u>.

expand [ek SPAND] *v.* to become larger
After a huge meal, our waistlines <u>expand</u>.

glinting [GLINT ing] *adj.* flashing with a small amount of light
We couldn't see well with the sun <u>glinting</u> off the windshield.

mere [MEER] *adj.* nothing more than; small or unimportant
Huge stars are so far away that they appear as <u>mere</u> dots of light.

mutations [myoo TAY shuhnz] *n.* changes in form of things in nature
The purple butterflies were <u>mutations</u> of the original blue ones.

outward [OWT wuhrd] *adv.* toward the outside
The lawn sprinkler shot water <u>outward</u> in all directions.

radiation [ray dee AY shuhn] *n.* invisible rays of light or heat that an object sends out
The sun's <u>radiation</u> is not constant but varies over time.

violence [VY uh luhns] *n.* great force
The tomato hit the ground with such <u>violence</u> that it splattered.

Word List B

asteroid [AS tuh royd] *n.* tiny planetlike object that moves around the sun
An <u>asteroid</u> from space landed in Arizona and made a huge hole.

astronomer [uh STRAH nuh mer] *n.* scientist who studies stars and planets in space
An <u>astronomer</u> explained the use of a radio telescope to study stars.

compact [kuhm PAKT] *adj.* taking up little space
Jay rolled and squeezed a slice of bread into a <u>compact</u> ball.

desolate [DES uh lit] *adj.* having no people or activity
When the mine closed, the nearby town became a <u>desolate</u> spot.

doling [DOHL ing] *v.* giving out little by little
Ann is that girl at the dessert table, <u>doling</u> out the cake so it lasts.

galactic [guh LAK tik] *adj.* relating to large groups of stars
I love looking up at that <u>galactic</u> wonder, the Milky Way.

heaving [HEEV ing] *adj.* rising and falling
The <u>heaving</u> waves nearly tossed us overboard.

vaporize [VAY puh ryz] *v.* to turn into a gas
If you boil water long enough, it will <u>vaporize</u> in the air.

"Science and the Sense of Wonder" by Isaac Asimov
Vocabulary Warm-up Exercises

Exercise A *Fill in each blank in the paragraph below with an appropriate word from Word List A. Use each word only once.*

In a typical science fiction story, harmful [1] _____ from atomic waste causes strange [2] _____ in harmless frogs. They [3] _____ rapidly, growing to a huge size. From [4] _____ frogs that can fit easily in the palm of your hand, they become giants. They wander [5] _____ from their pond, now too small to contain them. Wherever they go, they create [6] _____. They are either squashing everything in their path or [7] _____ their deadly radioactive breath. Humans are at a loss to stop the frogs, which grow bigger and tougher. Finally, someone comes up with a simple, obvious solution. The rays of the sun [8] _____ off a mirror dry up the moist-skinned troublemakers. Peace rules.

Exercise B *Decide whether each statement below is true or false. Circle T or F. Then, explain your answer.*

1. An <u>astronomer</u> may study an <u>asteroid</u>.
   T / F _____

2. <u>Heaving</u> water is calm water.
   T / F _____

3. Our sun is not part of any <u>galactic</u> system.
   T / F _____

4. Water can <u>vaporize</u> from either a <u>compact</u> container or a giant one.
   T / F _____

5. A busy building by day might be a <u>desolate</u> place by night.
   T / F _____

6. People <u>doling</u> out their money are generous.
   T / F _____

Name _____ Date _____

"Science and the Sense of Wonder" by Isaac Asimov
Reading Warm-up A

Read the following passage. Pay special attention to the underlined words. Then, read it again, and complete the activities. Use a separate sheet of paper for your written answers.

Jamie had always refused to believe that humans were the only living creatures in the universe. He had also refused to believe that space was full of strange mutations of people like the aliens in most science-fiction movies. So, he was totally shocked by what happened to him one weekend evening.

He was walking home from the movies, a mere three short blocks from his house. The street was well lit. There had never been any violence along this route that Jamie knew of, so he felt safe.

Suddenly, Jamie spied what looked like a square coin on the sidewalk, glinting in the light of the streetlamp. As he stooped to pick it up, the strangest thing happened: The coin began to expand on all sides. Slowly at first, it seemed to be gathering speed as it spread outward.

Jamie glanced around him to see if this action had attracted any attention, but he realized he was alone. Backing up to avoid the edge of the rapidly expanding coin, Jamie collided with the side of a building.

Now the coin seemed to be developing features: a face, limbs, and a trunk. It was glowing, too. Jamie held his breath in case the thing was giving off any harmful radiation. Luckily, it only seemed to be inhaling and exhaling the night air.

Suddenly, Jamie found himself in a conversation with the thing, and he hadn't said a word. Yes, like aliens in the movies, it was reading his thoughts.

"Of course I'm not a coin," it responded, "although I do feel *minty* fresh."

"Wow," thought Jamie, "it has a sense of humor."

"Why not?" responded the creature. "Why do humans think they're the only ones who can make jokes?"

"Hmm," thought Jamie, "if it played a comedy club, I wonder if it would knock the audience dead."

1. Underline the words that give you a clue to the meaning of <u>mutations</u>. Then, write a sentence for **mutations**.

2. Circle the words that hint at the meaning of <u>mere</u>. Write about an exchange of money that includes the word **mere**.

3. Circle the word that hints at the opposite of the meaning of <u>violence</u>. Write a sentence that describes one effect of **violence**.

4. Underline the words that help to understand <u>glinting</u>. Write a sentence about something you've seen **glinting**.

5. Circle the word that names what began to <u>expand</u>. Explain how you might cause an object to **expand**.

6. Circle the words in the paragraph that help you understand <u>outward</u>. Name something that opens **outward**.

7. Underline the word that describes <u>radiation</u>. Describe one harmful effect of **radiation** from the sun.

8. Circle the word that is the opposite of <u>exhaling</u>. Use **exhaling** in a sentence.

Name _____ Date _____

Read the following passage. Pay special attention to the underlined words. Then, read it again, and complete the activities. Use a separate sheet of paper for your written answers.

Compared with the huge size of a star, an <u>asteroid</u> might seem ridiculously <u>compact</u>. However, asteroids, those small objects that travel around the sun, mostly between Mars and Jupiter, are no laughing matter. Many an <u>astronomer</u> spends hours and hours studying the size, structure, and paths of those tiny parts of our solar system.

Studying asteroids may not seem as exciting as studying stars. Collecting <u>galactic</u> data—information about star systems—is on a much grander scale. Who knows what one might find in the bright, swelling, <u>heaving</u> center of a galaxy? However, scientists who collect data about asteroids know that their work may someday have a great impact upon what happens on Earth.

In fact, several asteroids have already crash-landed here. That was many, many years ago. Oh, bits of space rock so small that they go unseen are always landing on Earth. However, we're talking about a chunk sixty or eighty feet wide. What would happen if something like that dropped from the sky?

That is just what happened in Arizona thousands of years ago. Like that asteroid, any new one would leave a hole about three-quarters of a mile wide and <u>vaporize</u> anything unlucky enough to be in its way. There is certainly nothing cheerful about instantly turning to gas.

How likely is that scenario? It is nothing you have to worry about when you wake up in the morning. Thousands or millions of years from now, another large asteroid might fall. Asteroids are like that, <u>doling</u> out their danger little by little over the centuries. For now, most asteroids will continue to orbit in the <u>desolate</u> regions between Mars and Jupiter. Those that cross the path of Earth's orbit will continue to do so, too. Still, they won't come close enough to scare us—or even make us run for cover!

1. Underline the words that explain what an <u>asteroid</u> is. How might you feel if you saw an *asteroid* fall to Earth?

2. Circle a word in the next sentence that helps you to understand <u>compact</u>. Describe someone you know who is *compact*.

3. Circle the words in this sentence that tell you what an <u>astronomer</u> does. Write your own sentence, describing something an *astronomer* does.

4. Underline the words that hint at the meaning of <u>galactic</u>. Write a question you would like to have answered about *galactic* space travel.

5. Circle the word that is a synonym for <u>heaving</u>. Then, use *heaving* in your own sentence.

6. Underline the words in the next sentence that define <u>vaporize</u>. Describe a scientific experiment, using the word *vaporize*.

7. Circle the words that provide a clue to <u>doling</u>. Then, use *doling* in your own sentence.

8. Underline the words that hint at the meaning of <u>desolate</u>. Describe a place that is *desolate*.

Name _____ Date _____

"Science and the Sense of Wonder" by Isaac Asimov
Writing About the Big Question

How much information is enough?

Big Question Vocabulary

accumulate	challenge	decision	development	discrimination
explanation	exploration	factor	global	inequality
quality	quantity	reveal	statistics	valuable

A. *Use a word from the list above to complete each sentence.*

1. Science is more than facts and _____.

2. Scientists' _____ of knowledge about the world continues to grow.

3. Do you think there will come a time when there is a(n) _____ for everything?

B. *Follow the directions in responding to each of the items below.*

1. What two scientific developments would you like to learn more about?

   _____

   _____

2. How might you learn more about these scientific developments? Use at least two list words in your answer.

   _____

   _____

   _____

   _____

C. *Complete the sentence below. Then, write a short paragraph in which you connect this answer to the Big Question.*

The knowledge we gain from space exploration shows us _____

_____

_____

_____

_____

_____

"Science and the Sense of Wonder" by Isaac Asimov
Reading: Use Support for Fact and Opinion

A **fact** is information that can be proved. An **opinion** is a person's judgment or belief. As you read nonfiction, ask questions to evaluate an author's support for his or her opinions.

- A *valid opinion* can be supported by facts or by expert authority.
- A *faulty opinion* cannot be supported by facts. Instead, it is supported by other opinions and may contradict the facts. Faulty opinions often show *bias*, an unfair preference or dislike for something.

In "Science and the Sense of Wonder," Isaac Asimov draws on facts and opinions to support his ideas about the limitations of Walt Whitman's poetic view of the stars. He claims that scientific knowledge is necessary to fully appreciate nature's beauty.

The following statement from the essay tells a fact. It can be proved by scientists.

Those other bright spots, which are stars rather than planets, are actually suns.

The following statement is an opinion because it is a judgment or belief.

The trouble is that Walt Whitman is talking through his hat, but the poor soul didn't know any better.

Asimov supports his opinion with scientific descriptions and explanations about our universe.

DIRECTIONS: *Read the following statements of opinion from the selection. Complete the chart with Asimov's statements of support for each opinion. Then, decide whether you think the opinion is adequately supported, or valid.*

Opinion	Support	Adequately Supported?
1. "That is a very convenient point of view since it makes it not only unnecessary, but downright aesthetically wrong, to try to follow all that hard stuff in science."		
2. "There are worlds with thick atmospheres of carbon dioxide and sulfuric acid; . . . each with a weird and unearthly beauty that boils down to a mere speck of light if we just gaze at the night sky."		
3. "Some of them are of incomparable grandeur, each glowing with the light of a thousand suns like ours; some of them are merely red-hot coals doling out their energy stingily."		

"Science and the Sense of Wonder" by Isaac Asimov
Literary Analysis: Use Word Choice to Convey Ideas

An author's **word choice** can help him or her convey a certain idea or feeling. An author might choose words that are formal or informal, simple or complex. Factors that influence an author's word choice include the following:

- the author's intended audience and purpose
- the **connotations** of words—the negative or positive ideas associated with them

In this passage from his essay about the wonders of science, Isaac Asimov chooses words that he hopes will appeal to his listeners and spark their interest in learning about the science behind our universe.

> That is a very convenient point of view since it makes it not only unnecessary, but downright aesthetically wrong, to try to follow all that hard stuff in science. Instead, you can just take a look at the night sky, get a quick beauty fix, and go off to a nightclub.

By using language such as *all that hard stuff* and *get a quick beauty fix*, Asimov creates an informal feeling in his essay. He gets the attention of his audience—as a result, his readers are more likely to continue reading.

DIRECTIONS: *Read the following passages from the selection. Decide whether the underlined words create a formal feeling or an informal feeling. Then, explain the effect of each passage on readers.*

1. "I . . . have in my time <u>spread out</u> on a hillside for hours looking at the stars and being awed by their beauty (and <u>receiving bug-bites</u> whose marks took weeks to go away)."

   _____

   _____

   _____

2. "There are stars that <u>pulsate endlessly</u> in a great <u>cosmic breathing</u>; and others that, having <u>consumed</u> their fuel, expand and redden until they <u>swallow up</u> their planets. . . ."

   _____

   _____

   _____

3. "And some stars explode in a <u>vast cataclysm</u> whose <u>ferocious blast</u> of cosmic rays . . . reaches across thousands of light years."

   _____

   _____

   _____

Name _____ Date _____

"Science and the Sense of Wonder" by Isaac Asimov
Vocabulary Builder

Word List

awed   cataclysm   conceivable   contraction   exultantly   radiation

A. DIRECTIONS: *Write the letter of the word that means the* opposite *of the word in* CAPITAL LETTERS.

____ 1. EXULTANTLY
    A. miserably   C. happily
    B. thankfully   D. hopefully

____ 2. CONTRACTION
    A. disappearing   C. shrinking
    B. expansion   D. brightening

____ 3. AWED
    A. scared   C. amused
    B. nervous   D. unimpressed

____ 4. RADIATION
    A. revolving   C. absorption
    B. brightness   D. growth

____ 5. CATACLYSM
    A. success   C. party
    B. challenge   D. event

____ 6. CONCEIVABLE
    A. unimaginable   C. fertile
    B. forgotten   D. initial

B. WORD STUDY The Latin root *-tract-* means "pull or drag." The following questions have words containing the root *-tract-*. Use the meaning of *-tract-* to help you answer the questions.

1. If something *contracts*, is it still or does it move?

_____

2. Can a *distraction* lure people away from their work?

_____

Unit 3 Resources: Types of Nonfiction
© Pearson Education, Inc. All rights reserved.
191

"Science and the Sense of Wonder" by Isaac Asimov
Enrichment: Basic Questions of Astronomy

Both Walt Whitman and Isaac Asimov refer to astronomers in their writing about the beauty of the night sky. Astronomers gather and study information about the planets, suns, stars, and galaxies in our universe. Many people who do not become astronomers are nevertheless fascinated by the sky. Thousands of amateur astronomers around the world observe the planets, suns, and stars through telescopes they set up in their backyards. They have created networks of communication for sharing their techniques and observations.

Listed below are some of the most common questions people have about what they see in the night sky. Use sources such as the Internet and encyclopedias to find answers to them. Then, add a question of your own, and find its answer.

1. Why do stars flicker or twinkle?

   _____

   _____

2. Why do stars appear to change color?

   _____

   _____

3. What are constellations, and how did they get their names?

   _____

   _____

4. How can someone tell the difference between a star and a planet?

   _____

   _____

   _____

from **"Sharing in the American Dream"** by Colin Powell
"Science and the Sense of Wonder" by Isaac Asimov
Integrated Language Skills: Grammar

Prepositions

A **preposition** relates the noun or pronoun following it to another word in the sentence. Commonly used prepositions are listed in the box below.

about	behind	during	off	to
above	below	except	on	toward
across	beneath	for	onto	under
after	beside	from	opposite	underneath
against	besides	in	out	until
along	between	inside	outside	up
among	beyond	into	over	upon
around	but	like	past	with
at	by	near	since	within
before	down	of	through	without

The group of words beginning with the preposition and ending with the noun or pronoun is called a **prepositional phrase.** The noun or pronoun that follows the preposition is called the **object of the preposition.** Read the following example, and then notice that when identifying the object of a preposition, you do not include any modifiers of the noun or pronoun.

I chased my cat around the house.

Around is the preposition, and *house* is the object of the preposition.

A. PRACTICE: *Underline each preposition, and circle its object.*

1. The teacher enjoyed reading aloud to the class.
2. I watched my dog jump over the fence.
3. If you look through the window, you will see a cardinal sitting on a branch.
4. Of all my friends, Jenny is the funniest.
5. Tom placed his backpack behind the tree.

B. Writing Application: *Choose at least three of the prepositional phrases in the preceding exercise, along with any others you want to include, and write a paragraph using them. Underline the prepositional phrases.*

_____

_____

_____

from "**Sharing in the American Dream**" by Colin Powell
"**Science and the Sense of Wonder**" by Isaac Asimov

Integrated Language Skills: Support for Writing a Response to Literature

from "Sharing in the American Dream"

To prepare for writing a **response** to Colin Powell's statement about volunteering, answer the following questions.

1. What is Colin Powell asking the people in his audience to do for thirty minutes or an hour, once a week?

   _____

2. Could you spare thirty minutes or an hour a week to help another person in some way? If you could spare the time, what are some things you might volunteer to do?

   _____

   _____

3. Do you, or does someone you know, volunteer weekly? If so, doing what?

   _____

4. Does your school have a student organization for community service? If not, how might you start one?

   _____

   Now, use your answers to write your response.

"Science and the Sense of Wonder"

To prepare for writing a **response** to Isaac Asimov's idea that a scientist's way of appreciating nature is just as valid as a poet's, answer the following questions.

1. Isaac Asimov's main objection to Walt Whitman's reaction to stars is that it limits one's appreciation of the night sky. Do you agree or disagree with Asimov?

   _____

2. Why do you agree or disagree? _____

   _____

3. Describe any experiences you have had looking at stars.

   _____

   _____

4. Would you describe your response to nature's beauty as more similar to Asimov's or to Whitman's? Explain.

   _____

   _____

   Now, use your answers to write your response.

from **"Sharing in the American Dream"** by Colin Powell
"Science and the Sense of Wonder" by Isaac Asimov
Integrated Language Skills: Support for Extend Your Learning

Listening and Speaking: *from* **"Sharing in the American Dream"**

Before you begin writing your speech commemorating the founding of a volunteer organization, gather more information about its history and mission. Use Internet and library resources to find supporting details for your speech. Use the lines below to record information.

Volunteer organization: _____

_____

Mission / purpose of the organization: _____

_____

Examples of its work: _____

_____

Benefits to the community: _____

_____

Lively adjectives you can use in your description: _____

_____

Listening and Speaking: **"Science and the Sense of Wonder"**

Before you begin writing your speech honouring the acheivements of a famous astronomer or astronaut, use Internet or library resources to choose your subject. Consult a librarian if you need help making a decision. Gather information about your subject. Try to include supporting details that will interest your audience. Use the lines below to record information you find.

Your subject (astronomer / astronaut): _____

_____

Background: _____

_____

Accomplishments: _____

_____

Anecdotes: _____

_____

Impact on his or her field: _____

_____

Lively adjectives you can use in your description: _____

"Science and the Sense of Wonder" by Isaac Asimov
Open-Book Test

Short Answer *Write your responses to the questions in this section on the lines provided.*

1. In the beginning of "Science and the Sense of Nature," Asimov imagines people responding exultantly to Whitman's poem about "the learn'd astronomer." Why would people respond exultantly? Focus on Whitman's message and the meaning of the word *exultantly* in your response.

   _____

   _____

   _____

   _____

2. In the second paragraph of "Science and the Sense of Wonder," Asimov refers to "all that hard stuff in science." What feeling does he create with that phrase? Explain.

   _____

   _____

   _____

3. In the fourth paragraph of "Science and the Sense of Wonder," Asimov says, "I don't deny that the night sky is beautiful." With that statement, is he expressing a fact or an opinion? How can you tell?

   _____

   _____

4. In the fourth paragraph of "Science and the Sense of Wonder," Asimov mentions the insect bites he got while stargazing. What feeling does he convey with this observation, and how does he create it?

   _____

   _____

   _____

5. Toward the beginning of "Science and the Sense of Wonder," Asimov voices the opinion that the stars are "not all the beauty there is." Is that a valid opinion? That is, can it be supported by facts or by expert authority? Is it instead a faulty opinion, one that cannot be supported by facts? Explain your answer.

   _____

   _____

   _____

   _____

6. In "Science and the Sense of Wonder," Asimov describes planets as "worlds of red-hot liquid" and "worlds with volcanoes puffing plumes of dust." What feeling about space is he trying to convey with those words?

   _____

   _____

7. In "Science and the Sense of Wonder," Asimov speaks of stars exploding "in a vast cataclysm." Are such explosions minor events or major events? How can you tell? Base your answer on the definition of *cataclysm.*

   _____

   _____

8. Asimov uses facts to support his opinion about the wonders of science. In this chart, write two facts from "Science and the Sense of Wonder" that support Asimov's opinion. Then, on the line below, state whether Asimov's opinion is valid or faulty. Explain your answer.

   ┌──┐
   │ The study of stars is as amazing as their beauty.│
   └──┘

   ┌─────────────────────────┐   ┌─────────────────────────┐
   │ **Fact:**   │   │ **Fact:**   │
   │   │   │   │
   │   │   │   │
   └─────────────────────────┘   └─────────────────────────┘

   _____

9. In "Science and the Sense of Wonder,"Asimov tries to convince readers that an understanding of science increases one's appreciation of nature's beauty. How does Asimov try to convince readers of his opinion?

   _____

   _____

10. In "Science and the Sense of Wonder," Asimov describes his appreciation of the beauty of the night sky. At the beginning of the essay, he says he has enjoyed the sky by spreading a blanket on the ground and looking at the stars. By the end of the essay, it is clear that he has also come to appreciate the sky in another way. What is that other way in which Asimov has come to appreciate the stars?

   _____

   _____

Essay

Write an extended response to the question of your choice or to the question or questions your teacher assigns you.

11. Read this sentence about stars from "Science and the Sense of Wonder":

    Some of them are of incomparable grandeur, each glowing with the light of a thousand suns like ours; some are merely red-hot coals doling out their energy stingily.

    In an essay, tell how Asimov's choice of words makes you feel. Refer to at least two words or phrases from the sentence above.

12. Asimov uses many descriptions of the night sky to support his opinion. Which of those descriptions had the greatest effect on you? In an essay, describe the effect of the description you chose. Tell how it made you feel, and explain how the author's use of language contributed to that effect.

13. At the end of "Science and the Sense of Wonder," Asimov notes that everything he has described was discovered after Walt Whitman's time. Imagine that Whitman had known about all those discoveries. Would he have felt differently about astronomy? In an essay, respond to that question. State your opinion, and cite details from the essay to support your points.

14. **Thinking About the Big Question: How much information is enough?** In "Science and the Sense of Wonder," Isaac Asimov argues with Walt Whitman's attitude toward the study of astronomy. In an essay, evaluate the effectiveness of Asimov's argument. Does Asimov succeed in convincing you that the appreciation of nature can be increased by an understanding of "hard" science? Do you instead agree with Whitman that one need not study "hard" science to appreciate the beauty in nature or even that the study of science can take away from that appreciation? Refer to Asimov's essay to support your viewpoint.

Oral Response

15. Go back to question 5, 6, or 9 or to the question your teacher assigns you. Take a few minutes to expand your answer and prepare an oral response. Find additional details in "Science and the Sense of Wonder" that support your points. If necessary, make notes to guide your oral response.

Name _____ Date _____

"Science and the Sense of Wonder" by Isaac Asimov
Selection Test A

Critical Reading *Identify the letter of the choice that best answers the question.*

____ 1. Asimov quotes a poem at the beginning of his essay, "Science and the Sense of Wonder." What does the speaker in the poem do after listening to the astronomer?
   A. He signs up for another class.
   B. He asks several challenging questions.
   C. He goes out alone to look at the stars.
   D. He acquires a telescope.

____ 2. Asimov says that the poet is "talking through his hat." What kind of statement is this?
   A. a conclusion
   B. a fact
   C. an opinion
   D. a generalization

____ 3. What feeling about space does Asimov want to create by describing planets as "worlds of red-hot liquid" and "worlds with volcanoes puffing plumes"?
   A. boredom
   B. anger
   C. happiness
   D. fascination

____ 4. What fact does Asimov give about our galaxy?
   A. Our galaxy is called the Milky Way.
   B. Our galaxy is beautiful.
   C. Our galaxy is called Pinwheel.
   D. Our galaxy is called Andromeda.

____ 5. How will the sun destroy Earth in billions of years?
   A. The sun will burn it into a gas.
   B. The sun will die, and Earth will freeze.
   C. The sun will crash into Earth.
   D. A black hole will suck in Earth.

Unit 3 Resources: Types of Nonfiction
© Pearson Education, Inc. All rights reserved.
199

____ 6. What support does Asimov call on to justify his sense of wonder about stars and planets?
A. opinions
B. facts
C. poems
D. observations

____ 7. What feeling does the author give the essay with phrases like "all that junk" and "a quick beauty fix"?
A. informal
B. romantic
C. formal
D. scholarly

____ 8. In space, what event causes a blast of cosmic rays, according to Asimov?
A. A planet explodes.
B. A star explodes.
C. Earth changes position.
D. A new galaxy forms.

____ 9. When did humans discover most of the scientific knowledge that Asimov describes in "Science and the Sense of Wonder"?
A. before the poet he quoted was born
B. in early civilization
C. in the five years before he wrote
D. in the twenty-five years before he wrote

____ 10. In what way did Asimov come to appreciate the beauty of the night sky?
A. He watched stars and studied science.
B. He only watched stars from his yard.
C. He read poetry.
D. He taught poetry.

____ 11. What does Asimov think of the speaker in Whitman's poem?
A. The speaker takes scientists too seriously.
B. The speaker should respect scientists.
C. The speaker lacks intelligence.
D. The speaker is a "learn'd" astronomer.

Vocabulary and Grammar

___ **12.** In which sentence is *desolate* used correctly?
  A. We crossed the lush, desolate landscape.
  B. The flat desert was silent and desolate.
  C. We were desolate for our team to win.
  D. The noisy amusement park was desolate.

___ **13.** Which word is a preposition in this sentence?
     The colorful snake wound itself neatly around the branch.
  A. colorful   C. around
  B. itself   D. branch

___ **14.** Which word is the best definition of *exultantly*?
  A. joyfully   C. quickly
  B. timidly   D. sadly

___ **15.** Which is *not* a prepositional phrase?
  A. before sunrise   C. in a shrill voice
  B. for his ferret   D. eating quickly

Essay

16. Read this sentence about stars from "Science and the Sense of Wonder."

   Some of them are of incomparable grandeur, each glowing with the light of a
   thousand suns like ours; some are merely red-hot coals doling out their energy
   stingily.

In a brief essay, tell how Asimov's choice of words makes his readers feel. Refer to at
least two words or phrases from the sentence above.

17. Write a short essay in which you explain the poet's attitude toward scientific knowledge and tell why Asimov objects to the poet's attitude. Then, include at least two
pieces of scientific information Asimov offers to counter the poet's attitude.

18. **Thinking About the Big Question: How much information is enough?** In "Science and the Sense of Wonder," Isaac Asimov argues with Walt Whitman's attitude
toward the study of astronomy. In an essay, evaluate the effectiveness of Asimov's
argument. Does Asimov convince you that learning "hard" science can help you
appreciate nature more? Explain your answer in an essay supported by details and
examples from the essay.

"Science and the Sense of Wonder" by Isaac Asimov
Selection Test B

Critical Reading *Identify the letter of the choice that best completes the statement or answers the question.*

_____ 1. What feeling does Asimov create in readers when he talks about insect bites he got while he was stargazing?
   A. anger
   B. disinterest
   C. boredom
   D. humor

_____ 2. How does the speaker in the poem quoted by Asimov react to the astronomer's lessons?
   A. The speaker becomes tired and sick.
   B. The speaker becomes more interested in learning about stars.
   C. The speaker is inspired to become a teacher.
   D. The speaker is upset about his lack of scientific knowledge.

_____ 3. What feeling does Asimov create by using the phrases "all that hard stuff in science" and "talking through his hat"?
   A. intense
   B. informal
   C. formal
   D. respectful

_____ 4. How would you categorize the following statement by Asimov?
   But what I see—those quiet, twinkling points of light—is not all the beauty there is.
   A. a valid opinion
   B. a faulty opinion
   C. a fact
   D. bias

_____ 5. In which years were most of the discoveries that Asimov describes made?
   A. in the mid 1800s
   B. in the past ten years
   C. in the twenty-five years before Asimov wrote
   D. before the poet's death

_____ 6. What does Asimov predict will happen to Earth in billions of years?
   A. It will be burned up by the sun.
   B. Its population will increase.
   C. It will shrink slightly in size.
   D. It will change position in the galaxy.

____ 7. How long does it take light to travel from one end of the Milky Way to the other, according to Asimov?
  A. a hundred years
  B. about a year
  C. No one knows exactly.
  D. a hundred thousand years

____ 8. How big is the Andromeda galaxy in relation to the Milky Way?
  A. the same size
  B. three times as big
  C. twice as big
  D. half as big

____ 9. Asimov uses phrases like "puffing plumes," "unearthly beauty," and "cosmic breathing" to describe stars and planets. What feeling do these expressions create in readers?
  A. fear
  B. fascination
  C. intimidation
  D. boredom

____ 10. In contrast to the poet, Asimov's appreciation for stars and planets is based on
  A. opinions of others.
  B. an inspirational professor.
  C. observation and a wealth of facts.
  D. observation only.

____ 11. What does Asimov do to convince readers that understanding science increases appreciation of nature's beauty?
  A. He describes advanced college classes.
  B. He provides vivid descriptions.
  C. He tells about famous scientists.
  D. He criticizes all nature poems.

____ 12. Asimov says that the poet saw "a stultified and limited beauty" when looking at the night sky. What kind of statement is Asimov making?
  A. a fact
  B. an exaggeration
  C. an opinion
  D. an overgeneralization

____ 13. What is Asimov's main idea in this essay?
  A. Space is best appreciated through poetry.
  B. Poetry and science can work together.
  C. The universe is more than beauty.
  D. Scientific knowledge is always advancing.

Vocabulary and Grammar

____ 14. A place that is *desolate* could also be described as
  A. swampy.
  B. green and lush.
  C. barren.
  D. well-populated.

____ 15. Which word means the opposite of *exultantly*?
  A. hopefully
  B. sadly
  C. strictly
  D. joyfully

____ 16. Which sentence does *not* contain a prepositional phrase?
  A. The quilt's bright patterns are lovely.
  B. I went swimming before sunrise.
  C. Luke looked under the rug for his ferret.
  D. Sherry spoke to me in a shrill voice.

____ 17. A synonym for *cosmic* is
  A. unusual.
  B. large.
  C. frightening.
  D. limitless.

____ 18. What is the object of the preposition in the following sentence?
    The cowboy rode the wild bull until he was bucked to the ground.
  A. cowboy
  B. bull
  C. he
  D. ground

Essay

19. Write an essay in which you evaluate the effectiveness of Asimov's argument against Whitman. Does Asimov succeed or not succeed in convincing you that scientific knowledge adds to an appreciation of nature? Give reasons for your conclusion about Asimov's success or failure.

20. Which of Asimov's descriptions of the night sky made the greatest impact on you? What did you learn that surprised you? Choose one of these topics, and write a brief essay about the author's effective use of language.

21. **Thinking About the Big Question: How much information is enough?** In "Science and the Sense of Wonder," Isaac Asimov argues with Walt Whitman's attitude toward the study of astronomy. In an essay, evaluate the effectiveness of Asimov's argument. Does Asimov succeed in convincing you that the appreciation of nature can be increased by an understanding of "hard" science? Do you instead agree with Whitman that one need not study "hard" science to appreciate the beauty in nature or even that the study of science can take away from that appreciation? Refer to Asimov's essay to support your viewpoint.

"Emancipation" *from* **Lincoln: A Photobiography** by Russell Freedman
"Brown vs. Board of Education" by Walter Dean Myers
Vocabulary Warm-up Word Lists

Study these words from the selections. Then, complete the activities.

Word List A

absurd [uhb SERD] *adj.* completely unreasonable; ridiculous
It is <u>absurd</u> to think you can fly if you build big enough wings.

authority [uh THAWR i tee] *n.* the power someone has because of his or her position
The employee did not have the <u>authority</u> to open the company safe.

equality [i KWAHL i tee] *n.* everyone having the same rights and opportunities
The civil rights movement has fought for <u>equality</u> of the races.

honorable [AHN uhr uh buhl] *adj.* proper and moral; deserving respect
The <u>honorable</u> thing is to confess your guilt and apologize.

legal [LEE guhl] *adj.* allowed by law
The <u>legal</u> speed limit varies from state to state.

outlaw [OWT law] *v.* to say officially that something is against the law
City officials decided to <u>outlaw</u> skateboarding in parking lots.

slavery [SLAY vuh ree] *n.* a system of one person owning another
<u>Slavery</u> has existed in many societies, especially when one nation has taken prisoners of war.

Union [YOON yuhn] *n.* the states in the North during the Civil War
Sometimes one brother fought for the <u>Union</u> and the other for the Confederacy.

Word List B

abolitionist [ab uh LISH uh nist] *n.* someone who wanted to do away with slavery
In the town square, the <u>abolitionist</u> spoke out against slavery.

captors [KAP terz] *n.* people holding others as prisoners
The prisoners were afraid that their <u>captors</u> would treat them badly.

decree [di KREE] *n.* official order or decision
The mayor signed a <u>decree</u> against using the park at night.

enlist [en LIST] *v.* to join the army
When war broke out many people decided to <u>enlist</u> in the army.

inferior [in FIR ee er] *adj.* not as good as someone or something else
His worn-out shoes made him feel <u>inferior</u>.

intentions [in TEN shuhnz] *n.* things one means to do
Your <u>intentions</u> may be good, but you must follow through on them.

referred [ri FERD] *v.* had to do with; related to
Tim's essay about "the law" <u>referred</u> to his uncle Bob, the sheriff.

segregation [seg ri GAY shuhn] *n.* the practice of keeping groups apart
A century after the Civil War, there was still <u>segregation</u> in America.

Name _____ Date _____

"Emancipation" *from* **Lincoln: A Photobiography** by Russell Freedman
"Brown vs. Board of Education" by Walter Dean Myers
Vocabulary Warm-up Exercises

Exercise A *Fill in each blank in the paragraph below with an appropriate word from Word List A. Use each word only once.*

It took an amendment to the Constitution to [1] _____ the inhumane
system known as [2] _____ in the United States. With the
[3] _____ and the South joined again as one nation, it was no longer
[4] _____ for one person to own another anywhere. There was no plan,
however, to help former slaves achieve [5] _____ with the rest of the
nation's people. They needed jobs and education. It would be [6] _____
to think these things could happen in a short period of time. Therefore, the
[7] _____ thing would have been for the government to help out more
than it did. No one, however, had or took the [8] _____ to do so. As a
result, achieving rights was a long, hard struggle for the families of former slaves.

Exercise B *Decide whether each statement below is true or false. Circle T or F. Then, explain your answer.*

1. An <u>abolitionist</u> was a person who fought against <u>segregation</u>.
   T / F _____

2. If you have good <u>intentions</u>, it means you're great at doing things.
   T / F _____

3. If you <u>enlist</u> in the army, you join by signing up.
   T / F _____

4. The word <u>captors</u> once <u>referred</u> to people who were held against their will.
   T / F _____

5. A king, a queen, or a president may issue a <u>decree</u>.
   T / F _____

6. A house built of <u>inferior</u> materials is likely to stand for hundreds of years.
   T / F _____

Name _____ Date _____

"Emancipation" *from* **Lincoln: A Photobiography** by Russell Freedman
"Brown vs. Board of Education" by Walter Dean Myers
Reading Warm-up A

Read the following passage. Pay special attention to the underlined words. Then, read it again, and complete the activities. Use a separate sheet of paper for your written answers.

Many people believe that Abraham Lincoln freed the slaves during the Civil War, on January 1, 1863. That is only partly true. On that day, he boldly declared that the slaves in the southern states were free.

However, Lincoln had no <u>authority</u> over the eleven southern states that had pulled out of, or seceded from, the <u>Union</u>. They had their own laws, their own government, and their own president. As a result, Lincoln's action had no effect in those areas right away.

Did Lincoln's action immediately <u>outlaw</u> <u>slavery</u> in the North? No, it didn't. Slaves in the so-called border states—Delaware, Maryland, Kentucky, and Missouri—were still bound to their masters. Lincoln was afraid that setting slaves free in the border states would turn their slave owners against the Union.

In view of all this, does Lincoln's declaration seem <u>absurd</u>? In fact, Lincoln's action was quite sensible. It encouraged free blacks and escaped slaves to join the northern army. With heavy losses, the Union army needed more and more soldiers. With the help of blacks, the North was able to win the war.

As Lincoln had hoped, the border states remained loyal to the Union. England and France, which depended on southern cotton, refused to help the South when the Civil War turned into a war against slavery.

Perhaps the most important and <u>honorable</u> event that Lincoln's action prompted was the Thirteenth Amendment to the Constitution, which passed on December 18, 1865. From that time forward, slavery was not <u>legal</u> anywhere in the Union. Former slaves now could begin walking down that long road toward <u>equality</u>. They could hope that someday their children's children would enjoy the same rights that others took for granted.

1. Circle the text that explains why Lincoln's word had no <u>authority</u> in the South. Write a sentence about a person of *authority* in your life.

2. Circle the words that describe the opposite of the <u>Union</u>. Name four states mentioned that were part of the *Union*.

3. Underline the places where Lincoln did not <u>outlaw slavery</u>. Rewrite the sentence in which *outlaw slavery* appears, replacing the phrase with words that have the same meaning.

4. Circle the word in the next sentence that is an antonym for <u>absurd</u>. Tell about something *absurd* in your own life.

5. Circle the smaller word, or base word, of <u>honorable</u>. Then, write your own sentence for *honorable*.

6. What was no longer <u>legal</u> after the Thirteenth Amendment was passed? Write your own sentence, using the word *legal*.

7. Underline the words in the next sentence that define <u>equality</u>. Tell what *equality* means to you.

"Emancipation" *from* **Lincoln: A Photobiography** by Russell Freedman
"Brown vs. Board of Education" by Walter Dean Myers
Reading Warm-up B

Read the following passage. Pay special attention to the underlined words. Then, read it again, and complete the activities. Use a separate sheet of paper for your written answers.

Before the Civil War, it was against the law in southern states to teach African Americans to read and write. Slave owners were like <u>captors</u>, and slaves were their prisoners. In the North, there was no law against black people learning to read, but there were few schools they could attend. Most schools practiced <u>segregation</u>, a term that <u>referred</u> to keeping blacks out. Separate schools for black children were usually <u>inferior</u> to schools that whites attended, with poorer buildings and supplies.

The Civil War changed many things in our country. Black men by the thousands—including those who escaped slavery—decided to <u>enlist</u> in the armed forces to help the North. After the war, the Thirteenth Amendment to the Constitution finally set all slaves free.

The new law cheered <u>abolitionists</u>, but the freed slaves now needed jobs, and their children needed schools.

The United States government set up the Freedmen's Bureau to deal with these needs. It helped former slaves get jobs and own farms. It also issued a <u>decree</u> for free public schools for blacks in the South.

Starting schools to educate black children was full of good <u>intentions</u>. However, the schools had built-in segregation. As the years passed, most people in the South did not see any reason to change things. Segregation, not just in schools but also in other public places, became part of state laws.

In the North, no law existed against having schools where blacks and whites could learn together. Still, many schools remained segregated because of custom or geography. Children often went to the school nearest their home. If blacks and whites lived in separate neighborhoods, then it was likely they would attend separate schools.

Today, all the segregation laws are gone. However, we are still dealing with the reality of separate schools in some parts of the country. How would you solve this problem?

1. Circle the word that hints at the meaning of <u>captors</u>. Write your own definition of *captors*.

2. Underline the words that tell what <u>segregation referred</u> to. Then, explain what *segregation* and *referred* mean.

3. Circle the word that is a synonym for <u>inferior</u>. Write a sentence that compares two things, one *inferior* to the other.

4. Underline the places where black men could <u>enlist</u>. Tell why you think they did *enlist*.

5. Circle the words in the previous paragraph that explain why the Thirteenth Amendment cheered <u>abolitionists</u>. Describe an *abolitionist*.

6. Write a synonym for <u>decree</u>. Name another *decree* you know of.

7. Circle the sentences that tell what the good <u>intentions</u> of starting schools for blacks also led to. Tell about a time you had good *intentions*.

"Emancipation" *from* **Lincoln: A Photobiography** by Russell Freedman
"Brown vs. Board of Education" by Walter Dean Myers
Writing About the Big Question

How much information is enough?

Big Question Vocabulary

accumulate	challenge	decision	development	discrimination
explanation	exploration	factor	global	inequality
quality	quantity	reveal	statistics	valuable

A. *Use a word from list above to complete each sentence.*

1. Did emancipation mean the end of _____?

2. What is the _____ for Lincoln's emancipation of the slaves?

3. Not many children could face the _____ of being the first to integrate a school.

4. It took a long time for the Supreme Court to come to a _____ in *Brown vs. Board of Education*.

B. *Follow the directions in responding to each of the items below.*

1. Give two reasons that Lincoln's decision to emancipate the slaves was difficult for him.

   _____

   _____

2. In two or three sentences, explain what *Brown vs. Board of Education* meant for students. Use at least two list words in your explanation.

   _____

   _____

C. *These works each involve important historical events in the struggle for racial equality. Complete the sentence below. Then, write a short paragraph in which you connect this sentence to the Big Question.*

To learn about inequality in history, I would want to read about _____

because _____

_____

_____

Name _____ Date _____

Literary Analysis: Comparing Tone

The **tone** of a literary work is the author's attitude toward his or her audience and subject.

- Tone can often be described by a single adjective, such as *formal, informal, serious, playful, impersonal,* or *personal.*
- Tone is conveyed through an author's choice of words, sentence structure, and details. Tone may vary within a piece of writing.

Both "Emancipation" and "Brown vs. Board of Education" are nonfiction works that describe and explain key figures and events in American history. Both works are serious and aim to make a piece of history interesting. However, these two pieces do have subtle differences in tone, partly because the authors' purposes, or reasons for writing, are different.

DIRECTIONS: *Answer the following questions to discover more about the tone and purpose of the two essays.*

1. What words or details in "Emancipation" suggest the author's tone, or attitude toward his audience and subject?

   _____

   _____

2. What adjectives describe the author's tone, or attitude toward his audience and subject, in "Emancipation"?

   _____

   _____

3. What is the author's purpose, or reason, for writing "Emancipation"?

   _____

   _____

4. What words or details in "Brown vs. Board of Education" suggest the author's tone, or attitude toward his subject and audience?

   _____

   _____

5. What adjectives describe the author's tone, or attitude toward his subject and audience, in "Brown vs. Board of Education"?

   _____

   _____

Name _____ Date _____

"Emancipation" *from* **Lincoln: A Photobiography** by Russell Freedman
"Brown vs. Board of Education" by Walter Dean Myers
Vocabulary Builder

Word List

alienate	compensate	deliberating	humiliating
oppressed	predominantly	unconstitutional	

A. DIRECTIONS: *Write a complete sentence to answer each question. In each sentence, use a vocabulary word from the above Word List in place of the underlined word(s) with similar meanings.*

1. What could you do that would <u>make</u> someone <u>unfriendly</u> to you?

   _____

   _____

2. Based on what you have learned in history class, what action would be <u>not in accordance with or permitted by the U.S. Constitution</u>?

   _____

   _____

3. What group of people could be found <u>thinking and considering</u> something <u>carefully and fully</u>?

   _____

   _____

4. Have you ever done something that was <u>embarrassing</u> or <u>undignified</u>?

   _____

   _____

5. What group of people did slave owners <u>keep down by cruel and unjust power</u>?

   _____

   _____

6. Whom should you <u>repay</u>?

   _____

   _____

7. Are there <u>mainly</u> people under the age of twenty-one living in your neighborhood?

   _____

   _____

"Emancipation" *from* **Lincoln: A Photobiography** by Russell Freedman
"Brown vs. Board of Education" by Walter Dean Myers

Integrated Language Skills: Support for Writing to Compare Tone

Before you write your essay that compares the tone of "Emancipation" and the tone of "Brown vs. Board of Education," use the graphic organizer below to list details and to make notes about each essay.

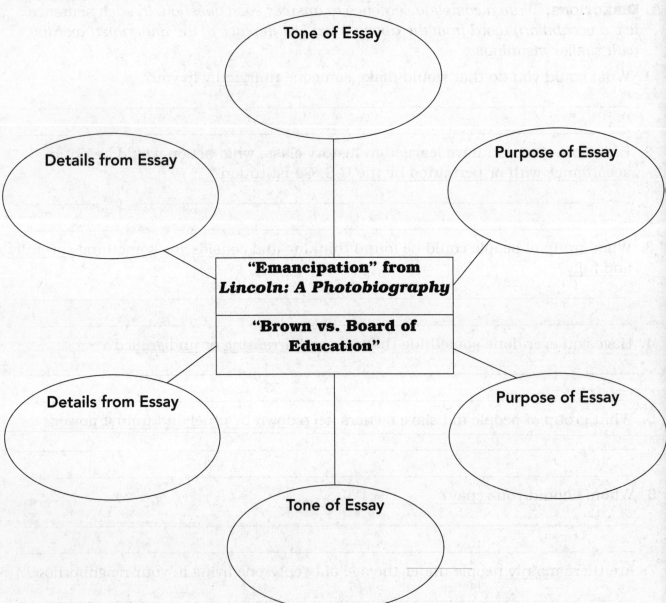

Now, use your notes to write your essay comparing the tone of these two works.

Name _____ Date _____

"Emancipation" *from* Lincoln: A Photobiography by Russell Freedman
"Brown vs. Board of Education" by Walter Dean Myers
Open-Book Test

Short Answer *Write your responses to the questions in this section on the lines provided.*

1. The tone of a work of literature is the author's attitude toward his or her audience and subject. How would you describe the tone of "Emancipation"? Explain.

   _____

   _____

2. In "Emancipation," the Republican senators argued that it was necessary to free the enslaved African Americans. Eventually President Lincoln became convinced that they were right. What was the senators' argument?

   _____

   _____

3. In "Emancipation," Russell Freedman makes a point about President Lincoln's decision to issue the Emancipation Proclamation. That is, Lincoln was advised that freeing the slaves in the Confederacy would help the Union army. How would emancipation help the army?

   _____

   _____

4. In the second section of "Brown vs. Board of Education," Myers writes about neighborhoods that were predominantly African American. In your own words, describe such a neighborhood. Base your answer on the definition of *predominantly*.

   _____

   _____

5. According to the third section of "Brown vs. Board of Education," Thurgood Marshall's father made sacrifices to send his sons to college. What does that information tell you about Marshall's father?

   _____

   _____

6. In the third section of "Brown vs. Board of Education," Myers discusses the way white southerners felt about ending legal segregation. He quotes a white southern congressman, who said that making segregation illegal would create a "gap between law and custom." What is the meaning of the congressman's words?

   _____

   _____

   _____

7. In "Brown vs. Board of Education," Myers describes laws that oppressed African Americans. What is one such law? Explain how it oppressed African Americans, and base your answer on the definition of *oppressed*.

_____

_____

_____

8. Although the tone of both "Emancipation" and "Brown vs. Board of Education" is formal, in one essay the tone is more formal than in the other. Use this chart to analyze the tone of the two essays. For each essay, provide two examples of words, phrases, or sentence structures that are typical of the essay's tone.

"Emancipation"	"Brown vs. Board of Education"

Which essay is more formal? What words, phrases, or sentence structures led you to make your choice?

_____

_____

9. The author of "Emancipation" and the author of "Brown vs. Board of Education" had similar purposes for writing their essays. For what purpose did they write these essays?

_____

_____

10. The essays "Emancipation" and "Brown vs. Board of Education" deal with similar topics. In what way are the topics similar?

_____

_____

Essay

Write an extended response to the question of your choice or to the question or questions your teacher assigns you.

11. Write an essay comparing the tone of "Emancipation" with the tone of "Brown vs. Board of Education." In your essay, consider the topic of each essay, each author's purpose for writing his essay, and the words, sentence structures, and details that characterize each one.

12. Both Lincoln's decision to free the enslaved African Americans and Thurgood Marshall's decision to fight legal battles on behalf of African Americans were influenced by other people. In an essay, discuss the people who influenced Lincoln and Marshall. Tell who they were and how they exerted their influence. Conclude your essay by describing how those influences have affected daily life in the United States today.

13. In "Brown vs. Board of Education," Myers acknowledges that even after the landmark decision, "the major struggle would be in the hearts and minds of people." In an essay, explain what Myers means by that statement. Use details from the essay and information from your own reading to support the accuracy of Myers's prediction.

14. **Thinking About the Big Question: How much information is enough?** Both "Emancipation" and "Brown vs. Board of Education" explain the history behind two ground-breaking decisions in American history. In an essay, discuss whether those essays provided you with enough information to understand Lincoln's decision to issue the Emancipation Proclamation and the Supreme Court's decision to rule that segregated schools could not be equal. If they did, briefly describe the information that made the decisions meaningful. If they did not, tell what information you felt was lacking.

Oral Response

15. Go back to question 2, 6, or 8 or to the question your teacher assigns you. Take a few minutes to expand your answer and prepare an oral response. Find additional details in "Emancipation" and "Brown vs. Board of Education" that support your points. If necessary, make notes to guide your oral response.

"Emancipation" *from* **Lincoln: A Photobiography** by Russell Freedman
"Brown vs. Board of Education" by Walter Dean Myers
Selection Test A

Critical Reading *Identify the letter of the choice that best answers the question.*

____ 1. What was the "toughest decision facing Lincoln" as president during the Civil War, according to "Emancipation"?

A. He had to decide what to do about rebels in the South.

B. He had to decide what to do about slavery.

C. He had to decide how to win battles.

D. He had to decide how to keep the border states loyal.

____ 2. Which statement best summarizes the main idea of "Emancipation"?

A. Lincoln's original reason for fighting the Civil War was to free the slaves.

B. Everyone in the North agreed with the Emancipation Proclamation.

C. The abolitionists were disappointed with Lincoln's Emancipation Proclamation.

D. Lincoln deserves to be remembered for the Emancipation Proclamation.

____ 3. According to some people mentioned in "Emancipation," how would freeing the slaves help the Union army, which did not have enough soldiers to fight the Confederacy?

A. Many former slaveowners would join the Union army.

B. Many people in the border states would join the Union army.

C. Many freed slaves would join the Union army.

D. Many soldiers would leave the Confederate army in protest.

____ 4. According to "Emancipation," what comment did Lincoln make when signing the Emancipation Proclamation?

A. "If my name ever goes into history, . . . it will be for this act."

B. "We of this congress and this administration, will be remembered in spite of ourselves."

C. "In giving freedom to the slave, we assure freedom to the free. . . . "

D. Emancipation was "a military necessity. . . . "

____ 5. According to "Brown vs. Board of Education," how did young Thurgood Marshall get involved in throwing punches with a stranger?

A. Marshall often picked fights.

B. Marshall was involved in a case of mistaken identity.

C. The stranger accused Marshall of disrespecting a white woman.

D. Marshall was reacting to bad news he had received at school that morning.

_____ 6. How did Professor Charles Hamilton Houston influence Thurgood Marshall, according to "Brown vs. Board of Education"?

   A. He encouraged Marshall to give up his study of predentistry and to pursue law.

   B. He had experienced discrimination in his professional life.

   C. He encouraged his students to use the law to help African Americans.

   D. He led the challenge to end school segregation.

_____ 7. Who led the N.A.A.C.P. attorneys in the challenge to segregation, according to "Brown vs. Board of Education"?

   A. Thurgood Marshall

   B. Charles Hamilton Houston

   C. Linda Brown

   D. Abraham Lincoln

_____ 8. Based on "Brown vs. Board of Education," how did segregation in the schools affect many African American children?

   A. It made them feel superior.

   B. It made them feel inferior.

   C. It caused them to want black dolls.

   D. It caused them to get better grades.

_____ 9. Which of the following words is another word for *tone*?

   A. attitude

   B. sincerity

   C. belief

   D. formality

_____ 10. What kind of tone can you find in both "Emancipation" and "Brown vs. Board of Education"?

   A. ironic

   B. humorous

   C. informal

   D. serious

_____ 11. In both "Emancipation" and "Brown vs. Board of Education," what was the author's purpose for writing his essay?

   A. to entertain an audience

   B. to persuade readers to take action

   C. to narrate a historical event

   D. to provide technical information

____ 12. What is similar about the topics of "Emancipation" and "Brown vs. Board of Education"?

  A. Both essays are about presidential decisions.

  B. Both essays are about the Supreme Court.

  C. Both essays are about segregation and its effects on children.

  D. Both essays are about how African Americans gained important freedoms.

Vocabulary

____ 13. Which word best completes the following sentence?

  You might _____ your teammates if you criticize them during a game.

  A. compensate   B. deliberate   C. alienate   D. console

____ 14. Which word or phrase is closest in meaning to the italicized word in this sentence?

  In *predominantly* African American areas, most students in the schools were African American.

  A. in a bossy way   B. in a biased way   C. slightly   D. mainly

____ 15. Which word or phrase is closest in meaning to the italicized word in this sentence?

  After the Brown decision, other laws that *oppressed* African Americans began to fall.

  A. uplifted

  B. kept down by unjust use of power

  C. worked in support of

  D. calmed

Essay

16. Write an essay comparing the tone of "Emancipation" with the tone of "Brown vs. Board of Education." What is each of the essays about? What is each author's purpose for writing the piece? Describe Freedman's tone. Describe Myers's tone.

17. All people, even great leaders, are influenced and guided by others. "Emancipation" tells of people who influenced Lincoln's decision to free the slaves. "Brown vs. Board of Education" tells of people who influenced Thurgood Marshall to become a lawyer. In an essay, discuss the people who influenced Lincoln and Marshall. Who were they? How did they influence Lincoln and Marshall?

18. **Thinking About the Big Question: How much information is enough?** Both "Emancipation" and "Brown vs. Board of Education" explain the history behind two groundbreaking decisions in American history. In an essay, discuss whether those essays provided you with enough information to understand Lincoln's decision to issue the Emancipation Proclamation and the Supreme Court's decision to rule that segregated schools could not be equal. Support your opinion with details from the selections.

"Emancipation" *from* **Lincoln: A Photobiography** by Russell Freedman
"Brown vs. Board of Education" by Walter Dean Myers
Selection Test B

Critical Reading *Identify the letter of the choice that best completes the statement or answers the question.*

____ 1. According to "Emancipation," what did President Lincoln originally think was the purpose of the Civil War?
  A. to punish the traitors who had formed the Confederacy
  B. to restore the Union, making the United States one nation again
  C. to emancipate, or free, the slaves in the Southern and border states
  D. to keep the loyal slaveholding border states in the Union

____ 2. According to "Emancipation," how would freeing the slaves help the North's war effort?
  A. Freed slaves could fight in the Union army.
  B. The slave owners in the Confederacy would allow the freed slaves to leave.
  C. Freeing the slaves would please the abolitionists.
  D. Freeing the slaves would guarantee victory for the North.

____ 3. Which sentence from "Emancipation" suggests why President Lincoln became convinced of the necessity to free the slaves?
  A. "Emancipation in the cotton states is simply an absurdity."
  B. The president must wait until the Union had won a decisive military victory in the East.
  C. Perhaps then the liberated slaves could be resettled in Africa or Central America.
  D. It was absurd, [Republican Senators] argued, to fight the war without destroying the institution that had caused it.

____ 4. According to "Emancipation," which argument convinced President Lincoln that he had the authority to abolish slavery, which was protected by law?
  A. The president must weaken the enemy. Ending slavery would reduce the enemy's power.
  B. Abolishing slavery was a moral action. The president was the moral leader of the country.
  C. Laws protecting slavery predated the Confederacy, so they no longer applied.
  D. The president had the power to abolish laws that he did not agree with.

____ 5. Which statement from "Emancipation" best summarizes Lincoln's hopes in freeing the slaves?
  A. "We shout for joy that we live to record this righteous decree."
  B. "In *giving* freedom to the *slave*, we *assure* freedom to the *free*. . . . "
  C. "We didn't go into the war to put down slavery, but to put the flag back."
  D. The Emancipation Proclamation would be "the last shriek on our retreat."

_____ 6. According to "Brown vs. Board of Education," why did black and white students in the North usually go to separate schools from the end of the Civil War to the early 1950s?
A. Laws forbade blacks to attend schools with whites.
B. The students lived in different neighborhoods and attended schools near their homes.
C. Northern schools were simply following the example set by Southern schools.
D. Black and white children and their parents preferred for them to attend separate schools.

_____ 7. According to "Brown vs. Board of Education," Thurgood Marshall's father made sacrifices to send his sons to college. What does this action tell you about the father?
A. He believed that education would help his sons achieve more than he was able to.
B. He was bitter because there had been no opportunities for him when he was a boy.
C. He hoped that people would admire him for having educated sons.
D. He thought his sons were intelligent.

_____ 8. According to "Brown vs. Board of Education," why did Charles Hamilton Houston want his students to have "absolute understanding of the law"?
A. He did not want white lawyers to win cases against African American lawyers.
B. He wanted his students to succeed in helping white Americans.
C. He believed that the law was a strong weapon in the civil rights movement.
D. He believed that African Americans could become great lawyers.

_____ 9. According to "Brown vs. Board of Education," the Supreme Court's ruling about schools in Topeka, Kansas, changed the struggle for civil rights by signaling that
A. laws oppressing African Americans would have to fall.
B. the struggle against racial prejudice was coming to an end.
C. the "gap between law and custom" would soon close.
D. African Americans would have no more legal battles.

_____ 10. What makes both "Emancipation" and "Brown vs. Board of Education" important essays?
A. Both essays tell the life stories of significant African Americans.
B. Both essays help young students easily understand presidential politics.
C. Both essays are about how segregation harmed children.
D. Both essays are about dramatic events that changed the nation.

_____ 11. The tone of a literary work is
A. its author's ability to hold readers' interest.
B. the general lesson that the work communicates.
C. its author's attitude toward the subject and audience.
D. the point of view of the narrator.

____ 12. The tone of all of "Emancipation" and much of "Brown vs. Board of Education" could be described as

A. playful.   B. preposterous.   C. prejudiced.   D. serious.

____ 13. Which is *least* likely to contribute to the tone of a literary work?

A. the author's purpose for writing
B. the author's choice of words
C. the author's writing process
D. the author's sentence structure

Vocabulary

____ 14. The honor student felt it was _____ to get a *B* on the final exam.

A. oppressed   B. humiliating   C. unconstitutional   D. compensate

____ 15. In which sentence is *alienate* used correctly?

A. My friend believes that there are alienate life forms on other planets.
B. She seems to alienate others because she is friendly.
C. You might alienate your teammates if you criticize them during a game.
D. Always try to alienate group members during cooperative activities.

____ 16. Which word or phrase is closest in meaning to the italicized word in this following sentence?

After *deliberating* for more than a year, the Supreme Court finally reached a decision.

A. listening
B. accidentally watching
C. thinking and talking
D. delaying

Essay

17. Write an essay comparing the tone of "Emancipation" with the tone of "Brown vs. Board of Education." In answering, consider the following questions: How is the subject matter of the two essays similar or different? What is each author's purpose for writing the piece? Does each essay have (1) a single tone or (2) a dominant tone *and* a secondary tone? What details in each essay suggest its tone or tones?

18. All people, even great leaders, are influenced and guided by others. Both Lincoln's decision to free the slaves and Thurgood Marshall's decision to fight legal battles on behalf of African Americans were influenced by other people. In an essay, discuss the people who influenced Lincoln and Marshall. Who were they? Specifically, in what ways did they influence Lincoln and Marshall? How did their influence on Lincoln and Marshall impact daily life in the United States today?

19. **Thinking About the Big Question: How much information is enough?** Both "Emancipation" and "Brown vs. Board of Education" explain the history behind two groundbreaking decisions in American history. In an essay, discuss whether those essays provided you with enough information to understand Lincoln's decision to issue the Emancipation Proclamation and the Supreme Court's decision to rule that segregated schools could not be equal. If they did, briefly describe the information that made the decisions meaningful. If they did not, tell what information you felt was lacking.

Name _____ Date _____

Prewriting: Narrowing Your Topic

Read newspapers and watch the local and national news to find possible topics for your persuasive editorial. Write down interesting issues covered in the media in the graphic organizer below. You will be able to choose one as the subject of your editorial.

Newspapers	Television News

Drafting: Using a Clear Organization

Use the following graphic organizer to create a strong organization of your ideas that will help make your editorial effective.

Effective Introduction:

Second-Strongest Point:

Another Argument:

Another Argument:

Strongest Point:

Strong Conclusion:

Writing Workshop—Unit 3, Part 2
Editorial: Integrating Grammar Skills

Revising Sentences by Combining With Conjunctions

Conjunctions connect words or groups of words. They can be used to combine sentences. **Coordinating conjunctions** can form a compound subject or a compound sentence.

Example:	Pablo takes dance lessons. June takes dance lessons.
Compound Subject:	Pablo and June take dance lessons.
Example:	Pablo takes dance lessons. He doesn't enjoy them.
Compound Sentence:	Pablo takes dance lessons, but he doesn't enjoy them.

Subordinating conjunctions create complex sentences. They show that one idea is dependent on the other.

Example:	June takes dance lessons. She wants to improve her grace.
Complex Sentence:	Because June wants to improve her grace, she takes dance lessons.

Common Conjunctions	
Coordinating	and, or, but, nor, so, yet, for
Subordinating	after, although, as, as soon as, because, before, if, since, unless, until, when, while, whenever

A. DIRECTIONS: *Underline the conjunction in each sentence. Then, write* compound subject, compound sentence, *or* complex sentence *to identify how the conjunction is used.*

1. Young people and adults like to solve crossword puzzles. _____

2. Working puzzles is good because it makes you use your brain cells.

   _____

3. As soon as I fill in one more word, I'll be ready to go with you. _____

4. I practice by playing word games whenever I can. _____

B. DIRECTIONS: *On the lines provided, revise the two short sentences. Write a compound subject, compound sentence, or complex sentence.*

1. Gymnastics builds muscles. Lifting weights builds muscles.

   _____

2. The competition is Saturday. Harry didn't qualify.

   _____

3. He hopes to make the finals next year. He plans to practice.

   _____

Name _____ Date _____

Unit 3 Vocabulary Workshop—1
Words With Multiple Meanings

A multiple-meaning word is a word that has more than one definition.

DIRECTIONS: *Write each pair of homophones next to their clues. Then, find and circle each one in the word search.*

1. a thick cloud/puzzled, bewildered   _____   _____
2. gratuity/to push over   _____   _____
3. land near the sea/sail, glide   _____   _____
4. a strip of metal/a flat dish   _____   _____
5. teach a skill/railroad cars   _____   _____
6. examine/summary, critique   _____   _____

c	o	a	s	t	r	s	d	e	r	w	a	n	f	v	r	r	t	c	o	y	r	m
v	i	h	b	o	h	r	e	y	h	u	p	p	o	s	c	o	a	r	s	e	y	u
n	w	t	f	a	u	d	h	i	t	h	c	r	g	i	k	j	n	m	y	h	u	s
a	r	a	c	b	y	o	e	o	z	z	s	w	c	r	e	v	i	e	w	e	c	s
n	f	o	i	h	j	d	i	r	l	z	c	h	e	o	t	p	e	e	y	u	v	l
c	u	v	t	s	x	c	w	n	t	e	o	u	r	c	t	i	o	l	z	x	r	l
i	l	m	m	s	g	a	z	w	u	e	s	r	u	o	c	p	o	u	r	s	e	
a	t	r	a	i	n	q	p	l	a	t	e	r	e	w	m	s	s	l	u	f	x	k
g	a	o	a	w	i	g	i	a	e	g	m	s	w	b	s	r	o	a	e	r	f	u

Unit 3 Vocabulary Workshop—2
Words With Multiple Meanings

We rely on context to help us determine the meaning of a multiple-meaning words. Without context, the written words are identical.

DIRECTIONS: *A story has been started below. Continue the story using at least 4 of the multiple-meaning words given. Every multiple-meaning word you use must be used twice, each time with a different meaning. Make sure the context of your sentences helps the reader determine the meaning of the multiple-meaning word. Be creative and use your imagination. You may use a dictionary if you are unsure of any definitions.*

positive	jam	nature	lean
match	horn	might	

> Noel couldn't **bear** the thought of seeing another **bear**.

Name _____ Date _____

Evaluating an Oral Presentation

Use this chart to help you evaluate an oral presentation.

Topic of presentation: _____

What is the main topic of the presentation?
What ideas and facts support the main idea?
How well did the speaker inform you about the topic?
Were the ideas presented clearly and in an organized way?
What impact did the presentation have on you?

Unit 3: Types of Nonfiction
Benchmark Test 6

MULTIPLE CHOICE

Reading Skill: Fact and Opinion *Read the selection. Then, answer the questions that follow.*

Until the twentieth century, women were denied the right to vote in Great Britain. The movement for women's rights began in England in 1792. Many women, known as suffragists, were sent to prison, where they continued to work for their cause by staging hunger strikes. Bill after bill was introduced to the British Parliament during the 1800s and early 1900s, with no success. Public support for women's voting rights slowly grew and, in 1918, an act was passed that allowed women age 30 or over to vote. In 1928, this age was lowered to 21, the same as for men. After more than a century, women finally achieved equal voting rights with men.

1. Which of the following statements is a fact?
   A. Women were treated unfairly.
   B. In 1928, the voting age for women was 21.
   C. Women were impatient.
   D. The British Parliament acted unjustly.

2. Which of the following is an opinion?
   A. Many bills were introduced in Parliament.
   B. Women achieved equal voting rights.
   C. By 1918 women 30 and over could vote.
   D. British Parliament was unfair.

3. Which of the following sentences contains a clue word indicating a judgment?
   A. Being denied the vote was the worst injustice.
   B. Because Parliament moved slowly, women grew impatient.
   C. Nothing was done for women for centuries.
   D. Women had always been treated unfairly.

4. Which of the following statements supports the opinion that women were treated unfairly?
   A. Many women fought for all women's right to vote.
   B. Women were not allowed to vote in Great Britain.
   C. Public support for women's rights grew.
   D. The movement for women's rights began in 1792.

Reading Skill: Analyze Proposition and Support Patterns

Read the selection. Then, answer the questions that follow.

On April 25, 1990, the crew of the space shuttle *Discovery* placed the most sophisticated telescope ever created in orbit around the Earth. The Hubble Space Telescope was named for Edwin Hubble, the most important American astronomer of the 20th century. Unlike telescopes on Earth, the Hubble telescope can see deep into space without the interference of Earth's atmosphere. The images received by Hubble are much brighter and clearer than anyone could have imagined. With the Hubble Space Telescope, people are able to clearly see the breathtaking beauty of the universe. We have taken an enormous step forward in our ongoing attempt to unlock the secrets of the universe.

Name _____ Date _____

5. Which of the following opinions could be supported by facts?
   A. The space shuttle crew performed a great service for humanity.
   B. It is important for scientists to see objects in outer space.
   C. Hubble is the most sophisticated telescope ever created.
   D. Hubble is a wonderful invention that will make the world better.

6. Which of the following statements can be considered a faulty opinion?
   A. People will benefit from Hubble by learning more about the universe.
   B. People on Earth are lucky to have the Hubble.
   C. The Hubble can help scientists learn much more about the universe.
   D. Most astronomers consider the Hubble an important invention.

7. Which of the following statements best describes the author's opinion of the Hubble Space Telescope?
   A. It is an important invention that will benefit science and humanity.
   B. The Hubble took a great effort to put in place, but it was worth it.
   C. It is a technologically advanced invention that will benefit scientists.
   D. Without the Hubble, scientists would know very little about the universe.

8. How does the author support his position?
   A. He asks questions, and then answers them.
   B. He presents an opposing fact, and then disproves it.
   C. He gives several reasons why the Hubble Telescope is important.
   D. He quotes people involved in placing the Hubble Telescope in orbit.

9. Which statement in the selection is used to directly support the author's position?
   A. The Hubble Space Telescope was placed in orbit on April 25, 1990.
   B. The telescope was placed in orbit by the crew of the *Discovery*.
   C. Edwin Hubble was the most important American astronomer of the 20th century.
   D. The Hubble Space Telescope will help us unlock the secrets of the universe.

10. Which of the following most accurately describes this selection?
   A. It is a telescope advertisement.
   B. It is a newspaper editorial.
   C. It is a company brochure.
   D. It is a political speech.

Literary Analysis: Persuasive Techniques *Read the selection. Then, answer the questions that follow.*

In 1960, President Kennedy challenged young people to join the Peace Corps. Why might someone want to join the Peace Corps? Peace Corp volunteers help people in developing nations. Peace Corps volunteers might counsel teens in Belize, launch a computer center in Armenia, or teach chemistry in a high school in Ghana. Since the 1960s, more than 178,000 Peace Corps volunteers have had the satisfaction of helping others and living in 138 countries around the world. Individuals who join the Peace Corps know that they have served their country, served humanity, and made a difference in the world.

11. What is the author attempting to persuade the reader of in this selection?
    A. President Kennedy wanted to bring world peace with the Peace Corps.
    B. People should work for world peace by doing volunteer work.
    C. Peace Corps volunteers serve humanity and the cause of peace.
    D. Peace Corps volunteers can bring world peace.

12. How is the rhetorical question in this selection answered?
    A. by listing the countries to which Peace Corps volunteers travel
    B. by describing how Peace Corps volunteers help others around the world
    C. by explaining what Peace Corps volunteers do in Belize and Ghana
    D. by explaining the numbers of volunteers who have joined the Peace Corps

13. To which emotions does the phrase "served their country, served humanity" appeal?
    A. pride and a desire for peace
    B. pride and patriotism
    C. pride and a desire to help others
    D. patriotism and a desire to help others

Literary Analysis: Word Choice *Read the selection. Then, answer the questions that follow.*

The civil rights movement was a remarkable time in American history. Using nonviolent demonstrations, African Americans brought attention to the injustice of their situation. For generations they had been segregated, or kept apart from the white population. The "sit-in" movement was begun by young black people, who insisted on being served at a lunch counter in Greensboro, North Carolina. These courageous demonstrators suffered abuse, physical violence, and even the threat of death. Yet they remained firm and succeeded in achieving desegregation across the nation. Their courage, and the courage of all those who participated in the civil rights movement, helped awaken the conscience of white Americans and bring justice to those who had been oppressed.

14. Which of the following phrases from this selection best conveys a positive feeling?
    A. The "sit-in" movement was begun by young African Americans.
    B. For generations, African Americans had been segregated.
    C. African Americans brought attention to the injustice of their situation.
    D. Their courage helped awaken the conscience of Americans.

15. Which of the following words from this selection has negative connotations?
    A. participated   C. nonviolent
    B. oppressed   D. desegregation

16. Which word in the following sentence helps convey the author's attitude of admiration?
    These courageous demonstrators suffered abuse, physical violence, and even the threat of death.

    A. courageous   C. abuse
    B. demonstrators   D. threat

Literary Analysis: Tone

17. In a discussion of literature, to what does the term *tone* refer?
    A. the sources the author uses to do research before writing
    B. the author's attitude toward his or her subject and audience
    C. the organizational pattern in which information is presented
    D. the use of various techniques to emotionally affect the reader

18. What is the overall tone of the author in this selection?
    A. admiring   C. impersonal
    B. playful   D. critical

19. Which of the following details best conveys the author's tone?
    A. The "sit-in" movement was begun by young people.
    B. Their courage helped awaken the conscience of white Americans.
    C. They brought attention to the injustice of their situation.
    D. They succeeded in achieving desegregation.

Vocabulary: Roots

20. Which word has the same root as *rebellion*?
    A. bellicose
    B. doorbell
    C. belief
    D. label

21. What is the definition of *pervading* in the following sentence?

    When our team lost, there was a sense of defeat pervading the school.

    A. absent from
    B. forbidden in
    C. officially declared at
    D. present everywhere in

22. Which word has the same root as *compassionate*?

    Meg was a good nurse and her patients liked her because she was compassionate.

    A. passenger
    B. compass
    C. passion
    D. desperate

23. Which of the following sentences correctly uses the word *contraction*?
    A. Before agreeing to the business arrangement, I made sure I signed a contraction.
    B. Fred wanted to have dinner with Ruth because he felt a strong contraction to her.
    C. Feeling the contraction in his stomach, all Alex could think about was eating.
    D. Sorry for what he said, the movie star quickly made a public contraction.

Unit 3 Resources: Types of Nonfiction
230

24. Which definition best fits the word *belligerent* in the following sentence?

Most people at school avoided Marvin because he was usually belligerent.

    A. having or showing joy or hopefulness

    B. tending to or showing anger or aggression

    C. easy going

    D. lazy

25. Which word has the same root as *distract*?

    A. desert

    B. detract

    C. trackage

    D. demonstrate

Grammar

26. Which of the following sentences contains a conjunction?

    A. Everyone in the club wanted to go to the home team's opening game.

    B. There were not enough tickets for all of them to go to the game.

    C. It rained in the morning, but the sun came out in the afternoon.

    D. It was a great day for the opening of the baseball season.

27. Which of the following is a true statement about prepositions?

    A. They can join two sentences or sentence parts together.

    B. They can change the meaning of a sentence.

    C. They can separate two complete sentences.

    D. They are used to add information to sentences.

28. Which of the following sentences contains a prepositional phrase?

    A. Many people attempted to win the tournament.

    B. Bad weather forced the tournament to be postponed.

    C. When the tournament finally resumed, most spectators had left.

    D. The judge presented flowers to the winner.

29. Which of the following sentences contains a subordinating conjunction?

    A. Because the closest star is so far away, humans will probably never travel there.

    B. Many people believe that there is undiscovered life on other planets in our galaxy.

    C. There are billions of stars in our galaxy, and our galaxy is only one of millions.

    D. Scientists continue to listen for messages sent by intelligent life on other planets.

30. Identify the prepositional phrase in the following sentence.

Sitting at his computer and briefly thinking, Dan began typing as fast as his fingers could move.

    A. at his computer

    B. and briefly thinking

    C. Dan began typing

    D. as fast as his fingers

31. Which coordinating conjunction is used to join similar or related ideas?
    A. and
    B. but
    C. or
    D. so

32. Which coordinating conjunction is used to show cause and effect?
    A. and
    B. but
    C. or
    D. so

Spelling: Homophones

33. Which of the following pairs of words are homophones?
    A. bored / bared
    B. like / dislike
    C. bored / board
    D. fair / fair

34. Which of the following sentences contains a homophone of the word *allowed*?
    A. He was very proud to be one of the players on the team.
    B. They were not permitted to attend the game.
    C. Members of the losing team behaved in an aloof manner.
    D. The names of the winners were read aloud.

ESSAY

Writing

35. What current issue do you feel strongly about? Issues at school? Curfew? The environment? Write a brief editorial stating and defending your opinion on the issue. Be sure to include reasons and evidence to support your opinion. Don't forget to use persuasive techniques.

36. Think of a short piece of nonfiction that you have read recently in which the author has made an argument for or against something. It might be a letter to an editor of your newspaper or an article in a magazine or textbook. Write a brief response to the idea, explaining whether you agree or disagree with it.

37. What techniques does your favorite commercial use to persuade you to buy a product? Write a brief evaluation of a commercial. Describe the persuasive techniques, including repetitions or rhetorical questions, used in the piece. Evaluate its overall effectiveness.

Name _____ Date _____

Vocabulary in Context

Identify the answer choice that best completes the statement.

1. When I was still outside the kitchen, my nose sensed wonderful _____ .
   A. aromas
   B. benefits
   C. refuse
   D. delicious

2. They had collected the wood and were _____ it into smaller pieces.
   A. swaying
   B. sawing
   C. drifting
   D. bulging

3. As the puppy tried to chase them, the girls' sad faces turned to _____ .
   A. grins
   B. fearful
   C. gleams
   D. squints

4. By morning, the grass will be covered with _____ .
   A. thickets
   B. dioxide
   C. muck
   D. dew

5. As the sun set by the water, we were attacked by a _____ of biting insects.
   A. cruelty
   B. shimmer
   C. swarm
   D. peril

6. Snakes like to move in the grass in a very _____ way.
   A. dart
   B. steed
   C. stiffen
   D. slithery

7. A large crowd came to hear him speak, and he loudly addressed the _____ .
   A. masses
   B. images
   C. authority
   D. relationships

8. Instead of walking, let's take the _____ up to the fifth floor.
   A. latticework
   B. radiator
   C. elevator
   D. casement

9. Much vegetation was burned during the flow of the _____ down the mountain.
   A. undergrowth
   B. cedars
   C. lava
   D. volcano

10. To keep warm, they put on their heavy _____ .
    A. parkas
    B. thatch
    C. soot
    D. naked

11. I will be able to help you because my chores will take only another _____ .
    A. delayed
    B. moment
    C. hasten
    D. metric

12. We are not seeking general ideas but want some very _____ plans.
    A. humorous
    B. mournful
    C. teeming
    D. concrete

13. The water in the sea was so blue that it was almost an _____ color.
    A. aura
    B. aqua
    C. maple
    D. absolutely

14. He gave away his money to follow his dream, although some thought this was _____ .
    A. folly
    B. bonanza
    C. treason
    D. claimed

15. The wind blew through the pine trees, creating a sad and_____ tune.
   A. critical
   B. nightmare
   C. mournful
   D. battered

16. We watched a flock of_____ fly away from the shore.
   A. herons
   B. furies
   C. perch
   D. salmon

17. I checked this spelling in the dictionary, so I am_____ sure that it is right.
   A. approving
   B. individually
   C. occasionally
   D. absolutely

18. Not being able to find her puppy gave her a feeling of such_____ .
   A. desolate
   B. petition
   C. anguish
   D. imperative

19. For its religious meaning, many people read the_____ .
   A. biography
   B. Bible
   C. commercial
   D. vocabularies

20. The military leader told the troops to report to the_____ in their home state.
   A. vigilance
   B. fugitives
   C. garrison
   D. voluntary

Diagnostic Tests and Vocabulary in Context
Use and Interpretation

The Diagnostic Tests and Vocabulary in Context were developed to assist teachers in making the most appropriate assignment of *Prentice Hall Literature* program selections to students. The purpose of these assessments is to indicate the degree of difficulty that students are likely to have in reading/comprehending the selections presented in the *following* unit of instruction. Tests are provided at six separate times in each in each grade level—a *Diagnostic Test* (to be used prior to beginning the year's instruction) and a *Vocabulary in Context,* the final segment of the Benchmark Test appearing at the end of each of the first five units of instruction. Note that the tests are intended for use not as summative assessments for the prior unit, but as guidance for assigning literature selections in the upcoming unit of instruction.

The structure of all Diagnostic Tests and Vocabulary in Context in this series is the same. All test items are four-option, multiple-choice items. The format is established to assess a student's ability to construct sufficient meaning from the context sentence to choose the only provided word that fits both the semantics (meaning) and syntax (structure) of the context sentence. All words in the context sentences are chosen to be "below-level" words that students reading at this grade level should know. All answer choices fit *either* the meaning or structure of the context sentence, but only the correct choice fits *both* semantics and syntax. All answer choices—both correct answers and incorrect options—are key words chosen from specifically taught words that will occur in the subsequent unit of program instruction. This careful restriction of the assessed words permits a sound diagnosis of students' current reading achievement and prediction of the most appropriate level of readings to assign in the upcoming unit of instruction.

The assessment of vocabulary in context skill has consistently been shown in reading research studies to correlate very highly with "reading comprehension." This is not surprising as the format essentially assesses comprehension, albeit in sentence-length "chunks." Decades of research demonstrate that vocabulary assessment provides a strong, reliable prediction of comprehension achievement—the purpose of these tests. Further, because this format demands very little testing time, these diagnoses can be made efficiently, permitting teachers to move forward with critical instructional tasks rather than devoting excessive time to assessment.

It is important to stress that while the Diagnostic and Vocabulary in Context were carefully developed and will yield sound assignment decisions, they were designed to *reinforce*, not supplant, teacher judgment as to the most appropriate instructional placement for individual students. Teacher judgment should always prevail in making placement—or indeed other important instructional—decisions concerning students.

Diagnostic Tests and Vocabulary in Context
Branching Suggestions

These tests are designed to provide maximum flexibility for teachers. Your *Unit Resources* books contain the 40-question **Diagnostic Test** and 20-question **Vocabulary in Context** tests. At *PHLitOnline*, you can access the Diagnostic Test and complete 40-question Vocabulary in Context tests. Procedures for administering the tests are described below. Choose the procedure based on the time you wish to devote to the activity and your comfort with the assignment decisions relative to the individual students. Remember that your judgment of a student's reading level should always take precedence over the results of a single written test.

Feel free to use different procedures at different times of the year. For example, for early units, you may wish to be more confident in the assignments you make—thus, using the "two-stage" process below. Later, you may choose the quicker diagnosis, confirming the results with your observations of the students' performance built up throughout the year.

The **Diagnostic Test** is composed of a single 40-item assessment. Based on the results of this assessment, make the following assignment of students to the reading selections in Unit 1:

Diagnostic Test Score	Selection to Use
If the student's score is 0–25	more accessible
If the student's score is 26–40	more challenging

Outlined below are the three basic options for administering **Vocabulary in Context** and basing selection assignments on the results of these assessments.

1. For a one-stage, quicker diagnosis using the *20-item* test in the *Unit Resources:*

Vocabulary in Context Test Score	Selection to Use
If the student's score is 0–13	more accessible
If the student's score is 14–20	more challenging

2. If you wish to confirm your assignment decisions with a *two-stage* diagnosis:

Stage 1: Administer the 20-item test in the *Unit Resources*	
Vocabulary in Context Test Score	Selection to Use
If the student's score is 0–9	more accessible
If the student's score is 10–15	(Go to Stage 2.)
If the student's score is 16–20	more challenging

Stage 2: Administer items 21–40 from *PHLitOnline*	
Vocabulary in Context Test Score	Selection to Use
If the student's score is 0–12	more accessible
If the student's score is 13–20	more challenging

3. If you base your assignment decisions on the full 40-item **Vocabulary in Context** from *PHLitOnline:*

Vocabulary in Context Test Score	Selection to Use
If the student's score is 0–25	more accessible
If the student's score is 26–40	more challenging

Name _____ Date _____

Grade 8—Benchmark Test 5
Interpretation Guide

For remediation of specific skills, you may assign students the relevant Reading Kit Practice and Assess pages indicated in the far-right column of this chart. You will find rubrics for evaluating writing samples in the last section of your Professional Development Guidebook.

Skill Objective	Test Items	Number Correct	Reading Kit
Reading Skill			
Main Idea	1, 2, 3, 4, 5, 6, 7		pp. 102, 103
Analyze Treatment, Scope, and Organization of Ideas	8, 9, 10		pp. 104, 105
Literary Analysis			
Biography and Autobiography	11, 12, 13		pp. 106, 107, 108, 109
Types of Organization	14, 15, 16		pp. 110, 111
Vocabulary			
Roots and Suffixes -ly, -ance, -val-, -nym-	17, 18, 19, 20, 21, 22		pp. 112, 113
Grammar			
Adjectives and Articles	23, 24, 25		pp. 114, 115
Adverbs	26, 27, 28		pp. 116, 117
Comparative and Superlative Forms	29, 30, 31		pp. 118, 119
Writing			
How-to Essay	32	Use rubric	pp. 120, 121
Biographical sketch	33	Use rubric	pp. 122, 123
Reflective Essay	34	Use rubric	pp. 124, 125

Unit 3 Resources: Types of Nonfiction

Name _____ Date _____

Grade 8—Benchmark Test 6
Interpretation Guide

For remediation of specific skills, you may assign students the relevant Reading Kit Practice and Assess pages indicated in the far-right column of this chart. You will find rubrics for evaluating writing samples in the last section of your Professional Development Guidebook.

Skill Objective	Test Items	Number Correct	Reading Kit
Reading Skill			
Fact and Opinion	1, 2, 3,		pp. 126, 127
Analyze Proposition and Support	4, 5, 6, 7, 8, 9, 10		pp. 128, 129
Literary Analysis			
Persuasive Techniques	11, 12, 13		pp. 130, 131
Word Choice	14, 15, 16		pp. 132, 133
Tone	17, 18, 19		pp. 134, 135
Vocabulary			
Roots –bellum-, -vad-, -pass-, -tract-	20, 21, 22, 23, 24, 25		pp. 136, 137
Grammar			
Conjunctions	26, 29		pp. 138, 139
Prepositions and Prepositional Phrases	27, 28, 30		pp. 140, 141
Combining Sentences With Conjunctions	31, 32		pp. 142, 143
Spelling			
Homophones	33, 34		pp. 144, 145
Writing			
Editorial	35	Use rubric	pp. 146, 147
Response	36	Use rubric	pp. 148, 149
Evalution	37	Use rubric	pp. 150, 151

Unit 3 Resources: Types of Nonfiction

ANSWERS

Big Question Vocabulary—1, p. 1

Sample Answers

A. 1. gather; scatter
2. growth; deterioration
3. prejudice; fairness
4. expose; hide
5. treasured; worthless

B. 1. development
2. accumulate
3. valuable
4. discrimination
5. reveal

Big Question Vocabulary—2, p. 2

Sample Answers

A. 1. challenge
2. inequality
3. decision
4. exploration
5. explanation

B. Answers will vary, but should address the question of inequality. Use of the Thematic Vocabulary words should be encouraged.

Big Question Vocabulary—3, p. 3

Sample Answers

A. Proposals will vary but should attempt to persuade Ferdinand and Isabella to fund the voyage, and should contain all five Thematic Vocabulary words.

B.
1. I believe that a quantity of three should be enough.
2. I challenge their knowledge on that issue. Let me prove them wrong!
3. It could have global significance. In fact, it might prove that the world IS global and not flat.

"Making Tracks on Mars" by Andrew Mishkin

Vocabulary Warm-up Exercises, p. 8

A. 1. Exploration
2. spacecraft
3. solar
4. panels
5. software
6. critical
7. operations
8. meteor

B. Sample Answers
1. The *diagnosis* was great; Sam would *regain* his health.

2. The program *director* gave orders to the office workers.
3. I received written *confirmation* that my application had arrived.
4. In the juice department of a supermarket, there are many *alternatives* to orange juice.
5. When the radio station's roof *collapsed*, the *transmitter* that had been positioned there was damaged.

Reading Warm-up A, p. 9

Sample Answers

1. (on the red planet); I would love to travel into outer space on a *spacecraft* so that I could look back at Earth.
2. (increasing knowledge of this cold, rocky wasteland); An *exploration* that I will always remember was going into an amazing cave during one of my spelunking classes.
3. streaking through the sky, crashed and left deep craters; A *meteor* that crashed on Earth could leave a large hole in the surface. If it landed in a populated area, it could kill a lot of people.
4. (have developed a strategy); *Operations* managers at an ice-cream factory would make sure all the machines are working, that they are clean, and that the ice cream was of a good quality.
5. These collect sunlight and change it to the electricity the spacecraft needs; *Solar panels* are sheets of sun-sensitive material that collect sunlight.
6. (A mission might have to end early.); If a hospital patient becomes *critical*, his or her life is in danger.
7. (computer program); *Software* I have used includes word-processing programs, games, and an electronic calculator.

Reading Warm-up B, p. 10

Sample Answers

1. a whole section of the wall of the service module; The roof of a house *collapsed* because no one removed a heavy layer of snow from it.
2. analyzed the situation; A *diagnosis* is important when someone is ill.
3. (lowest-level worker); A movie has a *director*.
4. unbelievable; It is *incredulous* to me that we can send a spacecraft to the outer planets.
5. (its course to the moon); *Regain* means "to get back something."
6. (control system in the lunar module . . . could remove dangerous carbon dioxide gas from the astronauts' cabin); I had to choose between two *alternatives* for an after-school activity: band and soccer.
7. that their idea worked; A written *confirmation* is necessary when you make a plane reservation.
8. (television); Because the radio *transmitter* was not very strong, I could never get the station very clearly on the car radio.

Listening and Viewing, p. 11

Sample Answers

Segment 1. Mishkin writes about the Mars rover missions that he participated in. Students may say that a challenge for Mishkin is making descriptions of technical projects understandable to and exciting for the general reader.

Segment 2. Mishkin decided to write the book because he wanted to tell about all the people who helped make the mission a success and show the importance of working with a team. The essays that Mishkin wrote every day, in the form of a Web log describing the details of the mission, were important to the development of his book because he turned them into a journal that he then used as a reference when he was writing the book.

Segment 3. Mishkin has other people, like his wife and his friends, look over his drafts to see whether the scientific content is accessible to general readers. Students may suggest that revision is important because it allows writers to correct their mistakes and refine their language.

Segment 4. Mishkin hopes that his book will inspire readers to take on difficult projects and work with others. Students may say that it is important to learn the different stories that contribute to a single event and the ways in which people can meet difficult objectives by working together.

Learning About Nonfiction, p. 12

A. 1. autobiography
   2. Web log
   3. essay or article
   4. letter
   5. media account
   6. memoir
   7. biography
   8. journal

B. formal; The writer appears to be addressing teachers or a professional audience.

"Making Tracks on Mars" by Andrew Mishkin

Model Selection: Nonfiction, p. 13

A. 1. Each entry is dated, and the dates show that the entries are presented in time order.
   2. The subheads tell what each entry is about.
   3. It is informal. The writer seems to be addressing the audience in a friendly way.
   4. The journal tracks a 2003–2004 mission to explore the surface of Mars.
   5. Mishkin was responsible for planning the activities of the rover *Spirit*.

B. Students should conclude that the mission appears to have been successful. As evidence, they might point out that *Spirit* survives its landing, does not tip over when leaving its "lander platform," and transmits data after a temporary problem is solved.

Open-Book Test, p. 14

Short Answer

1. The author is using chronological order.
   Difficulty: *Easy*   **Objective:** *Literary Analysis*
2. You are analyzing the author's tone.
   Difficulty: *Average*   **Objective:** *Literary Analysis*
3. You are focusing on the writer's voice.
   Difficulty: *Average*   **Objective:** *Literary Analysis*
4. You are reading expository writing.
   Difficulty: *Average*   **Objective:** *Literary Analysis*
5. The author says he has a "sick feeling," he says that he thinks the *Beagle 2* mission has failed, and he imagines wreckage. Those remarks suggest that he is in a pessimistic mood.
   Difficulty: *Challenging*   **Objective:** *Interpretation*
6. The blog is organized in chronological order.
   Difficulty: *Easy*   **Objective:** *Literary Analysis*
7. Students should say that the blog is informal or friendly. They should cite any of the exclamations (like "We can drive here!" "We were off!" and "Jackpot!"), the references to popular culture (the theme song from *Rawhide* and the remark about a repairman who makes house calls), and any other relevant evidence.
   Difficulty: *Challenging*   **Objective:** *Literary Analysis*
8. The correct order of events is 3, 2, 1, 4. After the fourth event, the reader is left wondering whether *Spirit* will be repaired.
   Difficulty: *Average*   **Objective:** *Literary Analysis*
9. The author's use of *we* shows that he feels close to the other scientists and engineers. The fact that he writes as if he were on Mars himself shows how deeply involved in the mission he is.
   Difficulty: *Challenging*   **Objective:** *Interpretation*
10. Students should recognize that the exclamation is affirmation of the rover's successful landing. They may also note that it is acknowledgment of the good luck that the rover has landed on terrain that is unlike anything else the scientists have seen on Mars.
    Difficulty: *Average*   **Objective:** *Interpretation*

Essay

11. Students should recognize that a journal is a record of an experience that is written as the experience takes place. Therefore, they should say that the primary method of organization will be chronological. They should use a single adjective to describe the tone they will take. They should explain that they will include insights about the importance of the experience to make the journal reflective.
    Difficulty: *Easy*   **Objective:** *Essay*
12. Students should recognize that a blog is a journal that is posted online. Therefore, it contains the kind of information a journal contains: a record of events as well as reflections on the meaning of those events. In

naming topics that are well suited to a blog, they might mention a political campaign, a trip to a place the writer has never visited before, or a new job. Students should refer to "Making Tracks on Mars" to support their points.

Difficulty: *Average*   **Objective:** *Essay*

13. Students who find the journal format effective might point out that the updates create suspense and that the informal tone helps readers feel involved. Students who do not find the journal format effective may say that it prolongs description unnecessarily and sacrifices hard facts to personal reflection.

Difficulty: *Challenging*   **Objective:** *Essay*

14. Students who feel the journal provided enough information should explain how the information gave them a complete explanation of the events. Students who want more information should explain what they feel is lacking or what they did not understand completely.

Difficulty: *Average*   **Objective:** *Essay*

Oral Response

15. Oral responses should be clear, well organized, and well supported by appropriate examples from the blog.

Difficulty: *Average*   **Objective:** *Oral Interpretation*

express an understanding that a journal contains descriptive information as well as personal thoughts and reflections.

Difficulty: *Easy*

Objective: *Essay*

17. Students should include examples of the team's reactions to such events as *Spirit*'s landing (they are tense and then scream and cheer with relief). They might point out other descriptions of emotions (such as waiting with a "sick feeling" to learn the fate of *Spirit*), direct questions about worries and uncertainties ("Will we have better luck?"), sentences that end with exclamation points ("We can drive here!"), the informal name the engineers give to the waiting period ("the six minutes of terror"), and the description of the Flight Director playing the theme from *Rawhide*.

Difficulty: *Easy*

Objective: *Essay*

18. Students who feel the journal provided enough information should explain how it gave them a complete explanation of the events. Students who want more information should explain what they feel is lacking or what they did not understand completely.

Difficulty: *Average*

Objective: *Essay*

Selection Test A, p. 17

Learning About Nonfiction

1. ANS: D	DIF: Easy	OBJ: Literary Analysis
2. ANS: A	DIF: Easy	OBJ: Literary Analysis
3. ANS: D	DIF: Easy	OBJ: Literary Analysis
4. ANS: B	DIF: Easy	OBJ: Literary Analysis
5. ANS: A	DIF: Easy	OBJ: Literary Analysis

Critical Reading

6. ANS: A	DIF: Easy	OBJ: Comprehension
7. ANS: B	DIF: Easy	OBJ: Interpretation
8. ANS: D	DIF: Easy	OBJ: Comprehension
9. ANS: C	DIF: Easy	OBJ: Interpretation
10. ANS: C	DIF: Easy	OBJ: Comprehension
11. ANS: B	DIF: Easy	OBJ: Comprehension
12. ANS: A	DIF: Easy	OBJ: Comprehension
13. ANS: B	DIF: Easy	OBJ: Interpretation
14. ANS: B	DIF: Easy	OBJ: Literary Analysis
15. ANS: A	DIF: Easy	OBJ: Literary Analysis

Essay

16. Students should recognize that a journal is an ongoing record of an experience as it unfolds. They should

Selection Test B, p. 20

Learning About Nonfiction

1. ANS: B	DIF: Average	OBJ: Literary Analysis
2. ANS: C	DIF: Average	OBJ: Literary Analysis
3. ANS: D	DIF: Challenging	OBJ: Literary Analysis
4. ANS: D	DIF: Average	OBJ: Literary Analysis
5. ANS: A	DIF: Average	OBJ: Literary Analysis
6. ANS: C	DIF: Average	OBJ: Literary Analysis

Critical Reading

7. ANS: D	DIF: Average	OBJ: Literary Analysis
8. ANS: A	DIF: Average	OBJ: Comprehension
9. ANS: C	DIF: Average	OBJ: Comprehension
10. ANS: A	DIF: Challenging	OBJ: Comprehension
11. ANS: D	DIF: Average	OBJ: Comprehension
12. ANS: A	DIF: Average	OBJ: Literary Analysis
13. ANS: C	DIF: Challenging	OBJ: Interpretation
14. ANS: A	DIF: Challenging	OBJ: Comprehension
15. ANS: D	DIF: Challenging	OBJ: Interpretation
16. ANS: D	DIF: Average	OBJ: Comprehension
17. ANS: B	DIF: Challenging	OBJ: Comprehension
18. ANS: B	DIF: Average	OBJ: Literary Analysis
19. ANS: A	DIF: Challenging	OBJ: Literary Analysis

Essay

20. Students might cite the engineers and scientists' tension ("the six minutes of terror") as they await reports of the landing and their reaction when they learn that the landing has been achieved (screams, cheers, fists thrust in the air). They also might refer to the author's "sick feeling" as he awaits news of the fate of *Spirit*, his direct questions ("Will we have better luck?"), his exclamations ("We were on Mars!"), and the description of the Flight Director playing the theme from *Rawhide*.

    Difficulty: *Average*

    Objective: *Essay*

21. Students should recognize that a Web log is merely an online journal, and so contains the kind of information a journal contains—personal thoughts and reflections as well as descriptions of events. Students should suggest topics that are well suited to a blog, such as a political campaign, an unusual trip, a significant job (such as Mishkin's with the rover mission), or simply one's everyday life. Students should cite two examples from the selection to support their points.

    Difficulty: *Average*

    Objective: *Essay*

22. Students who find the journal format effective might point out that daily or periodic updates create suspense—for example, in "Making Tracks on Mars," by keeping readers interested in the progress of the *Spirit*—and that the informal tone helps readers feel involved. Students who do not find the journal format effective may say that it unnecessarily prolongs a description and sacrifices hard facts to personal reflection.

    Difficulty: *Challenging*

    Objective: *Essay*

23. Students who feel the journal provided enough information should explain how the information gave them a complete explanation of the events. Students who want more information should explain what they feel is lacking or what they did not understand completely.

    Difficulty: *Average*

    Objective: *Essay*

"Baseball" by Lionel G. García

Vocabulary Warm-up Exercises, p. 24

A.
1. exception
2. professional
3. fielder
4. ignorance
5. scheme
6. complicate
7. standard
8. exhausted

B. Sample Answers

1. The kids' chatter, which was *idle*, drifted though the window making it hard for me to concentrate.

2. After the fight *erupted*, the police came, but everyone *evaded* capture.
3. We stood in the *expanse* of green that made up the *outfield*.
4. Paul Bunyan strode *mightily* through the northern forests.
5. On our mock quiz show, we decided to *rotate* being emcee and panelists.
6. My *option* is to save all my money for college or to use a part of it for a summer vacation.

Reading Warm-up A, p. 25

Sample Answers

1. (ballplayers); It takes a lot of hard work to become a *professional* athlete.
2. It, too, was in need of players; There is no *exception* to detention if you got to class after the late bell.
3. (plan); Wrigley's *scheme* was to start a women's softball league to keep interest in baseball alive.
4. (pitcher, catcher, and fielder); A *fielder* is any baseball player other than the pitcher or catcher.
5. (trained hard); I was *exhausted* after taking a ten-mile hike.
6. they also had to travel; I hoped the bad weather wouldn't *complicate* our plans for getting to the game.
7. (softball rules): *Standard* means "usual."
8. Out of *ignorance*, I almost gave my dog some chocolate. Luckily, my brother told me that chocolate can actually kill a dog.

Reading Warm-up B, p. 26

Sample Answers

1. (chose); I have an *option* to take Spanish or French.
2. (huge); The botanical gardens covered quite an *expanse* in the heart of the city.
3. (Beyond the second-to-third baseline was a huge expanse of street); The batter hit a strong line drive into the outfield.
4. (hit); The batter swung *mightily* at the ball and missed.
5. had to be on constant lookout for cars; had to be ready for a ball; *Idle* means "having no purpose."
6. capture; I tried to get the cat into its carrier, but it *evaded* me.
7. No one had to play outfield for long.; We would *change positions in a set order.*
8. (arguments and fights); Mount St. Helens, a volcano, *erupted* and sent smoke into the air.

Writing About the Big Question, p. 27

A.
1. explanation
2. global
3. accumulate
4. inequality

B. Sample Answers

1. I made the decision to attend Houston Magnet School. That decision was important because it will affect the rest of my education.
2. One **factor** in my **decision** was the **challenge** I would face at Houston. **Statistics** show that Houston students get really good grades and most go to college.

C. Sample Answer

Children's games should be fun and easy to learn. Game instructions need to have just the right amount of information—if there is too much information, the instructions are too hard to follow, and if there is not enough, kids won't understand them.

Reading: Use Details to Identify the Main Idea, p. 28

Sample Answers

2. A few leaders decided the rules.
3. The playing field extended through the town.
4. The players enjoyed chasing each other.
5. The author loved the freedom of their large field.

Main idea of the selection: Both the players and the neighborhood spectators enjoyed the youngsters' unique version of baseball.

Literary Analysis: Narrative Essay, p. 29

Sample Answers

1. The games take place in the children's neighborhood.
2. The children could hear Father Zavala laugh with enjoyment.
3. The game's unusual rules made it fun and active for all the players, so it didn't matter so much who was at bat.
4. The players could chase the batter all over town.
5. The author probably did not let Uncle Adolfo's negative comment upset him.

Vocabulary Builder, p. 30

Sample Answers

A. 1. C; 2. A; 3. D; 4. A; 5. B; 6. A; 7. C;
B. 1. fuss
2. regret
3. struggle

Enrichment: Outlining, p. 31

Sample Answers

I. The name of the game might indicate something about the equipment needed to play or the way the game is played.
II. Equipment or materials might include balls, nets, boards, dice, or spinners, for example.
III. The goal might be to score the most or the fewest points, or to outlast another opponent in some way.

IV. Students should present their steps in chronological order.
V. Students should mention special rules not already covered and/or special situations.

"Baseball" by Lionel G. García

Open-Book Test, p. 32

Short Answer

1. His laughter reveals that he is fun-loving and does not mind when people do not play a game by the rules.
   Difficulty: *Easy* **Objective:** *Literary Analysis*
2. He means that they made the rules for the games they played, and no one could challenge them.
   Difficulty: *Average* **Objective:** *Interpretation*
3. When they could not avoid being hit, they were out.
   Difficulty: *Average* **Objective:** *Vocabulary*
4. *Details:* They rotated positions. They chased players across town. They threw balls at players. Students should recognize that the boys had a carefree life and were not concerned with the rules of organized sports.
   Difficulty: *Average* **Objective:** *Reading*
5. Father Zavala's enjoyment of the boys' games adds to the author's enjoyment of the memory of the games.
   Difficulty: *Challenging* **Objective:** *Interpretation*
6. He is surprised and displeased by the way they play.
   Difficulty: *Easy* **Objective:** *Interpretation*
7. He means that Uncle Adolfo was surprised that the children did not know how baseball should be played.
   Difficulty: *Easy* **Objective:** *Vocabulary*
8. Students should recognize that the narrator cherishes his memory of the game, which for some reason is very important to him.
   Difficulty: *Average* **Objective:** *Literary Analysis*
9. "Baseball" tells about real people and real events, and it tells a story.
   Difficulty: *Average* **Objective:** *Literary Analysis*
10. The author and his friends loved to play their version of baseball.
    Difficulty: *Challenging* **Objective:** *Reading*

Essay

11. Students should describe Father Zavala's laughter and his enjoyment of the games. They should recognize that the narrator's focus on Father Zavala suggests that he was an important figure in the narrator's childhood and might even have been a role model. They should also recognize that Father Zavala's enjoyment of the children's games appears to have validated the narrator's sense that they were having a great deal of fun.
    Difficulty: *Easy* **Objective:** *Essay*
12. Students should identify examples of how the games were fun for everyone, not just those who batted. They might mention the rule allowing anyone who caught the

ball to throw it at the batter, the rule allowing players to chase the batter, and the fact that the players had an appreciative audience in Father Zavala.

Difficulty: *Average*   **Objective:** *Essay*

13. Students should point out that Uncle Adolfo had been a professional baseball player and that he had given the children the baseball they played with. They should recognize that he apparently viewed their game with disdain. He might have thought that his gift of the baseball was being wasted. Students should point out that the children were ignorant of the official rules. Uncle Adolfo, however, seems to be ignorant of the value of fun. He doesn't recognize that the children are enjoying the game in part because it is their own invention.

Difficulty: *Challenging*   **Objective:** *Essay*

14. Students should base their response on the rules of the children's baseball game. They should cite details in the narrative to support their opinion of whether the author provides enough information to explain his enjoyment of the game.

Difficulty: *Average*   **Objective:** *Essay*

Oral Response

15. Oral responses should be clear, well organized, and well supported by appropriate examples from the essay.

Difficulty: *Average*   **Objective:** *Oral Interpretation*

"Baseball" by Lionel G. García

Selection Test A, p. 35

Critical Reading

1. ANS: D	DIF: Easy	OBJ: Comprehension
2. ANS: C	DIF: Easy	OBJ: Comprehension
3. ANS: B	DIF: Easy	OBJ: Comprehension
4. ANS: A	DIF: Easy	OBJ: Comprehension
5. ANS: A	DIF: Easy	OBJ: Reading
6. ANS: C	DIF: Easy	OBJ: Comprehension
7. ANS: B	DIF: Easy	OBJ: Literary Analysis
8. ANS: D	DIF: Easy	OBJ: Literary Analysis
9. ANS: C	DIF: Easy	OBJ: Reading
10. ANS: A	DIF: Easy	OBJ: Interpretation
11. ANS: B	DIF: Easy	OBJ: Interpretation

Vocabulary and Grammar

12. ANS: C	DIF: Easy	OBJ: Grammar
13. ANS: D	DIF: Easy	OBJ: Vocabulary
14. ANS: A	DIF: Easy	OBJ: Vocabulary
15. ANS: A	DIF: Easy	OBJ: Grammar

Essay

16. Students should briefly describe at least two rules the children used in their games. For example: there was a

rotation system for batting in which the outfielders never batted; if a ball hit the ground, the outfielder was expected to chase the batter anywhere; the distance from the batter to first base varied. These rules allowed for any number of unexpected outcomes, which made the game different each time.

Difficulty: *Easy*

Objective: *Essay*

17. Students should include in their essays a description of Father Zavala's hearty laughter and general enjoyment of the children's games. These descriptions add to the author's main idea that the games were fun—even for the spectators.

Difficulty: *Easy*

Objective: *Essay*

18. Students should cite details from the narrative to support their opinion of whether the author provides enough information to explain his enjoyment of the game.

Difficulty: *Average*

Objective: *Essay*

Selection Test B, p. 38

Critical Reading

1. ANS: C	DIF: Average	OBJ: Literary Analysis
2. ANS: A	DIF: Average	OBJ: Interpretation
3. ANS: C	DIF: Average	OBJ: Interpretation
4. ANS: B	DIF: Challenging	OBJ: Comprehension
5. ANS: D	DIF: Average	OBJ: Comprehension
6. ANS: A	DIF: Average	OBJ: Comprehension
7. ANS: C	DIF: Challenging	OBJ: Reading
8. ANS: B	DIF: Challenging	OBJ: Literary Analysis
9. ANS: D	DIF: Average	OBJ: Interpretation
10. ANS: C	DIF: Average	OBJ: Comprehension
11. ANS: B	DIF: Challenging	OBJ: Interpretation
12. ANS: A	DIF: Challenging	OBJ: Literary Analysis
13. ANS: D	DIF: Challenging	OBJ: Interpretation
14. ANS: A	DIF: Average	OBJ: Reading

Vocabulary and Grammar

15. ANS: A	DIF: Average	OBJ: Grammar
16. ANS: C	DIF: Average	OBJ: Vocabulary
17. ANS: D	DIF: Average	OBJ: Vocabulary
18. ANS: B	DIF: Average	OBJ: Grammar

Essay

19. Students' essays should identify at least two examples of how the baseball games were fun for everyone, not just for those who batted. For example, the rules allowed whoever caught the ball to throw it *at* the batter, everyone got involved in chasing the batter, and there was an appreciative audience watching.

Difficulty: *Average*
Objective: *Essay*

20. According to the author, Father Zavala laughed loudly from his seat on the rectory porch. In addition, the author imagines that Father Zavala had never seen any other kind of baseball game, and it must have been very entertaining for him to watch the chase. Students should point out that these details support the story's main idea that the children had a lot of fun playing the game in an unconventional way. The games were not only fun for the players but also enjoyable for observers.

Difficulty: *Average*
Objective: *Essay*

21. Students' essays should note that Uncle Adolfo, as a former professional baseball player, must have viewed the children's game with amusement and, perhaps, disdain. To him, official rules would be an important matter, but the children were ignorant of them. However, the children had a lot of fun making up and playing by their own rules. Uncle Adolfo seems to be ignorant of the value of fun, even at the expense of official rules.

Difficulty: *Challenging*
Objective: *Essay*

22. Students should base their response on the rules of the children's baseball game. They should cite details in the narrative to support their opinion of whether the author provides enough information to explain his enjoyment of the game.

Difficulty: *Average*
Objective: *Essay*

from "Harriet Tubman: Conductor on the Underground Railroad"
by Ann Petry

Vocabulary Warm-up Exercises, p. 42

A. 1. underground
2. serenity
3. hysterical
4. sufficient
5. reluctance
6. succession
7. vicinity
8. husky

B. Sample Answers
1. F. A plan can be *crystallized*, but concealed from others.
2. T. By maintaining proper *vigilance*, a guard can usually keep criminals *imprisoned*.
3. F. Party hosts usually want their guests to be in good moods and talkative, rather than *sullen*.
4. T. If you *lingered* at the party, you probably had a good time, unless you only stayed because you had to wait for your ride home.
5. T. A great speaker *invariably* has *eloquence*, but may not have the best manners when dealing with people.

Reading Warm-up A, p. 43

Sample Answers
1. burning desire for freedom; I have a *reluctance* to get out of bed on Monday morning.
2. (only two days); For a proper campfire, make sure you have *sufficient* wood.
3. (stations); When our teacher was out, we had four substitutes in *succession*.
4. Then, Matilda explained that underground meant "secret" in this case.; My brother's *underground* band doesn't play in public.
5. (outward excitement); The *serenity* seems unnatural because the escape is exciting and possibly dangerous, which would make it difficult for someone to be calm.
6. (hid it well); A *hysterical* person might cry and scream and act totally out of control.
7. (nearby); I was in the *vicinity* of the mall today, so I dropped by the video store.
8. The author contrasts the sound of *husky* voices with the sound of frogs in the spring.

Reading Warm-up B, p. 44

Sample Answers
1. an unexpected gift filled him with hope; My cousin Ed walks around with a frown on his face, which makes him look *sullen*.
2. (out of jail); For their part in the break-in, they were *imprisoned* for two years.
3. An understanding of what an isosceles triangle is finally became *crystallized* in my mind.
4. (hatred for slavery); Someone would show *unconcealed* hatred through their nasty actions and through horrible things he or she would say.
5. *always*; If given a choice of yogurt flavors, I *invariably* choose peach.
6. speech so stirred listeners; Rosa's *eloquence* as a graduation speaker really moved me.
7. (watch); With *vigilance*, we were able to keep all the newborn chicks alive.
8. I *lingered* at the dance because I was having so much fun.

Writing About the Big Question, p. 45

A. 1. quality
2. decision
3. global
4. discrimination

B. Sample Answers
1. Slavery was more common in the South because of one **factor**, the **development** of big cotton plantations, which used slaves from Africa who could work hard in the heat.
2. It will be a **challenge**, but even though we will probably always have **discrimination** of one kind or another, the people of the world should eventually get rid of slavery forever.

C. Sample Answer

The situation of slaves in the United States was harsh and unjust. Slaves were considered property not people. We have more than enough information from firsthand sources such as diaries and interviews, sales documents, runaway slave notices, and so on to prove that this was true.

Reading: Use Details to Identify the Main Idea, p. 46

Sample Answers

2. Tubman took big risks because she believed in freedom for all.
3. Tubman encouraged her group with hopeful stories, even when she felt unsure.
4. Tubman was prepared to shoot someone in order to protect the others.
5. Tubman earned people's total trust.

Literary Analysis: Narrative Essay, p. 47

Sample Answers

1. Tubman tells stories of how other slaves endured great difficulties in order to escape to freedom.
2. She probably would be hanged.
3. They walk at night and sleep during the day. It is very cold for much of the trip.
4. She tells stories about how wonderful Canada is.
5. He is always kind and always helps people. He gives every fugitive a new pair of shoes.
6. She rents a house for herself and the fugitives, and finds work for everyone.

Vocabulary Builder, p. 48

A. Sample Answers

1. Fugitives are trying to escape and do not want to be seen.
2. Employees might get a free or reduced membership.
3. He or she might look untidy and disorganized.
4. He or she might refuse to do assignments and might ignore instructions.
5. It would look clean and orderly.
6. A person might dispel a rumor by ignoring it.
7. Every class has different kinds of people, invariably including a person who can't stop talking.
8. No, I think the desert is beautiful in its own way.

B. 1. how
2. how often
3. how

Enrichment: Defining by Example, p. 49

Sample Answers

A. 2. You may alienate the students who are doing the teasing.

3. You must overcome the fear of failure.
4. You may lose the classmate as a friend. He or she may not help you when you need help.

B. Students should be as specific as possible in pointing out the courageous aspects of the person's life.

Sample response: a grandparent who fled oppression in his or her homeland and took a chance on the unknown in the United States.

from "Harriet Tubman: Conductor on the Underground Railroad" by Ann Petry "Baseball" by Lionel G. García

Integrated Language Skills: Grammar, p. 50

A. 1. *many* modifies *games*
2. *the* modifies *games*
3. *These* modifies *rules; complex* modifies *rules*
4. *One* modifies *game; unique* modifies *version*
5. *this* modifies *game; fifty* modifies *feet; the* modifies *seeker*
6. *a* and *big* modify *scarf*
7. *All* modifies *players; soft* modifies *sounds; the* modifies *seekers*
8. *long* and *fun* modify *Games*

B. Sample Answers

1. agile
2. dry
3. six
4. that

from "Harriet Tubman: Conductor on the Underground Railroad" by Ann Petry Open-Book Test, p. 53

Short Answer

1. She needed to see the star in order to know which direction to travel in.
   Difficulty: *Easy* **Objective:** *Interpretation*
2. The word *underground* suggests that it was secret. The word *railroad* suggests that it was a route with stations along the way.
   Difficulty: *Challenging* **Objective:** *Interpretation*
3. Among Garrett's traits that students might describe are his size and strength in contrast to his gentleness and the great kindness he showed to all fugitive slaves. They should mention that he helped fugitives by providing them with shoes, which were essential in their journey north by foot and in the cold weather they encountered.
   Difficulty: *Average* **Objective:** *Literary Analysis*
4. They might have rebelled against Tubman. They might have refused to go on, and Tubman might have shot them in order to keep them from returning and betraying the secrets of the Underground Railroad.
   Difficulty: *Average* **Objective:** *Vocabulary*
5. She wanted to inspire them by showing that other people like them had made the difficult journey successfully.
   Difficulty: *Average* **Objective:** *Interpretation*

6. *Implied main idea:* Harriet Tubman took risks when she helped fugitives escape to freedom.

Sample answer: Tubman deeply believed in the importance of freedom.

Difficulty: *Average* **Objective:** *Reading*

7. It reveals that they trusted her to bring them to safety and that they had come to believe that it was more important to risk their lives to be free than to return to the South, where they might be a little comfortable but they were not free.

Difficulty: *Challenging* **Objective:** *Literary Analysis*

8. Students might cite the runaway who found the journey so difficult he wanted to return to slavery; others might point to the great distances they covered on foot, the difficulty they had sleeping, and the very cold weather they encountered.

Difficulty: *Average* **Objective:** *Reading*

9. The trips show that Tubman was very brave (or very committed to freeing all the slaves she could). The fact that she risked her life on every trip is evidence of her bravery (or her determination).

Difficulty: *Easy* **Objective:** *Literary Analysis*

10. Tubman settled in Canada because African Americans there had freedoms that they did not have in the United States.

Difficulty: *Average* **Objective:** *Interpretation*

Essay

11. Students should describe three of these details: the cold weather, the risk of being discovered, Tubman's unfamiliarity with the route to Canada, the discouragement of some members of the group, and the uncertainty of the future.

Difficulty: *Easy* **Objective:** *Essay*

12. In their essays, students should include an example of sacrifices made or risks taken for the sake of freedom. They should refer to someone they know or someone they have read or heard about. Students who hold that no one today is so heroic should explain that they are aware of no such instances of heroism.

Difficulty: *Average* **Objective:** *Essay*

13. In their essays, students should recognize that Tubman believed that if a fugitive returned to the South, he or she would be forced to reveal the secrets of the Underground Railroad and therefore get the people who had helped them in trouble and make it difficult for other people living in slavery to escape. Students should recognize that Tubman might have believed that the cause of freedom was so great it was worth killing for. They may also point out that Tubman might have thought that her killing a mutinous fugitive would keep other fugitives from rebelling. Some students may agree that those reasons are justifiable. Others may say that the taking of a life can never be justified.

Difficulty: *Challenging* **Objective:** *Essay*

14. Students who think that the information provided is adequate to explain Tubman's motivations should point out that the essay touches on the horrors of slavery and mentions some of the freedoms that the enslaved people were deprived of. Students who say they need more information might mention that not much is told about Tubman's own life in slavery and that that information might help them understand her actions more fully.

Difficulty: *Average* **Objective:** *Essay*

Oral Response

15. Oral responses should be clear, well organized, and well supported by appropriate examples from the essay.

Difficulty: *Average* **Objective:** *Oral Interpretation*

Selection Test A, p. 56

Critical Reading

1. ANS: C	DIF: Easy	OBJ: Comprehension
2. ANS: C	DIF: Easy	OBJ: Interpretation
3. ANS: A	DIF: Easy	OBJ: Comprehension
4. ANS: D	DIF: Easy	OBJ: Comprehension
5. ANS: B	DIF: Easy	OBJ: Interpretation
6. ANS: B	DIF: Easy	OBJ: Literary Analysis
7. ANS: C	DIF: Easy	OBJ: Comprehension
8. ANS: C	DIF: Easy	OBJ: Reading
9. ANS: B	DIF: Easy	OBJ: Literary Analysis
10. ANS: D	DIF: Easy	OBJ: Comprehension
11. ANS: C	DIF: Easy	OBJ: Reading

Vocabulary and Grammar

12. ANS: B	DIF: Easy	OBJ: Vocabulary
13. ANS: A	DIF: Easy	OBJ: Grammar
14. ANS: C	DIF: Easy	OBJ: Vocabulary
15. ANS: A	DIF: Easy	OBJ: Grammar

Essay

16. Students' essays should include several examples of difficulties. For example, they could cite the increasingly cold weather, the continued risk of being discovered, the unfamiliarity of the territory, the discouragement of some members of the group, and the uncertainty of the future.

Difficulty: *Easy*

Objective: *Essay*

17. Students' essays should give examples, such as the following, of Tubman's courage, intelligence, determination, and unselfishness: her encouraging stories of escape, her careful attention to planning, her friendships with people along the Underground Railroad, her commitment to finding housing and work for the runaways when they got to Canada.

Difficulty: *Easy*

Objective: *Essay*

18. Students who think that the information provided is adequate might point out that the essay touches on the horrors of slavery and mentions some of the freedoms that the enslaved people were deprived of. Students who say they need more information might mention that not much is told about Tubman's own life in slavery and that such details might help them understand her actions more fully.

Difficulty: *Average*

Objective: *Essay*

Selection Test B, p. 59

Critical Reading

1. ANS: B	DIF: Average	OBJ: Comprehension
2. ANS: C	DIF: Average	OBJ: Comprehension
3. ANS: A	DIF: Challenging	OBJ: Interpretation
4. ANS: D	DIF: Challenging	OBJ: Interpretation
5. ANS: A	DIF: Average	OBJ: Interpretation
6. ANS: B	DIF: Average	OBJ: Comprehension
7. ANS: A	DIF: Average	OBJ: Reading
8. ANS: C	DIF: Challenging	OBJ: Interpretation
9. ANS: C	DIF: Challenging	OBJ: Literary Analysis
10. ANS: B	DIF: Average	OBJ: Literary Analysis
11. ANS: B	DIF: Average	OBJ: Comprehension
12. ANS: C	DIF: Challenging	OBJ: Reading
13. ANS: C	DIF: Average	OBJ: Interpretation
14. ANS: D	DIF: Average	OBJ: Reading
15. ANS: A	DIF: Challenging	OBJ: Comprehension

Vocabulary and Grammar

16. ANS: D	DIF: Average	OBJ: Vocabulary
17. ANS: B	DIF: Average	OBJ: Grammar
18. ANS: A	DIF: Average	OBJ: Grammar
19. ANS: A	DIF: Average	OBJ: Vocabulary
20. ANS: C	DIF: Average	OBJ: Vocabulary

Essay

21. Students' essays should include at least one example of sacrifices people have made or risks they have taken to attain freedom. Such examples may pertain to students' own experiences or to historical experiences ranging from the French Revolution to the 2005 free election in Iraq.

    Difficulty: *Average*

    Objective: *Essay*

22. Students' essays should include at least two qualities of Tubman's that contributed to her success. For example, Tubman was courageous, intelligent, determined, kind, and unselfish. Examples include her encouraging stories of escape, her careful attention to planning, her many friendships with people along the Underground Railroad, her commitment to finding housing and work for everyone once they got to Canada, and so forth.

    Difficulty: *Average*

    Objective: *Essay*

23. Students' essays should include at least two possible reasons for Tubman's feeling justified: Tubman felt that the cause of freedom was worth killing for; she knows firsthand about the struggles that former slaves endured to gain freedom; she was unwilling to risk the lives of all those involved in the Underground Railroad; she hoped to discourage other fugitives from retreating. Examples should include brief descriptions of actions and words that illustrate Tubman's commitment to shepherding the fugitives to safety.

    Difficulty: *Challenging*

    Objective: *Essay*

24. Students who think that the information provided is adequate to explain Tubman's motivations should point out that the essay touches on the horrors of slavery and mentions some of the freedoms that the enslaved people were deprived of. Students who say they need more information might mention that not much is told about Tubman's own life in slavery and that that information might help them understand her actions more fully.

    Difficulty: *Average*

    Objective: *Essay*

"Always to Remember: The Vision of Maya Ying Lin" by Brent Ashabranner

Vocabulary Warm-up Exercises, p. 63

A. 1. attending
2. architect
3. site
4. durable
5. political
6. appropriate
7. response
8. tribute

B. Sample Answers

1. News that is broadcast *nationally* is about things that people all over the country would be interested in, not just local events.
2. When a person *relates* well to someone, he or she connects with that person in some way. They may share the same ideas and outlook on life.
3. No, a skyscraper reaches up toward the sky rather than lying level to the ground in a *horizontal* way.
4. Once you are *enrolled* in a class, you should attend it and do the work.
5. *Sculpture* would not usually result in art for a wall because the artist creates things that have form and shape.

6. The *merits* of my favorite television show are that it makes me laugh, covers topics that happen in my life, and holds my attention.

7. The most *distinguished* adult I know is my teacher, Ms. Herrera, who won Teacher of the Year in our state last year.

8. A sofa that is in *harmony* with a room would fit in well with the other furniture and the colors in the room and would be pleasing to look at.

Reading Warm-up A, p. 64

Sample Answers

1. designed the Vietnam Veterans Memorial; An *architect* designs buildings for a living.

2. (the land, other memorials); The best building designs help the *site* become part of the whole area and require *appropriate* materials that blend in with the surroundings.

3. let their emotions show, stunned; I was surprised recently by my *response* to the National Anthem because I got choked up when I heard it.

4. (the Vietnam War); *Political* means "relating to government actions and policies."

5. the men and women who served our country; A *tribute* can be given, spoken, or done.

6. (When the weather is bad, the objects are picked up more often.); Some less *durable* objects left at the wall might be photographs, letters, poems written on paper, and fresh flowers.

7. special events; *Attending* means "being present at an event."

Reading Warm-up B, p. 65

Sample Answers

1. Pennsylvania; *Enrolled* means "officially joined a school or class."

2. Someone who is *distinguished* is very well known in lots of places and, therefore, has probably received attention *nationally*.

3. (with nature); *Harmony* means "the combination of parts to create a pleasing whole."

4. the larger area; *Relates* means "shows or proves a connection between things."

5. (round, polished, granite); In order for people to be able to stand on the stone, it had to be *horizontal*.

6. *simplicity*; The *merits* of my favorite spot in the woods are a running stream, beautiful trees, and quiet.

7. The Peace Chapel was made from stones carefully chosen and placed, and it has form and shape. So, it represents *sculpture*.

Writing About the Big Question, p. 66

A. 1. global
2. challenge
3. reveal

B. Sample Answers

1. I would like to honor Winsor McCay for the **quality** of his comics and animated films. His pioneering works **reveal** a great imagination, and he influenced artists and animators who came after him including Walt Disney.

2. Creating a memorial for Winsor McCay would be a **challenge**. Since "Gertie the Dinosaur" was his most famous cartoon character, one **decision** might be to create a playground with a Gertie the Dinosaur theme.

C. Sample Answer

Exploration of history requires a historian to accumulate a vast quantity of knowledge, much of it from primary sources. When the historian feels as though he or she can has explored all sides of a question, the person probably has enough information.

Reading: Make Connections Between Supporting Paragraphs and the Main Idea, p. 67

Sample Answers

1. *Supporting details:* Young Maya Lin made sculptures. Her home had a lot of books.

2. *Supporting details:* The gardens were sunny and light. Many people enjoyed the park's path and lake.

3. *Supporting details:* No names were attached to the entries. The winner met previously established criteria.

Literary Analysis: Biography and Autobiography, p. 68

Sample Answers

Accept all responses that give accurate information that reasonably belongs in each blank (sample answers are underlined here).

Maya Ying Lin

I. Background and education
  A. Background
    1. Childhood in Athens, Ohio
    2. Chinese American heritage
    3. Parents—artists and teachers
  B. Education
    Undergraduate at Yale University
II. The Vietnam Veterans Memorial contest
  A. Steps to winning
    1. Lin's entry: a class assignment
    2. 1,421 designs submitted
  B. Rewards
    1. $20,000 prize
    2. Recognition
III. The Vietnam Veterans Memorial
  A. Specifications
    1. Must contain names of all killed or missing
    2. Must make no political statement

3. Must be harmonious with setting
   B. Judges' reactions to winning entry
      1. Unanimous winner
      2. Surprise at youth of winner

Vocabulary Builder, p. 69

A. 1. criteria
2. eloquent
3. harmonious
4. unanimous
5. authorized
6. anonymously

B. 1. an acronym
2. a synonym
3. homonyms
4. anonymous

C. 1. homonym
2. acronym
3. synonym
4. homonym
5. acronym

Enrichment: Memorial Design, p. 70

Sample Answers

1. Students may think of national or local individuals or causes. They should support their selections with reasoned arguments.
2. Students should consider the size, shape, materials, and details of a monument.
3. Students might use comparison/contrast or description to get across a sense of a memorial that is not a physical structure.
4. Students might respond in terms of people's thoughts, emotions, resolutions, and so on.

Open-Book Test, p. 71

Short Answer

1. It is a biographical essay. It is written by Brent Ashabranner, but it is about Maya Lin.
   Difficulty: *Easy*   Objective: *Literary Analysis*
2. Americans had been bitterly divided by their opinions of America's involvement in the Vietnam War, and the memorial was intended to heal that division.
   Difficulty: *Challenging*   Objective: *Interpretation*
3. A record number of people submitted designs.
   Difficulty: *Easy*   Objective: *Reading*
4. Students should recognize that by setting criteria, or standards, the judges made sure that the designs that were submitted met the standards they had set. The judges would not have to waste time reviewing inappropriate designs.
   Difficulty: *Average*   Objective: *Vocabulary*

5. The planners did not want the judges to be influenced by the names, because the judges might have favored—or not favored—a designer whose work they were familiar with.
   Difficulty: *Average*   Objective: *Interpretation*
6. Possible answers: The report called Lin's design "the finest and most appropriate." The entries were judged anonymously. The decision was unanimous. The fact that the decision was unanimous suggests that most people would appreciate the design.
   Difficulty: *Average*   Objective: *Reading*
7. The judges wrote that the design was vividly expressive in the simplicity with which it brought together the names of the dead, the earth, and the sky.
   Difficulty: *Challenging*   Objective: *Vocabulary*
8. By describing Lin's background, the author shows the experiences that most likely had an influence on her and on her design for the Vietnam Veterans Memorial.
   Difficulty: *Average*   Objective: *Literary Analysis*
9. The strongest influence was probably Lin's father's career as a successful ceramicist. Students should recognize that both ceramics and architecture involve the creation of a structure.
   Difficulty: *Challenging*   Objective: *Literary Analysis*
10. Students should mention any two of the following ideas: Lin noticed the light, the beauty, and the people enjoying themselves. It was at the park that the idea for the memorial came to her: She realized that she wanted to design a monument that incorporated the beauty of the park and would make people feel safe yet remind them of the dead.
    Difficulty: *Average*   Objective: *Interpretation*

Essay

11. Students should cite two relevant details from Lin's background—for example, her family's involvement in Asian culture; her father's career as a ceramicist and his position as a dean of fine arts; her mother's work as a poet and her position as a professor of literature; and Lin's own interest in sculpture, fantasy, and European cemetery architecture. Students may also mention Lin's visit to the site of the memorial. They should make a clear connection between the details they choose and Lin's design.
    Difficulty: *Easy*   Objective: *Essay*
12. Students might mention Lin's job at McDonald's, her indecision about her major, and her interest in travel. They should point out that these details suggest Lin's broad interests, her willingness to work hard, and her curiosity, all of which may have contributed to her unusual design. Students might also say that these details present a fuller, more human, or more personal picture of Lin.
    Difficulty: *Average*   Objective: *Essay*
13. Students might mention, for example, two of these characteristics: It fit well in the setting; it honored the

veterans in a simple and quiet way; and its horizontal design seemed to symbolize the sense of harmony that the judges wished the design would convey. Finally, students should relate the judges' remarks to Lin's comments about her visit to the site of the memorial and its influence on her design.

Difficulty: *Challenging* **Objective:** *Essay*

14. Students may note that the photographs of the veterans at the memorial and the description of Lin's design as a "place of quiet reflection" and "an eloquent place where the simple meeting of earth, sky, and remembered names contain messages for all" are all they need to understand the memorial's impact. Students who feel they need more information may point out that the essay does not describe the memorial's impact on veterans.

Difficulty: *Average* **Objective:** *Essay*

Oral Response

15. Oral responses should be clear, well organized, and well supported by appropriate examples from the essay.

Difficulty: *Average* **Objective:** *Oral Interpretation*

"Always to Remember: The Vision of Maya Ying Lin" by Brent Ashabranner

Selection Test A, p. 74

Critical Reading

1. ANS: B	DIF: Easy	OBJ: Comprehension
2. ANS: C	DIF: Easy	OBJ: Comprehension
3. ANS: A	DIF: Easy	OBJ: Comprehension
4. ANS: A	DIF: Easy	OBJ: Interpretation
5. ANS: D	DIF: Easy	OBJ: Interpretation
6. ANS: C	DIF: Easy	OBJ: Comprehension
7. ANS: B	DIF: Easy	OBJ: Comprehension
8. ANS: B	DIF: Easy	OBJ: Literary Analysis
9. ANS: D	DIF: Easy	OBJ: Literary Analysis
10. ANS: A	DIF: Easy	OBJ: Comprehension
11. ANS: D	DIF: Easy	OBJ: Reading

Vocabulary and Grammar

12. ANS: B	DIF: Easy	OBJ: Grammar
13. ANS: A	DIF: Easy	OBJ: Vocabulary
14. ANS: C	DIF: Easy	OBJ: Grammar
15. ANS: B	DIF: Easy	OBJ: Vocabulary

Essay

16. Students' essays should include at least two specific characteristics of Maya Ying Lin's design that fit the competition requirements. For example, it was harmonious with the park location, it had artistic merit, it was made of materials that were easy to care for, and it was a simple design that allowed for quiet reflection.

Difficulty: *Easy*

Objective: *Essay*

17. Students' essays should include examples from Maya Ying Lin's background: her experiences growing up with artistic parents, her early success as a student, her accomplishments in art, her later interest in different kinds of architecture, and her travels to see cemeteries in Europe. All of these experiences contributed to her ability to imagine and execute a successful and appealing design. Some students may also mention Lin's experience of checking out the site before developing a design for the memorial.

Difficulty: *Easy*

Objective: *Essay*

18. Students may note that the photographs of the veterans at the memorial and the descriptions of Lin's design are all they need to understand why the memorial is so admired. Students who feel they need more information may point out that the essay does not describe the memorial's effect on veterans.

Difficulty: *Average*

Objective: *Essay*

Selection Test B, p. 77

Critical Reading

1. ANS: D	DIF: Average	OBJ: Comprehension
2. ANS: B	DIF: Average	OBJ: Reading
3. ANS: C	DIF: Average	OBJ: Comprehension
4. ANS: B	DIF: Challenging	OBJ: Interpretation
5. ANS: C	DIF: Average	OBJ: Comprehension
6. ANS: B	DIF: Challenging	OBJ: Comprehension
7. ANS: D	DIF: Average	OBJ: Literary Analysis
8. ANS: C	DIF: Average	OBJ: Interpretation
9. ANS: C	DIF: Challenging	OBJ: Interpretation
10. ANS: A	DIF: Challenging	OBJ: Literary Analysis
11. ANS: B	DIF: Average	OBJ: Interpretation
12. ANS: D	DIF: Challenging	OBJ: Comprehension
13. ANS: A	DIF: Average	OBJ: Interpretation
14. ANS: C	DIF: Average	OBJ: Literary Analysis

Vocabulary and Grammar

15. ANS: D	DIF: Average	OBJ: Vocabulary
16. ANS: C	DIF: Average	OBJ: Grammar
17. ANS: A	DIF: Average	OBJ: Grammar
18. ANS: B	DIF: Average	OBJ: Vocabulary
19. ANS: A	DIF: Average	OBJ: Grammar

Essay

20. Students' essays should include examples from Maya Ying Lin's background: her experiences growing up with

artistic parents, her early success as a student, her accomplishments in art, her later interest in different kinds of architecture, and her travels to see cemeteries in Europe. All of these experiences contributed to her self-confidence, broad design sense, and sensitivity toward the dead and to those who want to pay homage to the dead. Some students may also mention Lin's experience of visiting and evaluating the site before developing a design for the memorial.

Difficulty: *Average*

Objective: *Essay*

21. Students' essays should name three characteristics of Maya Ying Lin's design that impressed the judges. For example, it fit well in the park space, it honored the veterans in a simple and quiet way, and it was unusual in its horizontal shape.

Difficulty: *Average*

Objective: *Essay*

22. Students' essays might identify Lin's job at McDonald's, her indecision about her major, and her interest in travel as details about Maya Ying Lin's life that do not seem to bear directly on the war memorial design or contest. However, they do indicate Lin's broad interests, her willingness to work hard, and her curiosity—all attributes that may, indeed, have contributed to Lin's unusual solution to the design problem.

Difficulty: *Challenging*

Objective: *Essay*

23. Students may note that the photographs of the veterans at the memorial and the description of Lin's design as a "place of quiet reflection" and "an eloquent place where the simple meeting of earth, sky, and remembered names contain messages for all" are all they need to understand the memorial's impact. Students who feel they need more information may point out that the essay does not describe the memorial's impact on veterans.

Difficulty: *Average*

Objective: *Essay*

from **I Know Why the Caged Bird Sings**
by Maya Angelou

Vocabulary Warm-up Exercises, p. 81

A. 1. romantic
2. unexpected
3. essence
4. judgment
5. accurate
6. wiry
7. assured
8. Numerous

B. Sample Answers
1. *Staples* that I might collect for the homeless would include canned beans, bread, and other things that do not have to be kept in the refrigerator.
2. An *obsession* takes over a person's life while a hobby is just something that you do for fun in your free time.
3. I think the job of air traffic controller would require thinking with *clarity* all the time.
4. Police check to be sure people's statements are *valid* so they do not arrest the wrong person.
5. The *exotic* animal I have always wanted for a pet is the koala bear.
6. The judge is the person who should have *absolute* control in a courtroom.
7. I would take the following *provisions* as treats: cheese, nuts and raisins, and granola bars.
8. The moment of *enchantment* I remember is my fifth birthday and going to see "The Nutcracker" ballet.

Reading Warm-up A, p. 82

Sample Answers
1. drove a hot car, played numerous sports well, was the student body president, dark curly hair; *Essence* means "the most important quality of something."
2. The *numerous* sports Phillip might have played include soccer, baseball, football, and basketball.
3. (the girls); *Romantic* means "having to do with love."
4. when he was thirteen; Most people would find a friendship between a young boy and an old woman *unexpected*, and Phillip may have been surprised by it as well.
5. (wasn't afraid); *Wiry* means "thin but strong."
6. looked Phillip up and down; Having good *judgment* about people is thought to be difficult, so Miss Ruth would be proud of her ability.
7. (the college education of her grandchildren); *Assured* means "made certain something would happen."
8. what they said; I want people to say *accurate* things about me so that people will know what I am really like.

Reading Warm-up B, p. 83

Sample Answers
1. There was no question about it.; *Absolute* means "complete and total."
2. (supplies); People might shop weekly for *provisions* such as cereal, eggs, bread, meat, fruits, and vegetables.
3. (gossip); Gossip is not usually based on facts, but *valid* news would be based on information that has been proven to be true.
4. needed; *Staples* means "basic foods that are used often."
5. (the huge selection of candies); Children might have also found *enchantment* in a section of the store that displayed toys.

6. <u>new products such as fancy fabrics and canned foods from faraway places</u>; The most *exotic* thing I have seen in the grocery store is a mango.

7. When you hear different viewpoints, you can gain *clarity* about your own opinions.

8. (the old-fashioned general store); *Obsession* means "an interest in something that becomes all you think about."

Writing About the Big Question, p. 84

A. 1. statistics
2. accumulate
3. quality
4. exploration

B. Sample Answers

1. My grandfather came from a poor family, but he made a **decision** to go to college, and he worked after school and during the summers to **accumulate** enough money to go. I admire him because he liked a **challenge** and never let **discrimination** keep him from doing what he wanted to do.

2. I talk to my grandfather a lot, so I'd rate the **quality** and **quantity** of my information about him as excellent.

C. Sample Answer

The accumulation of knowledge is a good thing and continues throughout a person's life. So in a way, someone can never have too much information. But information alone is not enough to make a person wise. Wisdom comes from analyzing information and using it appropriately.

Reading: Make Connections Between Supporting Paragraphs and the Main Idea, p. 85

Sample Answers

1. *Supporting details:* Customers sat on the porch; travelers stopped there to rest and meet others.

2. *Supporting details:* Mrs. Flowers smiled often; the author wanted to thank Mrs. Flowers for smiling at her; Mrs. Flowers's smile was appealing.

3. *Supporting details:* Her voice sounded like singing; she seemed to be reading musical notes on a page.

Literary Analysis: Biography and Autobiography, p. 86

Sample Answers

1. Angelou thinks of the Store, in the morning, as exciting as an unexpected gift. She thinks of it as a person, tired at the end of the day.

2. Angelou appreciates that Mrs. Flowers pronounces her name in an appealing way. She admires how Mrs. Flowers uses language clearly.

3. Angelou feels that Mrs. Flowers's affection made a difference in her life. She enjoyed being respected for herself alone.

Vocabulary Builder, p. 87

A. Sample Answers

1. Our math teacher asked us to write a <u>fiscal</u> report summarizing our bake sale profits.

2. When the children offered to weed her garden, Jean responded with a <u>benign</u> look.

3. The plot was lighthearted, so the director asked the actors to <u>infuse</u> their lines with humor.

4. The impatient babysitter was <u>intolerant</u> of the children's loud games.

5. People used earplugs to block the <u>ceaseless</u> noise of the loud speakers.

6. His driver's license was <u>valid,</u> so the man did not get a ticket.

7. The best way to get good grades is through effort, not <u>enchantment</u>.

B. 1. value
2. valedictorian
3. valor

Enrichment: Mentoring, p. 88

Sample Answer

A. Qualities of Mentor

1. well read
2. wealthy

Benefits to Protégé

1. Can help me decide what to read
2. Can teach me about savings and investments

B. Teaching someone to respect people from different cultures; teaching someone a language.

"Always to Remember: The Vision of Maya Ying Lin" by Brent Ashabranner
from **I Know Why the Caged Bird Sings** by Maya Angelou

Integrated Language Skills: Grammar, p. 89

A. 1. *very* modifies *cautiously; cautiously* modifies *considered*
2. *exceedingly* modifies *important*
3. *clearly* modifies *required*
4. *quite* modifies *tirelessly; tirelessly* modifies *worked*
5. *generally* modifies *had remained*
6. *eventually* modifies *made*

B. Sample Answers

1. soon
2. very
3. graciously

from **I Know Why the Cased Bird Sings** by Maya Angelou

Open-Book Test, p. 92

Short Answer

1. It is an autobiographical essay. It is written by and about Maya Angelou.
   Difficulty: *Easy* **Objective:** *Literary Analysis*

2. Angelou means that the musicians' movements (their crawlings) were without end—the musicians were always on the move.
   Difficulty: *Average* **Objective:** *Vocabulary*

3. Many people who shopped at the Store did not have electricity. Those who did were thought by the narrator to be wealthy.
   Difficulty: *Average* **Objective:** *Interpretation*

4. Angelou found the Store exciting, like a gift.
   Difficulty: *Average* **Objective:** *Reading*

5. She means that Mrs. Flowers was the first person she met who helped her realize that her life was worthwhile.
   Difficulty: *Challenging* **Objective:** *Literary Analysis*

6. She means that speaking words aloud adds to their meaning.
   Difficulty: *Challenging* **Objective:** *Interpretation*

7. She means that Angelou should not judge a person simply because he or she cannot read and write.
   Difficulty: *Average* **Objective:** *Interpretation*

8. Mrs. Flowers's reading voice is rich and musical; it is full of expression.
   Difficulty: *Easy* **Objective:** *Reading*

9. *Grandmother:* respect; *Bailey:* love; *Mrs. Flowers:* admiration
   Students should recognize that the fact that Angelou's feelings are all positive suggests that she has a positive outlook on life.
   Difficulty: *Average* **Objective:** *Literary Analysis*

10. She learns to have confidence in herself.
    Difficulty: *Challenging* **Objective:** *Interpretation*

Essay

11. In their essays, students should include details about the Store's products, its importance to the community, and Angelou's feelings about it. Students should note that the author loved the Store and took pride in working there.
    Difficulty: *Easy* **Objective:** *Essay*

12. Students should note that the first part of the essay recalls Angelou's day-to-day life in the Store and the second part tells about the day when Mrs. Flowers showed Angelou the power of reading aloud. Students' titles should reflect the main idea of each part, such as "The Store" and "Finding My Voice."
    Difficulty: *Average* **Objective:** *Essay*

13. Students should recognize that Maya Angelou is in awe of Mrs. Flowers. She calls her "aristocratic" and describes her as godlike (for example, she is warm in winter and cool in summer; she speaks with unusual clarity). Students might mention any of a number of lessons Angelou learns from Mrs. Flowers (for example, about the power of the spoken word and the difference between ignorance and illiteracy). Perhaps most important, Angelou learns self-worth; she learns that someone likes and values her, and that knowledge made an important difference to her life.
    Difficulty: *Challenging* **Objective:** *Essay*

14. Students who say they had enough information should point out that the essay explains Angelou's first interaction with poetry and the beginning of her love of language. Students who feel they did not have enough information might say that they have learned how Angelou began to love reading and the spoken word, but lack the information that explains how that love was translated into the inspiration and motivation needed to become a poet.
    Difficulty: *Average* **Objective:** *Essay*

Oral Response

15. Oral responses should be clear, well organized, and well supported by appropriate examples from the essay.
    Difficulty: *Average* **Objective:** *Oral Interpretation*

Selection Test A, p. 95

Critical Reading

	ANS	DIF	OBJ
1.	D	Easy	Literary Analysis
2.	C	Easy	Interpretation
3.	A	Easy	Comprehension
4.	B	Easy	Literary Analysis
5.	A	Easy	Comprehension
6.	C	Easy	Comprehension
7.	B	Easy	Comprehension
8.	C	Easy	Reading
9.	A	Easy	Interpretation
10.	D	Easy	Literary Analysis
11.	A	Easy	Interpretation

Vocabulary and Grammar

	ANS	DIF	OBJ
12.	C	Easy	Vocabulary
13.	D	Easy	Grammar
14.	B	Easy	Vocabulary
15.	B	Easy	Grammar

Essay

16. Students' essays should include several examples of things the author notices about Mrs. Flowers, both before and during her visit. For example, the author comments on Mrs. Flowers's pretty dresses and hats, her slow smile, and

Mrs. Flowers's pretty dresses and hats, her slow smile, and her gracefulness. Mrs. Flowers's home is cool and pleasant, with fresh curtains and family photographs. The author admires Mrs. Flowers's reading voice, her kindness in offering books to borrow, and her lessons about intolerance.

Difficulty: *Easy*

Objective: *Essay*

17. Students' essays should include details in each of the three categories. For example, products in the Store include food for livestock, food for people, clothing items, and candy. The Store was the center of the town's activities in the Negro area. Travelers often stopped to rest there. The author loved the Store and took pride in working there; for example, she could measure grains accurately without a scale.

Difficulty: *Easy*

Objective: *Essay*

18. Students who say they had enough information might point out that the essay explains how Angelou got to know poetry and how she developed a love of language. Students who feel they did not have enough information might say that they might have liked to have more details about how she developed her love of poetry and language.

Difficulty: *Average*

Objective: *Essay*

Selection Test B, p. 98

Critical Reading

1. ANS: C	DIF: Average	OBJ: Comprehension
2. ANS: C	DIF: Average	OBJ: Interpretation
3. ANS: A	DIF: Challenging	OBJ: Literary Analysis
4. ANS: C	DIF: Average	OBJ: Comprehension
5. ANS: B	DIF: Average	OBJ: Literary Analysis
6. ANS: C	DIF: Average	OBJ: Reading
7. ANS: D	DIF: Challenging	OBJ: Reading
8. ANS: C	DIF: Average	OBJ: Interpretation
9. ANS: A	DIF: Challenging	OBJ: Interpretation
10. ANS: A	DIF: Average	OBJ: Comprehension
11. ANS: B	DIF: Challenging	OBJ: Interpretation
12. ANS: B	DIF: Challenging	OBJ: Comprehension
13. ANS: C	DIF: Average	OBJ: Literary Analysis
14. ANS: A	DIF: Average	OBJ: Literary Analysis
15. ANS: A	DIF: Challenging	OBJ: Literary Analysis

Vocabulary and Grammar

16. ANS: A	DIF: Average	OBJ: Vocabulary
17. ANS: B	DIF: Average	OBJ: Grammar
18. ANS: B	DIF: Average	OBJ: Grammar
19. ANS: C	DIF: Average	OBJ: Vocabulary

Essay

20. Students' answers should include a clear summary of each excerpt with specific examples of what the author finds memorable. For example, students might tell how the author liked working in the Store, and Mrs. Flowers's ways of dressing and speaking. Possible titles for the excepts include "The Store and I" and "My First Lifeline."

Difficulty: *Average*

Objective: *Essay*

21. Students' essays should refer to necessary products and supplies the Store provides as well as its value as a place for people to gather and socialize. For example, travelers often stopped there to rest, people could buy meals there, supplies for both people and livestock were available, and so on.

Difficulty: *Average*

Objective: *Essay*

22. Students' essays should include several specific examples of things the author notices and experiences during her visit with Mrs. Flowers. For example, the author is surprised that the woman cooks and eats like a normal person, notices that she has the luxury of ice for her lemonade, and has family photographs on the wall. Students should point out at least one lesson the author learns—for example, the importance of speaking words aloud, the importance of tolerance, the importance of respecting people as individuals.

Difficulty: *Challenging*

Objective: *Essay*

23. Students who say they had enough information should point out that the essay explains Angelou's first interaction with poetry and the beginning of her love of language. Students who feel they did not have enough information might say that they have learned how Angelou began to love reading and the spoken word but lack the information that explains how that love was translated into the inspiration and motivation needed to become a poet.

Difficulty: *Average*

Objective: *Essay*

"Forest Fire" by Anaïs Nin
"Why Leaves Turn Color in the Fall"
by Diane Ackerman
"The Season's Curmudgeon Sees the Light"
by Mary C. Curtis

Vocabulary Warm-up Exercises, p. 102

A. 1. sizzling
2. reminder
3. humid
4. alarmingly
5. venture
6. maneuver

7. unruly
8. mortar

B. Sample Answers
1. I'd expect to find an *abundance* of green *foliage* in the summer and spring in the Northeast because that's when trees have green leaves on them.
2. I might be *compelled* to follow a *pungent* odor of cooking to see what's for dinner.
3. To keep something *fragile* from getting broken, I'd wrap it in heavy paper or bubble wrap.
4. A painting with *spectacular splotches* of color would have amazing, irregular shapes, kind of like those resulting from an artist throwing the paint at the canvas.
5. Skydiving could be *dizzyingly* delightful because as you fall, you might spin through the air and not know exactly where you are, but it could be fun all the same.

Reading Warm-up A, p. 103

Sample Answers
1. what the neighborhood was like many years ago; Mom left me a note as a *reminder* to take my lunch to school.
2. (bricks); The workers covered each brick with a thick layer of *mortar*.
3. (in no order whatsoever); Delores had an *unruly* mop of hair.
4. thunderstorms; The weather in south Florida is often hot and *humid*.
5. (risk); I don't want to *venture* out into the blizzard.
6. bright or exciting; The colors of the new summer fashions were *sizzling*.
7. (warn); The roller coaster moved *alarmingly* fast.
8. movement; The stunt pilot performed one exciting *maneuver* after another.

Reading Warm-up B, p. 104

Sample Answers
1. hanging on the trees; The *foliage* in front of our house hides the porch.
2. (bloodstains); The finger paintings had *splotches* of bright colors.
3. A brown leaf fell from the tree in front of the school.; The plant was too large and too *fragile* to carry home on the seat of the car.
4. burning leaves; On the sidewalk we could smell the *pungent* odor of Indian spices.
5. It was as if something were pulling me there.; For some strange reason, every year on Groundhog Day, I feel *compelled* to check my shadow.
6. (suddenly struck with a sight); The parade was really *spectacular* this year, with some sixty floats.
7. (all their leafy); At Thanksgiving, we celebrate the *abundance* of the harvest.

8. My head almost spinning from gazing up at patterns of golden leaves against black-and-white trunks; The model train's *dizzyingly* complex run of track stretched across the whole room.

Writing About the Big Question, p. 105

A. 1. reveal
2. factor
3. explanation
4. exploration

B. Sample Answers
1. Spring is my favorite season. My **explanation** for this is that I love the fresh **quality** of the air and the promise of warmer weather.
2. Winter is my least favorite season. As the snow **accumulates**, **exploration** of the outdoors becomes more difficult, and I often make the **decision** to stay indoors.

C. Sample Answer
The part of nature that I value the most is rain forests because so many animals live there. I think it's important for people to have lots of information about what we can do to keep rain forests safe.

Literary Analysis: Comparing Types of Organization, p. 106

Sample Answers
1. Students should identify six events in the correct sequence. Sample events include:
   Event 1: The author sees the mountains on fire.
   Event 2: Mountain people are evacuated.
   Event 3: The author sees animals go back into the fire.
   Event 4: The author helps a neighbor's children.
   Event 5: All night, fire engines spray water over houses.
   Event 6: The fire near the author's house is contained in the morning.
   Event 7: Flames reach the cities below and burn houses quickly.
   Event 8: A week later, the fires are out and the danger is over.
   Event 9: In January, rains bring floods.
   Event 10: The author helps a ranger take pictures of the floods.
2. Chronological order is the best and most natural choice because the author is telling about actual events that occurred.
3. Less sunlight causes the tree to prepare for winter. To prepare, a tree pulls nutrients away from the leaves and back to the trunk and roots. This action forms a layer of cells that scar over at the petioles of the leaves, so the leaves are choked off. The undernourished leaves stop

producing chlorophyll, the chemical that gives the leaves their green color. When there is no more chlorophyll in the leaves, the other colors that are present in the leaves begin to show up more.

4. Cause-and-effect order helps readers see connections between the steps in a process.

5. In the first half, the author describes why she prefers fall and does not like spring. Later, she describes how she too hastily judged spring and did not give it a chance. Then, she lists all the reasons (which are in direct contrast with those in the first half of the essay) that she now likes spring.

6. The author's earlier feelings about spring are opposite and contrasting with her current feelings about spring, so comparison and contrast is a logical organization choice.

Vocabulary Builder, p. 107

A. Sample Answers

1. The principal is <u>consoling</u> the student by reassuring him that everything will be all right.

2. The children are <u>predisposed</u> to illness; they always get sick.

3. I call Lillian <u>capricious</u> because she changes her mind on the spur of the moment.

4. As the fire engine arrived, the <u>evacuees</u> left the movie theater quickly.

5. The stage set was <u>macabre</u> and gruesome.

6. Scott has a <u>tenacious</u> personality, so he seldom compromises.

B. 1. D; 2. B; 3. A; 4. C

Open-Book Test, p. 109

Short Answer

1. They are more afraid of the crowds of people watching the fire than of the fire itself.
   Difficulty: *Average*   **Objective:** *Interpretation*

2. Nin plans to save only her diaries. She apparently realizes that they cannot be replaced in the way that clothing and other possessions can be.
   Difficulty: *Challenging*   **Objective:** *Interpretation*

3. She does not become an evacuee because the fire never comes close to her home.
   Difficulty: *Average*   **Objective:** *Vocabulary*

4. The fire destroyed the trees on the mountains. Then, there was a heavy rain. Because the trees' roots could no longer hold on to the soil, the rain washed the soil away, creating the mud slides.
   Difficulty: *Challenging*   **Objective:** *Literary Analysis*

5. She is suggesting that observing nature carefully is as important to humans as observing its prey is to leopards.
   Difficulty: *Challenging*   **Objective:** *Literary Analysis*

6. The United States has colder nights and drier, sunnier days in fall than Europe does, and those conditions allow anthocyanin to be produced in great quantities.

Anthocyanin is the pigment that produces the bright red in the leaves.
   Difficulty: *Average*   **Objective:** *Literary Analysis*

7. Ackerman uses cause-and-effect organization. She shows how each event in a series causes the next one in the series until the leaves change color and fall from the tree.
   Difficulty: *Average*   **Objective:** *Literary Analysis*

8. She appreciates the season because it is the time for a fresh start.
   Difficulty: *Easy*   **Objective:** *Interpretation*

9. By comparing and contrasting spring and fall, Curtis realizes that spring, the season she had always disliked, has many positive aspects.
   Difficulty: *Challenging*   **Objective:** *Literary Analysis*

10. *"Forest Fire"*: chronological order; describes events relating to a forest fire in the order in which they occur
    "Why Leaves Turn Color": cause-and-effect order; explains the events that cause leaves to turn color
    "The Season's Curmudgeon": comparison and contrast; compares the author's feelings about spring and fall
    Difficulty: *Average*   **Objective:** *Literary Analysis*

Essay

11. Students who choose "Forest Fire" should note that Nin uses chronological order to describe a fire and its after-effects. The organization allows her to describe what she lived through so that others can understand it. Students who choose "Why Leaves Turn Color in the Fall" should note that Ackerman uses cause and effect to explain what causes leaves to change color and fall from a tree. This type of organization is useful in explaining a process. Students who choose "The Season's Curmudgeon Sees the Light" should mention that Curtis uses comparison and contrast to compare her feelings for spring and fall and to show how her feelings about spring change from negative to positive.
    Difficulty: *Easy*   **Objective:** *Essay*

12. The author of "Why Leaves Turn Color in the Fall" writes to explain what causes leaves to turn colors and fall from a tree. She achieves her purpose by providing a lot of facts. The author of "The Season's Curmudgeon Sees the Light" writes to tell how she learned to like spring. She may be hoping to convince others who dislike that season to see the positive things about it. She achieves her purpose by describing her thoughts on the topic. Students should provide evidence to support their choice of the more successful presentation. They might recognize that Curtis's topic is lighter than Ackerman's and that Curtis provides less support for her thesis than Ackerman does for hers.
    Difficulty: *Average*   **Objective:** *Essay*

13. Students should recognize that "Forest Fire" shows how fragile nature is and how people are affected by natural disasters. Students should recognize that "Why Leaves

Turn Color in the Fall" teaches readers to appreciate the scientific explanations for events in nature that they may take for granted. Students should recognize that "The Season's Curmudgeon Sees the Light" points out the importance of appreciating a season that may at first seem to have no positive features. Students should name the essay they preferred and provide a valid reason for their choice.

Difficulty: *Challenging*   **Objective:** *Essay*

14. Students should point out that the chronological order of "Forest Fire" or the cause-and-effect order of "Why Leaves Turn Color in the Fall" helped them understand the topics. Students will probably think that "Why Leaves Turn Color in the Fall" provides enough information to understand the topic. Those who think that "Forest Fire" does not provide enough information might wish to know how the fire started, how a forest fire progresses, or how nature heals itself after such a fire.

Difficulty: *Average*   **Objective:** *Essay*

Oral Response

15. Oral responses should be clear, well organized, and well supported by appropriate examples from the essays.

Difficulty: *Average*   **Objective:** *Oral Interpretation*

Selection Test A, p. 112

Critical Reading

1. ANS: A	DIF: Easy	OBJ: Comprehension
2. ANS: C	DIF: Easy	OBJ: Interpretation
3. ANS: D	DIF: Easy	OBJ: Interpretation
4. ANS: D	DIF: Easy	OBJ: Literary Analysis
5. ANS: B	DIF: Easy	OBJ: Interpretation
6. ANS: A	DIF: Easy	OBJ: Comprehension
7. ANS: B	DIF: Easy	OBJ: Literary Analysis
8. ANS: B	DIF: Easy	OBJ: Literary Analysis
9. ANS: C	DIF: Easy	OBJ: Comprehension
10. ANS: A	DIF: Easy	OBJ: Interpretation
11. ANS: C	DIF: Easy	OBJ: Literary Analysis
12. ANS: A	DIF: Easy	OBJ: Literary Analysis

Vocabulary and Grammar

13. ANS: D	DIF: Easy	OBJ: Vocabulary
14. ANS: C	DIF: Easy	OBJ: Vocabulary
15. ANS: C	DIF: Easy	OBJ: Vocabulary

Essay

16. If students choose "Forest Fire," they should note that the author uses chronological order to describe her experiences during first a forest fire and then mudslides. The details of the essay are given in the order that the author experienced them. This chronological order helps the author describe what she lived through so that others can understand it. If students choose "Why Leaves Turn Color in the Fall," they should men-

tion that the author uses cause-and-effect order to explain what causes leaves to change colors and then fall off trees. This type of organization is useful in explaining how a natural process works. If students choose "The Season's Curmudgeon Sees the Light," they should mention that the author uses comparison and contrast to describe her earlier negative feelings and later positive feelings about spring.

Difficulty: *Easy*
Objective: *Essay*

17. Students may mention that "Forest Fire" teaches how fragile nature is. The author experiences a forest fire and subsequent mudslides. The author ends her essay about these two destructive forces by saying that people caused the damage. Students may mention that "Why Leaves Turn Color in the Fall" teaches readers not only about the passing beauty of autumn but also, step by step, how leaves achieve that beauty. The author describes multiple scenes of fall and people enjoying it.

Difficulty: *Easy*
Objective: *Essay*

18. Students might note that the time order of "Forest Fire" or the cause-and-effect format of "Why Leaves Turn Color in the Fall" helped them understand the topics. Students will probably think that "Why Leaves Turn Color in the Fall" provides enough information to understand the topic. Those who think that "Forest Fire" does not provide enough information might wish to know how the fire started, how a forest fire progresses, or how nature heals itself after such a fire.

Difficulty: *Average*
Objective: *Essay*

Selection Test B, p. 115

Critical Reading

1. ANS: D	DIF: Average	OBJ: Interpretation
2. ANS: B	DIF: Average	OBJ: Interpretation
3. ANS: C	DIF: Challenging	OBJ: Interpretation
4. ANS: A	DIF: Average	OBJ: Literary Analysis
5. ANS: A	DIF: Average	OBJ: Literary Analysis
6. ANS: D	DIF: Challenging	OBJ: Interpretation
7. ANS: A	DIF: Average	OBJ: Literary Analysis
8. ANS: C	DIF: Challenging	OBJ: Literary Analysis
9. ANS: B	DIF: Challenging	OBJ: Comprehension
10. ANS: B	DIF: Challenging	OBJ: Interpretation
11. ANS: C	DIF: Average	OBJ: Literary Analysis
12. ANS: A	DIF: Average	OBJ: Comprehension
13. ANS: D	DIF: Average	OBJ: Interpretation
14. ANS: C	DIF: Challenging	OBJ: Literary Analysis

Vocabulary

15. ANS: B	DIF: Average	OBJ: Vocabulary
16. ANS: C	DIF: Average	OBJ: Vocabulary

17. ANS: D   DIF: Average   OBJ: Vocabulary
18. ANS: C   DIF: Challenging   OBJ: Vocabulary
19. ANS: B   DIF: Average   OBJ: Vocabulary

Essay

20. The author of "Why Leaves Turn Color in the Fall" is writing to explain what causes leaves to turn colors and fall from trees. She achieves her purpose by providing a lot of scientific data. That is, she describes how shorter days cause trees to choke off leaves from nutrients, how that effect causes leaves to stop producing chlorophyll, what then causes cells to divide at the stems of the leaves so that they become vulnerable to a soft breeze. In "The Season's Curmudgeon Sees the Light," the author's purpose for writing is to compare how she used to dislike spring with how she now has positive feelings about spring. The author gives easy-to-grasp examples (such as her previous concern about allergies and her current appreciation of fresh beginnings). Overall, Curtis's topic is lighter than Ackerman's topic, and Curtis's support for her thesis is not as complete as Ackerman's.

    Difficulty: *Average*

    Objective: *Essay*

21. Students may say that "Forest Fire" teaches a lesson about how fragile nature is and the part people play in natural disasters. Nin first reports a forest fire near her home. Then, she reports mudslides. The author ends her report with a statement that we cause the damage. Students may say that "Why Leaves Turn Color in the Fall" teaches readers to appreciate the quickly passing beauty of life and nature. The author describes the beauty of the fall leaves and explains how this phenomenon occurs. Students may state that they preferred the lesson of one essay over that of the other because of the relative complexity of the subject or the students' interest in the subject.

    Difficulty: *Average*

    Objective: *Essay*

22. Students should point out that the chronological order of "Forest Fire" or the cause-and-effect order of "Why Leaves Turn Color in the Fall" helped them understand the topics. Students will probably think that "Why Leaves Turn Color in the Fall" provides enough information to understand the topic. Those who think that "Forest Fire" does not provide enough information might wish to know how the fire started, how a forest fire progresses, or how nature heals itself after such a fire.

    Difficulty: *Average*

    Objective: *Essay*

Writing Workshop

How-to Essay: Integrating Grammar Skills, p. 119

A   1. closest; 2. better; 3. better; 4. more clearly

B   1. Fries and a soda make one of the least nutritious lunches of all.

2. For a healthier lunch than fries and a soda, try a salad.

3. Of all these desserts, carrot cake has the most calories.

4. To lose weight, you must exercise more seriously than you now do.

Benchmark Test 5, p. 120

MULTIPLE CHOICE

1. ANS: B
2. ANS: C
3. ANS: D
4. ANS: A
5. ANS: C
6. ANS: A
7. ANS: B
8. ANS: C
9. ANS: A
10. ANS: D
11. ANS: D
12. ANS: C
13. ANS: A
14. ANS: B
15. ANS: B
16. ANS: B
17. ANS: C
18. ANS: B
19. ANS: A
20. ANS: D
21. ANS: A
22. ANS: D
23. ANS: D
24. ANS: C
25. ANS: D
26. ANS: B
27. ANS: C
28. ANS: C
29. ANS: D
30. ANS: D
31. ANS: A

ESSAY

32. Students' essays should contain a clear step-by-step explanation of the process.

33. Students' essays should clearly state the event in a well-organized manner and why they admire the person for his or her actions.

34. Students' essays should mention the story or article that has impressed them and how it relates to them. They should use details to support their main points.

"The Trouble With Television"
by Robert MacNeil

Vocabulary Warm-up Exercises, p. 128

A.
1. prime
2. verbal
3. calculate
4. precision
5. cultivate
6. fare
7. perceived
8. crisis

B. Sample Answers
1. It is an *imperative* to develop *tolerance* for different personalities because it is important to get along with all different kinds of people.
2. I don't know anyone in a *perpetual* good mood because everybody has bad times.
3. E-mail has become *virtually* a *substitute* for letter writing.
4. One of the *assumptions* that *humanity* made was that the earth was flat.
5. It is important to watch weight-loss commercials *skeptically* because many of the claims are not scientific.

Reading Warm-up A, p. 129

Sample Answers
1. danger; I faced a *crisis* when my grandmother got sick and I had to call the paramedics.
2. (the number of viewers); He could *figure out* with *exactness* the number of viewers watching each of the network's programs.
3. a taste for a single one of the network's shows; I once tried to *cultivate* a liking for chess because my uncle liked it.
4. (menu of programs); My favorite television *fare* is mystery shows.
5. others; Although our English teacher is sometimes *perceived* as strict, she just wants to make sure we learn.
6. (viewing time); I think *prime* viewing time is in the early evening when most people are at home and watching television.
7. (spoke) I prefer *verbal* news because it is shorter and easier to understand.

Reading Warm-up B, p. 130

Sample Answers
1. that are not true, often think; An *assumption* I made when I was little was that people lived in my television set.
2. (replacement); A *substitute* is something or someone that takes the place of something or someone else.
3. people; A new cure for a disease benefits *humanity*.
4. (Becoming familiar); It's important to develop *tolerance* for others because people in the world need to get along together.
5. (every subject); It changes the meaning from "all" to "nearly all."
6. important point; It is an *imperative* for me to get good grades so I can play football and so I can go on to high school.
7. always; *Perpetual* motion means that something never stops. It might be possible in space, where there is no friction or gravity.
8. (grant); Critics may grant *doubtfully* that some viewers are lively and intelligent.

Writing About the Big Question, p. 131

A.
1. reveal
2. development
3. explanation

B. Sample Answers
1. I think the quality of television programming varies a lot. The biggest factor is which channels and which audiences the shows are intended for.
2. The **decision** to give up television would be a huge **challenge** for me. I don't really watch much, so the **quality** doesn't matter, but I like to have a TV on in the background when I do my homework.

C. Sample Answer

The exploration of ideas on TV news shows is usually brief and shallow. That's why you need to read a newspaper if you want to find out any details about important news stories. There is never enough hard news on TV news shows, but there is plenty of information about celebrities, sports, and weather.

Reading: Use Clue Words to Distinguish Fact From Opinion, p. 132

Sample Answers
1. Commercials and sitcoms offer "neat resolutions" to problems.
2. Locate on the Internet, or in another research tool, statistics on illiteracy rates in the United States.
3. The image of commandments, written in stone, is extreme. Also, the words *nothing* and *ever* signal an extreme statement.

Literary Analysis: Persuasive Techniques, p. 133

Sample Answers

1. A. food, ideas, an impatient public
   B. It equates television ("fast ideas") with food that studies show has a negative impact on consumers.
2. A. There has probably not been another time in history when one object got so much attention.
   B. Answers will vary; at least some students will say "surrendered so much leisure to one toy" makes them feel guilty for watching television and persuades them to support the author's argument.
3. A. The word *surrendered* implies giving something up, having no gumption—a negative trait that might make readers feel ashamed.
   B. Students who watch a lot of television may feel embarrassed; students who do not watch a lot of television may feel vindicated.

Vocabulary Builder, p. 134

A. Sample Answers

1. F; Concentrating requires focus, not distraction.
2. T; A trivial problem would not have a major impact on the way a car functions.
3. F; A smell that is spreading is likely to stay around awhile.
4. F; If you react skeptically, you doubt the truth of something.
5. T; Constructive criticism is intended to be helpful.
6. T; Passive people do not react actively.

B.
1. A home invader might be breaking into a house.
2. The person might be ashamed of having made the mistake.
3. A very strong smell could fill a large auditorium.

Enrichment: Television and Society, p. 135

Sample Answers

A.
1. Students should give examples of ways in which teenagers are portrayed on television. They should explain why they think these portrayals are realistic or unrealistic.
2. Students should give examples of ways they have seen schools portrayed on television. They should explain whether these portrayals are similar to or different from their own school experiences.
3. Students should give examples of ways families are portrayed on television and in what kinds of shows they appear. Students should explain whether or not they find these portrayals realistic.

B. Students should include in their answer the kind of show they envision (situation comedy, documentary, news show, etc.). They should describe details such as the characters they would include in their show, the location of the action, and some specific topics they would cover.

"The Trouble With Television"
by Robert MacNeil

Open-Book Test, p. 136

Short Answer

1. He thinks we should study a topic in depth, read serious works of literature, or perhaps walk around the world and write a book about the experience.
   Difficulty: *Easy*   **Objective:** *Interpretation*
2. MacNeil means that television distracts its viewers for no other purpose than to entertain or amuse them.
   Difficulty: *Challenging*   **Objective:** *Vocabulary*
3. MacNeil says that the values of television are spreading throughout the nation by giving Americans the impression that it is "fashionable" to think that ideas should be presented in a fast, shallow way.
   Difficulty: *Average*   **Objective:** *Vocabulary*
4. He is using repetition. He repeats the word *fast* to make readers think about how quickly everything moves on television.
   Difficulty: *Easy*   **Objective:** *Literary Analysis*
5. He thinks that because it provides little information, it makes stories seem "boring and dismissable."
   Difficulty: *Easy*   **Objective:** *Reading*
6. He means that like machine gun bursts, news stories are short and quick, and like scraps, they are not worth much.
   Difficulty: *Challenging*   **Objective:** *Interpretation*
7. He says that television contributes to and is an influence on illiteracy by providing simple answers to complex problems and by taking up the time that people might otherwise use to read.
   Difficulty: *Average*   **Objective:** *Interpretation*
8. The rhetorical question leads readers to agree with MacNeil's obvious and well-supported statement. Once they have agreed with that statement, they are more likely to agree with the main point of his argument.
   Difficulty: *Challenging*   **Objective:** *Literary Analysis*
9. Possible answer:
   Facts: By age 20, most people have watched 20,000 hours of television. "30 million adult Americans are illiterate."
   Opinions: Television discourages concentration. TV's appeal to short attention spans is "decivilizing."
   If students choose a fact, they should explain why or how it can be proved; if they choose an opinion, they should explain why it cannot be proved.
   Difficulty: *Average*   **Objective:** *Reading*
10. He is trying to persuade his readers to watch less television.
    Difficulty: *Average*   **Objective:** *Literary Analysis*

Essay

11. MacNeil's opinion is that we should watch less television. In their essays, students should clearly state whether they agree or disagree with MacNeil, and they should cite two pieces of evidence, from MacNeil's essay or from their own reading or experience, to support their opinion.

    Difficulty: *Easy* Objective: *Essay*

12. MacNeil is asking a rhetorical question. Students should recognize that he is acknowledging the brilliance of the medium's marketing technique. They should explain that by doing so, he gains credibility for his argument against television. That is, he makes a positive statement about television, one that readers are likely to agree with, and thereby shows that he is not excessively prejudiced against it. Then, when he expresses negative opinions about television, readers are more likely to trust that his judgment in those instances is similarly sound.

    Difficulty: *Average* Objective: *Essay*

13. In their essays, students should recognize that MacNeil's reference to the Declaration of Independence is an appeal to authority. Students might also realize that because the Declaration symbolizes America, MacNeil is also appealing to Americans' patriotism. He suggests that the Founders would have agreed with him that the nation ought to strive to achieve a much greater literacy rate. Then, by suggesting that illiteracy might be a consequence of the nation's television habit, he suggests that the nation is not living up to the standards set by the Founders.

    Difficulty: *Challenging* Objective: *Essay*

14. Students should point to MacNeil's use of statistics (the hours Americans spend watching television, the way that time might be better spent, and the illiteracy rate). Some students may find that evidence sufficient to convince them of MacNeil's viewpoint. Others may say that those facts do not support MacNeil's contention that television is to blame for the illiteracy rate and for a supposedly shortened attention span. They might wish to know about studies that have proved links between television viewing and various social problems.

    Difficulty: *Average* Objective: *Essay*

Oral Response

15. Oral responses should be clear, well organized, and well supported by appropriate examples from the essay.

    Difficulty: *Average* Objective: *Oral Interpretation*

Selection Test A, p. 139

Critical Reading

1. ANS: A   DIF: Easy   OBJ: Comprehension
2. ANS: C   DIF: Easy   OBJ: Interpretation
3. ANS: D   DIF: Easy   OBJ: Reading
4. ANS: C   DIF: Easy   OBJ: Interpretation

5. ANS: B   DIF: Easy   OBJ: Comprehension
6. ANS: D   DIF: Easy   OBJ: Reading
7. ANS: A   DIF: Easy   OBJ: Comprehension
8. ANS: C   DIF: Easy   OBJ: Literary Analysis
9. ANS: D   DIF: Easy   OBJ: Comprehension
10. ANS: A   DIF: Easy   OBJ: Reading

Vocabulary and Grammar

11. ANS: D   DIF: Easy   OBJ: Grammar
12. ANS: B   DIF: Easy   OBJ: Vocabulary
13. ANS: C   DIF: Easy   OBJ: Vocabulary
14. ANS: A   DIF: Easy   OBJ: Grammar

Essay

15. Students' essays should clearly state MacNeil's view that watching too much television is damaging. They should include at least two reasons from the selection. For example, MacNeil points out that television discourages concentration and wastes valuable time.

    Difficulty: *Easy*

    Objective: *Essay*

16. Students' essays should present a clear statement of whether they agree or disagree with MacNeil. They might use examples from television shows with which they are familiar.

    Difficulty: *Easy*

    Objective: *Essay*

17. Students should point to MacNeil's use of statistics (the hours Americans spend watching television, the way that time might be better spent, and the illiteracy rate). Some students may find that he provides enough evidence to convince them. Others may say that those facts do not support MacNeil's idea that television is to blame for the illiteracy rate and for a shortened attention span.

    Difficulty: *Average*

    Objective: *Essay*

Selection Test B, p. 142

Critical Reading

1. ANS: C   DIF: Average   OBJ: Literary Analysis
2. ANS: A   DIF: Average   OBJ: Comprehension
3. ANS: C   DIF: Challenging   OBJ: Reading
4. ANS: A   DIF: Challenging   OBJ: Reading
5. ANS: B   DIF: Average   OBJ: Interpretation
6. ANS: A   DIF: Average   OBJ: Interpretation
7. ANS: C   DIF: Average   OBJ: Literary Analysis
8. ANS: D   DIF: Average   OBJ: Reading
9. ANS: C   DIF: Challenging   OBJ: Reading
10. ANS: A   DIF: Average   OBJ: Comprehension
11. ANS: D   DIF: Average   OBJ: Comprehension
12. ANS: C   DIF: Average   OBJ: Literary Analysis

Vocabulary and Grammar

13. ANS: B   DIF: Average   OBJ: Vocabulary
14. ANS: D   DIF: Average   OBJ: Vocabulary
15. ANS: D   DIF: Average   OBJ: Grammar
16. ANS: C   DIF: Average   OBJ: Grammar
17. ANS: A   DIF: Average   OBJ: Vocabulary

Essay

18. Students' responses should note that in asking this particular rhetorical question, MacNeil is giving television credit where credit is due. He is acknowledging the brilliance of the medium in a certain context. By so doing, MacNeil actually gains credibility in his overall argument *against* television. Students should recognize that if MacNeil can find something positive to say about television, we probably also should pay attention to the negatives he outlines.

    Difficulty: *Average*

    Objective: *Essay*

19. Students' essays might focus on the contrast between the Founding Fathers' respect for literacy and the apparent disrespect that many Americans hold it in today, given the 30 million adult Americans who are functionally illiterate, according to MacNeil. The author of the essay goes on to suggest that watching too much television contributes to and is an influence on illiteracy.

    Difficulty: *Challenging*

    Objective: *Essay*

20. Students should point to MacNeil's use of statistics (the hours Americans spend watching television, the way that time might be better spent, and the illiteracy rate). Some students may find that evidence sufficient to convince them of MacNeil's viewpoint. Others may say that those facts do not support MacNeil's contention that television is to blame for the illiteracy rate and for a supposedly shortened attention span. They might wish to know about studies that have proved links between television viewing and various social problems.

    Difficulty: *Average*

    Objective: *Essay*

"On Woman's Right to Suffrage"
by Susan B. Anthony

Vocabulary Warm-up Exercises, p. 146

A.
1. rebellion
2. welfare
3. Downright
4. endured
5. federal
6. constitution
7. promote
8. supreme

B. Sample Answers

1. People who are *opponents* of laws that unfairly target one group want equal treatment for all, so that *discrimination* is a thing of the past.
2. Yes, rulers usually hope that there is *domestic* peace, or peace inside their country.
3. I would not sign an agreement that was *void* because then the agreement would not be legal.
4. Even though I worked hard on a paper, I would not be *entitled* to the *A*, nor should any grade be *guaranteed* because I'd only have a right to an *A* or other grade if the paper were well written and fulfilled the assignment.
5. No, you have to be eighteen years old to vote, or have *suffrage*.
6. Yes, laws that grant *immunities* against unfair searches are good things because officers should respect people's privacy.

Reading Warm-up A, p. 147

Sample Answers

1. war for freedom; A *rebellion* is a struggle or fight against people who rule.
2. written, new country; Without a *constitution*, there are no clear, written rules for how to run the country.
3. (government); Many offices of the *federal* government are in Washington, D.C.
4. (law of the land); It is of *supreme* importance to get enough sleep.
5. (improve); I would like to *promote* the cause of finding places for the homeless to live.
6. (well-being); A person's *welfare* includes food, shelter, clothing, education, exercise, a family, friends, and recreation.
7. laws that kept people from voting; My teacher says that sloppy homework is not to be *endured* in his class or any other class.
8. (that we can vote); I had a *downright* sense of pride after winning the half-mile run.

Reading Warm-up B, p. 148

Sample Answers

1. With no vote; Luckily, the new parking law made my parking ticket *void*.
2. None of the states allowed women to vote. The men who made the laws also did not allow women to own property, go to college, or enter the professions.; *Discrimination* is wrong in our country because everyone is supposed to have equal opportunities according to our laws.
3. (vote); *Suffrage* is important for all adult citizens so they can express their views and have a say in how the government should be run.
4. to vote; I feel *entitled* to my allowance because I do all my chores.

5. states, The men who made the laws; Overbrook and Northeast high schools were our *opponents* at a debate last month.
6. of the country; A *domestic* issue in our country today is homeland security.
7. protections; Criminals typically do not have any *immunities* from the law.
8. If we raised at least $100 at the car wash, we were *guaranteed* a matching amount by a generous customer.

Writing About the Big Question, p. 149

A. 1. global
   2. accumulate(s)
   3. challenge

B. Sample Answers
   1. Susan B. Anthony believed that **discrimination** against women was wrong. Her lifelong goal was to fight against **inequality** by gaining women the vote.
   2. I believe Anthony was successful, even though women didn't gain the vote until after her death. Her **decision** to **challenge discrimination** against women eventually changed history.

C. Sample Answer

Discrimination based on gender is unfair. The U.S. Constitution gives citizens equal rights, and women are citizens. Therefore, women should have equal rights.

Reading: Use Clue Words to Distinguish Fact From Opinion, p. 150

Sample Answers
1. Women are persons.
2. Look up *citizen* in the dictionaries mentioned.
3. *Mockery* is a word that states how the author feels about the situation.
4. *Every* is a word that signals an extreme statement.

Literary Analysis: Persuasive Techniques, p. 151

Sample Answers
1. A. The repetition of the word *half* followed by *whole* reminds readers of the unequal rights of women and men in America.
   B. Answers will vary.
2. A. Yes, women are persons.
   B. Answers will vary.
3. A. hateful, aristocracy, oligarchy
   B. The words give the impression that America's leadership is hateful and elitist.

Vocabulary Builder, p. 152

A. 1. C; 2. A; 3. C; 4. B; 5. A; 6. D
B. 1. fight
   2. unhappy people

Enrichment: Community Action, p. 153

Sample Answers

Goal Statement
   1. To involve people in a friendly project to aid home gardeners in recycling leaves into compost

Tasks to Reach Goal
   2. Design and distribute fliers to announce project
   3. Produce and distribute written directions on building a home compost bin
   4. Build a demonstration compost bin
   5. Collect leaves for demonstration bin and show how to make compost

People Who Can Assist
   6. County horticultural agent
   7. Experienced home gardener
   8. Friends and fellow club members

How to Evaluate Progress
   9. Feedback from homeowners
   10. Demonstration bins finished

"The Trouble With Television"
by Robert MacNeil
"On Woman's Right to Suffrage"
by Susan B. Anthony

Integrated Language Skills: Grammar, p. 154
Conjunctions

A. 1. and
   2. but
   3. whenever
   4. Neither; nor
   5. As

B. Sample Answer

My friends <u>and</u> I went to the school carnival this weekend. We enjoyed it <u>because</u> there were lots of games and rides. <u>After</u> we tried the balloon toss, we drove the miniature cars. Some people left early, <u>but</u> we stayed <u>until</u> the carnival closed.

"On Woman's Right to Suffrage"
by Susan B. Anthony

Open-Book Test, p. 157
Short Answer
1. She defines "the people" as including both men and women.

   Difficulty: *Average* **Objective:** *Interpretation*
2. Anthony is using repetition. It reinforces the idea that "we, the people" refers to all citizens of the United States.

3. Anthony is referring to the future generations of women.
   Difficulty: *Average*   **Objective:** *Vocabulary*

4. Anthony says that the Constitution gives all citizens the right to vote, and since women are citizens, they have that right. A law that is in violation of the Constitution is one that neglects or disregards a principle of that document.
   Difficulty: *Challenging*   **Objective:** *Vocabulary*

5. Anthony is stating an opinion, a statement that cannot be proved. A clue is her use of the words "most hateful."
   Difficulty: *Easy*   **Objective:** *Reading*

6. Anthony is asking a rhetorical question. Because the answer is obvious, it is clear that she does not expect the question to be answered.
   Difficulty: *Average*   **Objective:** *Literary Analysis*

7. She claims that because women are people, they are citizens, and that it is illegal to discriminate against citizens.
   Difficulty: *Easy*   **Objective:** *Literary Analysis*

8. She says that women are people, and so they are full citizens; therefore, discrimination against them is illegal.
   Difficulty: *Challenging*   **Objective:** *Interpretation*

9. Possible answer:
   Facts: Susan B. Anthony voted even though she did not have the legal right to vote. Women were denied the right to vote.
   Opinions: It is a "mockery" to say that women enjoy liberty. The government is "the most hateful aristocracy" in the world.
   If students choose a fact, they should explain why or how it can be proved; if they choose an opinion, they should explain why it cannot be proved.
   Difficulty: *Average*   **Objective:** *Reading*

10. Anthony's main point is that women have a legal right to vote.
    Difficulty: *Easy*   **Objective:** *Interpretation*

Essay

11. In their essays, students should state that Anthony was accused of voting illegally. They should include two reasons she used in her defense—for example, that the Constitution guarantees liberty for all, not just for some, and that as citizens women have the same rights as men.
    Difficulty: *Easy*   **Objective:** *Essay*

12. Students should focus on the idea that a democracy represents the views, and the votes, of all its citizens. Students should explain that because women were not allowed to vote, their views were not represented in the government, and therefore the government was not a democracy.
    Difficulty: *Average*   **Objective:** *Essay*

13. Students should note that the repetition of words and sentence structures makes the lines musical and therefore memorable. They may point out that the repetition of *we* is particularly effective because it makes listeners feel included and strengthens the idea that all Americans should be considered citizens.
    Difficulty: *Challenging*   **Objective:** *Essay*

14. Students who think that the speech contains enough information to support its message may point to the argument that citizens are defined as people, and women are people. Students who think that the speech was not persuasive may wish to know how other women felt about voting at the time and whether other groups in the country were denied the vote.
    Difficulty: *Average*   **Objective:** *Essay*

Oral Response

15. Oral responses should be clear, well organized, and well supported by appropriate examples from the speech.
    Difficulty: *Average*   **Objective:** *Oral Interpretation*

Selection Test A, p. 160

Critical Reading

1. ANS: A	DIF: Easy	OBJ: Comprehension
2. ANS: B	DIF: Easy	OBJ: Interpretation
3. ANS: D	DIF: Easy	OBJ: Comprehension
4. ANS: A	DIF: Easy	OBJ: Reading
5. ANS: B	DIF: Easy	OBJ: Interpretation
6. ANS: C	DIF: Easy	OBJ: Comprehension
7. ANS: A	DIF: Easy	OBJ: Comprehension
8. ANS: C	DIF: Easy	OBJ: Reading
9. ANS: A	DIF: Easy	OBJ: Comprehension
10. ANS: D	DIF: Easy	OBJ: Literary Analysis
11. ANS: B	DIF: Easy	OBJ: Interpretation

Vocabulary and Grammar

12. ANS: B	DIF: Easy	OBJ: Vocabulary
13. ANS: D	DIF: Easy	OBJ: Grammar
14. ANS: C	DIF: Easy	OBJ: Vocabulary

Essay

15. Students' essays should include a clear statement explaining that Anthony is accused of voting illegally. They should write about two reasons she uses in her defense—for example, that the Constitution guaranteed liberty for all, not just some, and that women are U.S. citizens just as much as men are.
    Difficulty: *Easy*
    Objective: *Essay*

16. Students' essays should include a clearly stated opinion about whether the speech is convincing. Students also should cite at least one argument Anthony puts forward, and explain how this argument is effective or ineffective.
    Difficulty: *Easy*
    Objective: *Essay*

17. Students who think that the speech contains enough information to support its message may cite the point that citizens are defined as people, and women are

people. Students who think that the speech was not persuasive may wish to know how other women felt about voting at the time and whether other groups in the country were denied the vote.

Difficulty: *Average*
Objective: *Essay*

Selection Test B, p. 163

Critical Reading

1. ANS: C	DIF: Average	OBJ: Comprehension
2. ANS: A	DIF: Average	OBJ: Comprehension
3. ANS: B	DIF: Average	OBJ: Comprehension
4. ANS: D	DIF: Average	OBJ: Interpretation
5. ANS: B	DIF: Average	OBJ: Reading
6. ANS: C	DIF: Average	OBJ: Comprehension
7. ANS: C	DIF: Challenging	OBJ: Literary Analysis
8. ANS: A	DIF: Average	OBJ: Interpretation
9. ANS: B	DIF: Challenging	OBJ: Reading
10. ANS: C	DIF: Challenging	OBJ: Interpretation
11. ANS: B	DIF: Average	OBJ: Literary Analysis
12. ANS: C	DIF: Average	OBJ: Comprehension
13. ANS: A	DIF: Challenging	OBJ: Reading

Vocabulary and Grammar

14. ANS: A	DIF: Average	OBJ: Grammar
15. ANS: C	DIF: Average	OBJ: Vocabulary
16. ANS: B	DIF: Average	OBJ: Vocabulary
17. ANS: C	DIF: Average	OBJ: Vocabulary

Essay

18. Students' essays should focus on the idea that a democracy represents the views, and votes, of all its citizens. A supporting example might include Anthony's point that women can't enjoy American liberties without having had a say in who is upholding these liberties.

Difficulty: *Average*
Objective: *Essay*

19. The effect of the repetition of individual words and of a grammatical structure is to make the lines musical and memorable. The repetition of *we*, in particular, also has the effect of making listeners feel included, welcome. Students may either use the term *parallelism* or acknowledge the technique without naming it per se.

Difficulty: *Challenging*
Objective: *Essay*

20. Students who think that the speech contains enough information to support its message may point to the argument that citizens are defined as people, and women are people. Students who think that the speech was not persuasive may wish to know how other women felt about voting at the time and whether other groups in the country were denied the vote.

Difficulty: *Average*
Objective: *Essay*

from "Sharing in the American Dream"
by Colin Powell

Vocabulary Warm-up Exercises, p. 167

A.
1. inhabit
2. secure
3. denied
4. achieve
5. union
6. task
7. syrupy
8. sags

B. Sample Answers
1. F. The runt would be the most *vulnerable* to sickness and attacks by prey.
2. T. During wedding vows I have heard, people *pledge* to love and take care of each other.
3. F. When you *commit* to something, you are promising that you will definitely do it.
4. T. Your *moral* sense helps you know the difference between right and wrong.
5. F. When you are in *pursuit* of a goal, you are actively doing things to reach it, not just thinking about all the things you might do.
6. F. All kind acts are based on *virtue*.
7. F. An *alliance* cannot be successful unless each member gives up some independence, and *despite* each member's goals, each must work for what is best for the whole group.

Reading Warm-up A, p. 168

Sample Answers
1. speaking to a group of students about their bad behavior; A *task* is a job to be done rather than something you do because you really enjoy it.
2. (speechmaker); *Secure* means "to get or bring about."
3. requests to appear on the college television station; My parents *denied* me the opportunity to go on vacation with my best friend.
4. (droopy); The middle of our living room couch *sags*; the hammock in the backyard *sags*, but it is supposed to!
5. to get the students fired up about being good; *Achieve* means "to succeed in doing something you want."
6. ("touchy-feely remarks"); *Sugary* words include "You are all very, very special people" and "I feel so lucky to know you."
7. jail cells; I think it would be awful to *inhabit* a tent with a leaky roof.
8. (these students, adults at our school); *Union* means "separate groups or states coming together for a purpose."

Unit 3 Resources: Types of Nonfiction

Reading Warm-up B, p. 169

Sample Answers

1. <u>to help those less fortunate</u>; One of my *moral* duties is to treat others the way I would like to be treated.
2. (the magazine, the Points of Light Foundation, actor Paul Newman); An *alliance* is a close connection among groups working together.
3. <u>a specific project that will help others</u>; *Commit* means "to say that you will definitely do something."
4. (promised); I would *pledge* money to any effort that helps battered women.
5. <u>good deeds</u>; A *virtue* is anything with goodness.
6. *Even though* we all lead busy lives . . . .
7. (a solution to a problem in your neighborhood); I would be in *pursuit* of a way to help people who don't know how to read.
8. <u>sick, poor</u>; *Vulnerable* means "easily hurt or harmed."

Writing About the Big Question, p. 170

A. 1. statistics
2. quantity,challenge
3. quality

B. Sample Answers
1. When someone volunteers, the person gets to know different people. That helps the volunteer recognize unfair **discrimination** and **reveals** the basic likenesses among people.
2. The **decision** to volunteer can **challenge** someone intellectually and emotionally. Volunteering can improve the **quality** of the volunteer's life.

C. Sample Answer
When there is inequity in society, we should fight against it and refuse to give up. That's where education comes in. People have to get good educations so that they have the information and skills to succeed in whichever battles they take on.

Reading: Use Support for Fact and Opinion, p. 171

Sample Answers

Support
1. Powell has already noted that 15 million children are at risk.
2. Powell identifies "simple needs": a caring adult, a safe place to learn, a healthy start, and marketable skills.
3. Powell goes on to outline how specific people will spread the message.

Adequately Supported?
Students' answers may vary. However, Powell has supported his opinions with facts that can be proved and/or reasonable assumptions.

Literary Analysis: Use Word Choice to Convey Ideas, p. 172

Sample Answers

1. Informal. By referring to those less fortunate as "our brothers and sisters," the author implies that the people who need help should be looked on as part of the American "family."
2. Informal. The words *commit* and *promise* convey the feeling that volunteering one's time and effort are honorable and worthy goals.
3. Informal. By suggesting that volunteers metaphorically "reach out and touch" those in need, the author reminds them that what they will be doing is personal.

Vocabulary Builder, p. 173

Sample Answers

A. 1. Synonym: *hopes*
   He has <u>hopes</u> of becoming an astronaut.
2. Synonym: *postponed*
   The meeting was <u>postponed</u> until after the holidays.
3. Synonym: *sympathetic*
   She was <u>sympathetic</u> toward those whose homes had been destroyed in the flood.
4. Synonym: *partnership*
   Because the business was a 50–50 <u>partnership</u>, the founders shared the profits equally.
5. synonym: *assailable*
   Sensitive people are very <u>assailable</u> to criticism.
6. synonym: *morality*
   People's senses of <u>morality</u> can differ greatly.

B. 1. One child had so much compassion that she donated all her presents.
2. After she saw the movie, she became so impassioned that she phoned her senator's office.
3. A dispassionate teacher usually grades opinion essays fairly.

Enrichment: Community Service Opportunities, p. 174

Sample Answers

Survey responses should be complete and clear. Students should include specific examples of volunteer activities where possible.

Open-Book Test, p. 175

Short Answer

1. He is referring to the men who volunteered to draft and sign the Declaration of Independence in Philadelphia in 1776. Students should recognize that Powell is referring to the founding of the country.
   Difficulty: *Average*   **Objective:** *Interpretation*

2. It is a dream of prosperity and success in America, and it has been put off or delayed for some people because they live in poverty. Students familiar with Langston Hughes's poem may add that the dream has also been deferred on account of racism.
   Difficulty: *Challenging*   **Objective:** *Vocabulary*

3. With the phrase "my friends," he wants his listeners to feel as if they had a relationship with him; with "our brothers and sisters," he wants them to feel as if they had a relationship with those he wants to help.
   Difficulty: *Challenging*   **Objective:** *Literary Analysis*

4. *Fact:* Up to 15 million American children are at risk. Powell wants his audience to conclude that they must act to help the children in need.
   Difficulty: *Average*   **Objective:** *Reading*

5. It is a fact. It states a statistic that can be proved.
   Difficulty: *Easy*   **Objective:** *Reading*

6. Powell wants his audience to feel that they are his friends or colleagues.
   Difficulty: *Average*   **Objective:** *Literary Analysis*

7. He wants the U.S. government, corporations, nonprofit organizations, "institutions of faith," and "especially . . . individual Americans" to form a group that will work toward a common goal.
   Difficulty: *Average*   **Objective:** *Vocabulary*

8. The words bring to mind enthusiasm and a positive, can-do attitude.
   Difficulty: *Easy*   **Objective:** *Literary Analysis*

9. He wants them to use their time and money to volunteer to help underprivileged children.
   Difficulty: *Easy*   **Objective:** *Interpretation*

10. His purpose was to persuade Americans to help people in need. He makes his purpose clear by giving information about people who need help and then asking his audience to reach out to them.
    Difficulty: *Challenging*   **Objective:** *Interpretation*

Essay

11. Students should describe Powell's plan as involving a massive effort by the government, major businesses, nonprofit organizations and religious institutions, and most especially, individual American citizens. According to his plan, those groups and individuals will form a "grand alliance" to contribute money and time to the task of improving the lives of the nation's many impoverished children. Students should mention at least two of the following benefits: receiving the attentions of a caring adult, having a safe place in which to learn, learning "marketable skills," and learning "the virtue of service."
    Difficulty: *Easy*   **Objective:** *Essay*

12. In their essays, students should recognize that the American Dream is an ideal of prosperity that is thought to be attainable by every American. Students should also realize that in referring to society's imperfection, Powell is referring to "those who are less fortunate." In particular, he is referring to the many children who live in poverty.
    Difficulty: *Average*   **Objective:** *Essay*

13. Students should recognize that the "dream deferred" in the poem refers to any dream that must be put off because of circumstances. (If they are familiar with Hughes, they might note that the circumstances refer in particular to racism during the pre-civil rights movement era). Hughes wonders if such a dream dries up, goes bad like rotten food, becomes a heavy load, or blows up. Students should recognize that Powell is saying that for children in poverty, the American dream is a dream deferred.
    Difficulty: *Challenging*   **Objective:** *Essay*

14. Students who think that the speech contains sufficient information for them to form an opinion of Powell's call to volunteerism should state their opinion of it and cite two details from the speech that support their opinion. Students who say that they need more information may wonder about the precise nature of the volunteerism Powell recommends or about the benefits that can be expected from the plan.
    Difficulty: *Average*   **Objective:** *Essay*

Oral Response

15. Oral responses should be clear, well organized, and well supported by appropriate examples from the speech.
    Difficulty: *Average*   **Objective:** *Oral Interpretation*

Selection Test A, p. 178

Critical Reading

1. ANS: B	DIF: Easy	OBJ: Comprehension
2. ANS: A	DIF: Easy	OBJ: Comprehension
3. ANS: C	DIF: Easy	OBJ: Reading
4. ANS: B	DIF: Easy	OBJ: Reading
5. ANS: B	DIF: Easy	OBJ: Interpretation
6. ANS: D	DIF: Easy	OBJ: Comprehension
7. ANS: A	DIF: Easy	OBJ: Literary Analysis
8. ANS: D	DIF: Easy	OBJ: Interpretation
9. ANS: A	DIF: Easy	OBJ: Comprehension
10. ANS: C	DIF: Easy	OBJ: Literary Analysis
11. ANS: C	DIF: Easy	OBJ: Comprehension

Vocabulary and Grammar

12. ANS: C	DIF: Easy	OBJ: Vocabulary
13. ANS: B	DIF: Easy	OBJ: Grammar
14. ANS: A	DIF: Easy	OBJ: Grammar
15. ANS: D	DIF: Easy	OBJ: Vocabulary

Essay

16. Students' essays should give a clear statement of Powell's plan for Americans to volunteer up to an hour a week of their time to help people in need. In explaining whether they think the plan is possible, students might evaluate the legitimacy of Powell's belief that listeners will spread the word successfully.

    Difficulty: *Easy*

    Objective: *Essay*

17. Students' essays should begin with a clear topic sentence stating that children will receive benefits from getting help from volunteers. They should include at least two of the specific benefits Powell cites in his speech, such as attention from a caring adult, a safe place to learn, marketable skills, or becoming inspired to help others in the future.

    Difficulty: *Easy*

    Objective: *Essay*

18. Students who think that the speech contains sufficient information for them to form an opinion should state their opinion of it and cite two details from the speech that support their view. Students who say that they need more information may wonder exactly what kind of volunteerism Powell recommends or what benefits are likely to result from the plan.

    Difficulty: *Average*

    Objective: *Essay*

Essay

18. Students should feel free to agree or disagree with Powell's belief that volunteerism can help America fulfill its promise. Some students may support Powell's belief because they enjoy meeting challenges, such as the challenge set not only by Powell but also, as he explains, by our forefathers; some students may disagree with Powell's faith in volunteerism because they may have had previous negative experiences with it.

    Difficulty: *Average*

    Objective: *Essay*

19. In their essays, students should begin with a clear sentence about what they interpret Powell's American Dream to be. They might include examples of needs Powell refers to, such as better educational opportunities, safer neighborhoods, more adult mentors, and so on.

    Difficulty: *Challenging*

    Objective: *Essay*

20. Students who think that the speech contains sufficient information for them to form an opinion of Powell's call to volunteerism should state their opinion of it and cite two details from the speech that support their opinion. Students who say that they need more information may wonder about the precise nature of the volunteerism Powell recommends or about the benefits that can be expected from the plan.

    Difficulty: *Average*

    Objective: *Essay*

Selection Test B, p. 181

Critical Reading

1. ANS: B	DIF: Average	OBJ: Interpretation
2. ANS: B	DIF: Average	OBJ: Comprehension
3. ANS: C	DIF: Average	OBJ: Comprehension
4. ANS: D	DIF: Average	OBJ: Comprehension
5. ANS: A	DIF: Challenging	OBJ: Reading
6. ANS: C	DIF: Average	OBJ: Comprehension
7. ANS: B	DIF: Average	OBJ: Literary Analysis
8. ANS: C	DIF: Challenging	OBJ: Reading
9. ANS: A	DIF: Average	OBJ: Literary Analysis
10. ANS: B	DIF: Average	OBJ: Reading
11. ANS: C	DIF: Challenging	OBJ: Literary Analysis
12. ANS: D	DIF: Average	OBJ: Interpretation

Vocabulary and Grammar

13. ANS: A	DIF: Average	OBJ: Vocabulary
14. ANS: B	DIF: Average	OBJ: Vocabulary
15. ANS: D	DIF: Average	OBJ: Grammar
16. ANS: C	DIF: Average	OBJ: Grammar
17. ANS: B	DIF: Average	OBJ: Vocabulary

"Science and the Sense of Wonder"
by Isaac Asimov

Vocabulary Warm-up Exercises, p. 185

A. 1. radiation
   2. mutations
   3. expand
   4. mere
   5. outward
   6. violence
   7. exhaling
   8. glinting

B. Sample Answers

1. T. An *astronomer* studies stars and planets in space, and an *asteroid* is an object in space.
2. F. If water is *heaving*, it is rising and falling.
3. F. Our sun is a star in the Milky Way Galaxy and so is part of a *galactic* system.
4. T. Water can turn to gas, or *vaporize*, whether it is in a small *compact* container or a large one.
5. T. Many people might work there during the day but not at night, so the building could be *desolate*.
6. T. People *doling* out money would be generous because they are giving their money to other people.

Reading Warm-up A, p. 186

Sample Answers

1. <u>strange . . . people like the aliens</u>; In the lab, the scientists developed several *mutations* of mice.
2. (three short blocks); He wanted to give me a *mere* ten dollars for my bike.
3. (safe); *Violence* in the neighborhood had made it an unsafe place to live.
4. <u>light of the streetlamp</u>; The light *glinting* off the brass lamp made a strange shape on the wall.
5. (coin); If you use an air pump, the beach float will *expand* quickly.
6. (on all sides, spread); My umbrella opens *outward*.
7. <u>harmful</u>; Too much harmful *radiation* could cause your skin to burn.
8. (inhaling); People are *exhaling* when they sigh.

Reading Warm-up B, p. 187

Sample Answers

1. <u>small objects that travel around the sun, mostly between Mars and Jupiter</u>; It would be frightening but exciting to see an *asteroid* fall to Earth.
2. (small): The guy who plays tackle might be *compact*, but he sure is strong.
3. (spends hours and hours studying the size, structure, and paths of those tiny parts of our solar system); The *astronomer* is developing a new telescope to study galaxies.
4. (star systems) Do you think we will ever be able to travel in space to some as yet unknown *galactic* destination?
5. (swelling); The ship was *heaving* as it sailed across the choppy waters.
6. <u>turning to gas</u>; In science class, we heat liquid in a beaker to *vaporize* it.
7. (little by little, over the centuries); The food bank, *doling* out its remaining provisions, was in need of more donations.
8. <u>regions between Mars and Jupiter</u>; The field behind the old gas station is a scary and *desolate* place.

Writing About the Big Question, p. 188

A. 1. statistics
2. quantity
3. explanation

B. Sample Answers

1. I would like to learn more about cloning living beings and black holes in the universe.
2. I could get a great **quantity** of information on the Internet, but the **challenge** would be to judge the **quality** of the information. For that reason I would probably make the **decision** to read appropriate books and magazines.

C. Sample Answer

The knowledge we gain from space exploration shows us that there is an endless amount of information yet to learn about our universe and beyond. We will never have enough information about this topic. Every new discovery scientists make just raises new questions to answer one day.

Reading: Use Support for Fact and Opinion, p. 189

Sample Answers

Support

1. Asimov proceeds to describe and explain the "hard stuff"—the scientific characteristics of stars, planets, suns, galaxies, and clusters of galaxies.
2. Asimov gives scientific details about what planets are made of—acid, hot liquid, craters, volcanoes, and deserts.
3. Asimov describes scientific details about the greatly varying sizes and shapes of suns in the universe.

Adequately Supported?

Students' answers may vary. Asimov has supported his opinions with facts that can be proved and/or reasonable scientific assumptions. However, all may not be in agreement as to whether this information increases one's personal enjoyment of looking at stars.

Literary Analysis: Use Word Choice to Convey Ideas, p. 190

Sample Answers

1. Informal. The author's words describe a casual, and partially unpleasant, experience of watching the stars. He implies that this way of watching the sky only touches the surface.
2. Informal. The author's words give vivid human characteristics of breathing, consuming, and swallowing to the stars instead of describing them in a more formally scientific manner.
3. Informal. The author's words emphasize the violence of exploding stars. He is being scientifically accurate, but his word choice is not usually found in a formal scientific description.

Vocabulary Builder, p. 191

A. 1. A; 2. B; 3. D; 4. C; 5. A; 6. A

B. Sample Answers

1. Something that <u>contracts</u> moves.
2. Yes, a <u>distraction</u> can lure people away from their work.

Enrichment: Basic Questions of Astronomy, p. 192

1. Stars seem to flicker because of turbulence in the atmosphere.
2. The reason stars near the horizon sometimes look as if they are changing color is that the atmosphere causes star color to "split," just as a prism causes light rays to split into colors.

3. Constellations are vast groupings of stars. Throughout history, people (especially the ancient Greeks and Romans) have named them after animals or common objects in nature that the groupings resemble.

4. Planets are usually brighter and appear more stationary than stars.

from "Sharing in the American Dream"
by Colin Powell
"Science and the Sense of Wonder"
by Isaac Asimov

Integrated Language Skills: Grammar, p. 193
Prepositions and Prepositional Phrases

A. 1. <u>to</u>, (class)
2. <u>over</u>, (fence)
3. <u>through</u>, (window); <u>on</u>, (branch)
4. <u>of</u>, (friends)
5. <u>behind</u>, (tree)

B. Sample Answer

I jumped <u>over the fence</u> and hid <u>behind the tree</u>. I hoped my brother wouldn't see me <u>through the window</u>. After he left, I climbed the tree, sat <u>on a branch</u>, and watched the sun set.

"Science and the Sense of Wonder"
by Isaac Asimov

Open-Book Test, p. 196
Short Answer

1. In his poem, Walt Whitman suggests that nature can be appreciated simply by observing it and that the scientific study of nature robs nature of its beauty. Asimov imagines that many people will respond to Whitman's poem triumphantly because it confirms their own beliefs.
   Difficulty: *Challenging* **Objective:** *Vocabulary*

2. With the phrase "all that hard stuff," and especially the word *stuff*, he creates a feeling of informality.
   Difficulty: *Average* **Objective:** *Literary Analysis*

3. He is expressing an opinion. The statement is a judgment and cannot be proved or disproved.
   Difficulty: *Easy* **Objective:** *Reading*

4. He creates a feeling of humor by contrasting serious scientific information and his awe at the wonders of space with a minor annoyance.
   Difficulty: *Challenging* **Objective:** *Literary Analysis*

5. Students will probably call this a valid opinion because most people will agree that even though everyone's definition of beauty is different, there are countless other examples of beauty in the world.
   Difficulty: *Challenging* **Objective:** *Reading*

6. He is trying to convey a feeling of fascination at the wonders of space.
   Difficulty: *Easy* **Objective:** *Literary Analysis*

7. Since a cataclysm is a massive violent event that causes a tremendous amount of damage, it is clear that Asimov is describing a major event.
   Difficulty: *Average* **Objective:** *Vocabulary*

8. Sample answers: Some stars explode, and their cosmic rays influence evolution. The Milky Way is made up of as many as 300 billion stars.
   Asimov's opinion is valid. It is supported by facts.
   Difficulty: *Average* **Objective:** *Reading*

9. He provides vivid descriptions of the solar system and the universe that are based on scientific fact.
   Difficulty: *Average* **Objective:** *Interpretation*

10. He has studied science.
    Difficulty: *Easy* **Objective:** *Interpretation*

Essay

11. Students should clearly state the emotions that the sentence evokes. They may describe a sense of awe, for example, or they may say that thoughts about the vastness of the universe leave them feeling immeasurably small. They should point out the words and phrases that create the emotion, such as "incomparable grandeur" and "doling out their energy stingily."
    Difficulty: *Easy* **Objective:** *Essay*

12. Students should quote a passage from Asimov's essay, explain the feelings it evokes in them, and describe how particular words and phrases in the passage affected them.
    Difficulty: *Average* **Objective:** *Essay*

13. Some students might say that if Whitman had been able to learn about and observe many of the wonders Asimov describes, he might not have considered astronomy to be a cold, dull science. They might point to the beauty and power of Asimov's descriptions to support their opinion. Other students may say that no matter what he learned, Whitman would still have found the experience of gazing at the night sky preferable to learning about it in a classroom. Students may support their opinion by pointing to Asimov's opening statement about the many people today who would agree with Whitman.
    Difficulty: *Challenging* **Objective:** *Essay*

14. Students should state their opinion of the effectiveness of Asimov's argument and cite passages from the essay to support their opinion.
    Difficulty: *Average* **Objective:** *Essay*

Oral Response

15. Oral responses should be clear, well organized, and well supported by appropriate examples from the essay.
    Difficulty: *Average* **Objective:** *Oral Interpretation*

"Science and the Sense of Wonder"
by Isaac Asimov

Selection Test A, p. 199
Critical Reading

1. ANS: C	DIF: Easy	OBJ: Comprehension
2. ANS: C	DIF: Easy	OBJ: Reading
3. ANS: D	DIF: Easy	OBJ: Literary Analysis
4. ANS: A	DIF: Easy	OBJ: Reading
5. ANS: A	DIF: Easy	OBJ: Comprehension
6. ANS: B	DIF: Easy	OBJ: Reading
7. ANS: A	DIF: Easy	OBJ: Literary Analysis
8. ANS: B	DIF: Easy	OBJ: Comprehension
9. ANS: D	DIF: Easy	OBJ: Comprehension
10. ANS: A	DIF: Easy	OBJ: Interpretation
11. ANS: B	DIF: Easy	OBJ: Interpretation

Vocabulary and Grammar

12. ANS: B	DIF: Easy	OBJ: Vocabulary
13. ANS: C	DIF: Easy	OBJ: Grammar
14. ANS: A	DIF: Easy	OBJ: Vocabulary
15. ANS: D	DIF: Easy	OBJ: Grammar

Essay

16. Students' essays should include a clear statement about the awe and surprise (or other emotions) that the sentence evokes. They should include references to words that cause awe—for example, "incomparable grandeur," "glowing . . . suns"—and to words that cause surprise—for example, "red-hot coals," "doling out their energy stingily." Alternatively, students may suggest other feelings that these words call up.
Difficulty: *Easy*
Objective: *Essay*

17. Students' essays should include a clear statement that acknowledges the poet's unappreciative attitude when listening to the astronomer's lessons and tells why Asimov objects to that attitude. One reason Asimov objects is that, from his point of view, the more you know about something, the more you can appreciate it. Students' essays should include at least two scientific facts about planets, suns, stars, galaxies, or clusters of galaxies.
Difficulty: *Easy*
Objective: *Essay*

18. Students should state their opinion of the effectiveness of Asimov's argument and cite passages from the essay to support their opinion.
Difficulty: *Average*
Objective: *Essay*

Selection Test B, p. 202
Critical Reading

1. ANS: D	DIF: Challenging	OBJ: Literary Analysis
2. ANS: A	DIF: Average	OBJ: Interpretation
3. ANS: B	DIF: Average	OBJ: Literary Analysis
4. ANS: A	DIF: Challenging	OBJ: Reading
5. ANS: C	DIF: Average	OBJ: Comprehension
6. ANS: A	DIF: Average	OBJ: Comprehension
7. ANS: D	DIF: Average	OBJ: Comprehension
8. ANS: C	DIF: Average	OBJ: Comprehension
9. ANS: B	DIF: Average	OBJ: Literary Analysis
10. ANS: C	DIF: Average	OBJ: Reading
11. ANS: B	DIF: Average	OBJ: Interpretation
12. ANS: C	DIF: Average	OBJ: Reading
13. ANS: C	DIF: Average	OBJ: Interpretation

Vocabulary and Grammar

14. ANS: C	DIF: Average	OBJ: Vocabulary
15. ANS: B	DIF: Average	OBJ: Vocabulary
16. ANS: A	DIF: Average	OBJ: Grammar
17. ANS: D	DIF: Average	OBJ: Vocabulary
18. ANS: D	DIF: Average	OBJ: Grammar

Essay

19. Students must clearly state whether Asimov is convincing or not, and they must tell how they came to their conclusion. They might say that they themselves find the details of science eye-opening and impressive. Or they might say that Asimov's details do not particularly move them to a greater appreciation of the night sky.
Difficulty: *Average*
Objective: *Essay*

20. Students' essays should include a clear and detailed description of one of the wonders of the night sky that Asimov describes. They also should be specific about the particular words and phrases from the essay that affected them.
Difficulty: *Challenging*
Objective: *Essay*

21. Students should state their opinion of the effectiveness of Asimov's argument and cite passages from the essay to support their opinion.
Difficulty: *Average*
Objective: *Essay*

"Emancipation" from *Lincoln: A Photobiography* by Russell Freedman
"Brown vs. Board of Education" by Walter Dean Myers

Vocabulary Warm-up Exercises, p. 206

A. 1. outlaw
2. slavery
3. Union
4. legal
5. equality
6. absurd
7. honorable
8. authority

B. Sample Answers

1. F. An *abolitionist* was someone who specifically fought against slavery, not *segregation*. Still, those people would probably be against *segregation*.
2. F. If you have good *intentions*, you mean to do good things.
3. T. If you *enlist*, you're not being forced into the army, but rather, sign up on your own.
4. F. The word *captors* has always *referred* to people who hold others against their will.
5. T. A *decree* is an official order.
6. F. A house made of *inferior* materials is likely to fall down more quickly because the materials are not as strong or good as others that could be used.

Reading Warm-up A, p. 207

Sample Answers

1. (eleven southern states that pulled out of, or seceded from, the Union. They had their own laws, their own government, and their own president.); My parents have *authority* over every aspect of my life.
2. (southern states); Four *Union* states were Delaware, Maryland, Kentucky, and Missouri.
3. border states; Did Lincoln's action immediately *make it against the law for one person to own another person* in the North?
4. (sensible); It is *absurd* that in winter I have to get up while it's still dark.
5. (honor); It is *honorable* to tell the truth.
6. Slavery was no longer *legal* once the Thirteenth Amendment was passed.; In some states it is *legal* to drive at the age of sixteen.
7. enjoy the same rights; To me, *equality* means that everyone has the right to enjoy the same freedoms and opportunities of our society, no matter their color, creed, or gender.

Reading Warm-up B, p. 208

Sample Answers

1. (prisoners); *Captors* are people who hold other people as captives, or prisoners.
2. keeping blacks out; *Segregation* means "keeping groups separate," in this case blacks and whites, and *referred* means "relates to or has to do with."
3. (poorer); Some people think that acrylic sweaters are *inferior* to cotton ones.
4. armed forces; Black men decided to *enlist* in the army to help defeat the South.
5. (finally set all slaves free); An *abolitionist* was a person who worked to end slavery.
6. official decision or order; There was a *decree* in our town that all bicycle riders have to wear helmets.
7. (However, the schools had built-in segregation. As the years passed, most people in the South did not see any reason to change things. Segregation, not just in schools but also in other public places, became part of state laws.); I had good *intentions* when I tried to make dinner, but I burned the lasagna.

Writing About the Big Question, p. 209

A. 1. discrimination, inequality
2. explanation
3. challenge
4. decision

B. Sample Answers

1. Lincoln's felt that his first duty was to win the Civil War. He was afraid freeing the slaves would anger Northerners who believed in slavery and slave-holding states still in the Union.
2. The *Brown vs. Board of Education* **decision** meant the end to racial **discrimination** in schools. The Court decided that the best way to overcome **inequality** was for African American and Caucasian students to attend school together.

C. Sample Answer

To learn about inequality in history, I would want to read about the civil rights movement because it is an important part of U.S. history. I think people should have a lot of information on what happened during this time in U.S. history.

Literary Analysis: Comparing Tone, p. 210

Sample Answers

1. Details signaling seriousness: "The toughest decision," "Lincoln pleaded," "war had become an endless nightmare of bloodshed," "must wipe out slavery," "As Union armies smashed their way into rebel territory, they would annihilate slavery once and for all."

2. Serious and dramatic, with great and consistent respect for Lincoln and the burden he shouldered

3. The author's purpose for writing "Emancipation" is (a) to teach the historical facts surrounding Lincoln's issuing of the decree, (b) to describe the emotions surrounding President Lincoln's decision to put forth the Emancipation Proclamation, and (c) to suggest the significance of the document.

4. Details signaling formality: "shadows of chains," "warriors in the cause of freedom," "decision in *Brown vs. Board of Education* signaled an important change in the struggle for civil rights," "prohibitions that oppressed"

   Details signaling informality: "Thurgood's frequent scrapes earned him a reputation as a young boy who couldn't be trusted to get along with the white folks."

5. Serious and dramatic, but not afraid to get personal and familiar

Vocabulary Builder, p. 211

Sample Answers

1. I could alienate someone by saying mean things about him or her.

2. To not hire someone because of his or her race would be unconstitutional.

3. A jury could be found deliberating a case that has been tried.

4. Tripping and falling in front of the class was humiliating to me.

5. Slave owners oppressed slaves.

6. I should compensate whoever does a favor for me.

7. There are predominantly people under the age of twenty-one living in my neighborhood.

Open-Book Test, p. 213

Short Answer

1. The tone is serious. It uses formal language to tell about a serious subject.

   Difficulty: *Easy*   **Objective:** *Literary Analysis*

2. The senators argued that it did not make sense to continue to fight the war without destroying the institution that had caused it.

   Difficulty: *Average*   **Objective:** *Interpretation*

3. The Union army needed more soldiers, and it was believed that many emancipated African Americans would join the army.

   Difficulty: *Easy*   **Objective:** *Interpretation*

4. A predominantly African American neighborhood is one in which most of the residents are African American.

   Difficulty: *Average*   **Objective:** *Vocabulary*

5. He believed that his son's future was more important than his own material comfort, and he believed that an education would help his sons do better than he had done.

   Difficulty: *Easy*   **Objective:** *Interpretation*

6. If segregation were legally prohibited, there would be a gap between what the law stated and how white people thought and acted.

   Difficulty: *Challenging*   **Objective:** *Interpretation*

7. Sample answer: The law that required segregated schools kept African Americans down unjustly by providing them with an education that was inferior to the education provided to white children.

   Difficulty: *Average*   **Objective:** *Vocabulary*

8. Sample answer: *"Emancipation":* "He was afraid to alienate"; "they would annihilate" *"Brown vs. Board of Education":* "young Linda"; "Suddenly he felt a violent tug"

   Students should point out that the tone of "Emancipation" is more formal than that of "Brown vs. Board of Education." They might point to the more formal vocabulary in "Emancipation" or the more colorful details in "Brown vs. Board of Education." Students might also find Freedman's essay more dramatic and Myers's essay more friendly.

   Difficulty: *Average*   **Objective:** *Literary Analysis*

9. Both authors wrote their essays to narrate a historical event relating to the history of African Americans.

   Difficulty: *Easy*   **Objective:** *Interpretation*

10. Both essays deal with the way in which African Americans gained their civil rights.

    Difficulty: *Easy*   **Objective:** *Interpretation*

Essay

11. Students should note that "Emancipation" tells about the events leading up to Lincoln's signing of the Emancipation Proclamation. Freedman's purpose is to narrate a historical event. "Brown vs. Board of Education" describes the Supreme Court decision to outlaw segregation. Myers's purpose is the same as Freedman's. Students should point to word choice and choice of details to support their points.

    Difficulty: *Easy*   **Objective:** *Essay*

12. Students may mention that Lincoln was influenced by members of his cabinet, congressmen, and abolitionists. They may note that Marshall was influenced by the white people who criticized him and denied him, his father, and his law professor their rights. They should recognize that the people who influenced Lincoln and Marshall have had an effect on daily life in the United States by helping to make full civil rights for African Americans a reality and by making the United States more racially harmonious.

    Difficulty: *Average*   **Objective:** *Essay*

13. Students should recognize that the larger battle still to be won involved enforcement and acceptance of the Supreme Court ruling. They may point to Myers's repetition of the quotation about "that gap between law and custom" as evidence that this was so. Students who are familiar with the history of the civil rights movement can point to the violence that followed the 1954 Supreme

Court ruling as evidence that Myers's prediction was accurate.

Difficulty: *Challenging*   **Objective:** *Essay*

14. Students should recognize the various influences on Lincoln's decision (abolitionists, northerners who supported slavery, the border-state congressmen, and the Republican congressmen) and the various influences on the Supreme Court decision (Marshall's argument, Kenneth Clark's evidence, and the Court's recognition that public education had changed since the time of the *Plessy* decision). Most students will say that both essays succeeded in providing the information necessary to understanding those decisions. Students who feel that not enough information was presented should clearly describe what they did not understand.

Difficulty: *Average*   **Objective:** *Essay*

Oral Response

15. Oral responses should be clear, well organized, and well supported by appropriate examples from the essays.

Difficulty: *Average*   **Objective:** *Oral Interpretation*

Selection Test A, p. 216

Critical Reading

1. ANS: B	DIF: Easy	OBJ: Comprehension
2. ANS: D	DIF: Easy	OBJ: Interpretation
3. ANS: C	DIF: Easy	OBJ: Interpretation
4. ANS: A	DIF: Easy	OBJ: Comprehension
5. ANS: C	DIF: Easy	OBJ: Comprehension
6. ANS: C	DIF: Easy	OBJ: Interpretation
7. ANS: A	DIF: Easy	OBJ: Comprehension
8. ANS: B	DIF: Easy	OBJ: Comprehension
9. ANS: A	DIF: Easy	OBJ: Literary Analysis
10. ANS: D	DIF: Easy	OBJ: Literary Analysis
11. ANS: C	DIF: Easy	OBJ: Literary Analysis
12. ANS: D	DIF: Easy	OBJ: Literary Analysis

Vocabulary

13. ANS: C	DIF: Easy	OBJ: Vocabulary
14. ANS: D	DIF: Easy	OBJ: Vocabulary
15. ANS: B	DIF: Easy	OBJ: Vocabulary

Essay

16. Students may mention that "Emancipation" tells about the events and emotions that led up to Lincoln's signing of the Emancipation Proclamation. The author's purpose is to narrate a historical event and make it interesting to readers. The tone of the selection is serious and formal throughout. "Brown vs. Board of Education" describes the people and circumstances surrounding the Supreme Court decision to declare segregation unconstitutional. Myers's purpose is the same as Freedman's. The tone of Myers's work, while generally serious and formal like Freedman's, also becomes personal and familiar—for

example, in the description of young Marshall's "frequent scrapes" and of his reputation "as a young boy who couldn't be trusted to get along with the white folks."

Difficulty: *Easy*

Objective: *Essay*

17. Students may mention that Lincoln was influenced by members of his cabinet who were advising him about emancipation for the slaves; he was influenced by congressmen, whom he did not want to alienate, in the border states; and he was influenced by the abolitionists, who made ending slavery a goal. All these influences led to how and when Lincoln issued the Emancipation Proclamation. Students may note that white people who criticized young Marshall influenced him by motivating him to eliminate such hostility; that his mother's profession as a teacher and his father's belief in the importance of education may also have influenced him; and that law professor Charles Hamilton Houston influenced him by stressing the need for lawyers to help African Americans. All these influences led to the role Marshall played in the *Brown vs. Board of Education* case and later as a justice on the Supreme Court.

Difficulty: *Easy*

Objective: *Essay*

18. Most students will say that both essays succeeded in providing the information necessary to understanding those decisions. Students might cite the issues that affected Lincoln's decision (abolitionists, northerners who supported slavery, the border-state congressmen, and the Republican congressmen) and the issues that affected the Supreme Court decision (Marshall's argument, Kenneth Clark's evidence, and changes in public education since the time of the *Plessy* decision). Students who feel that not enough information was presented should clearly describe what they did not understand.

Difficulty: *Average*

Objective: *Essay*

Selection Test B, p. 219

Critical Reading

1. ANS: B	DIF: Challenging	OBJ: Comprehension
2. ANS: A	DIF: Average	OBJ: Comprehension
3. ANS: D	DIF: Average	OBJ: Interpretation
4. ANS: A	DIF: Challenging	OBJ: Interpretation
5. ANS: B	DIF: Average	OBJ: Interpretation
6. ANS: B	DIF: Average	OBJ: Comprehension
7. ANS: A	DIF: Average	OBJ: Interpretation
8. ANS: C	DIF: Challenging	OBJ: Interpretation
9. ANS: A	DIF: Average	OBJ: Comprehension
10. ANS: D	DIF: Challenging	OBJ: Literary Analysis
11. ANS: C	DIF: Average	OBJ: Literary Analysis
12. ANS: D	DIF: Average	OBJ: Literary Analysis
13. ANS: C	DIF: Average	OBJ: Literary Analysis

Vocabulary

14. ANS: B   DIF: Average   OBJ: Vocabulary
15. ANS: C   DIF: Average   OBJ: Vocabulary
16. ANS: C   DIF: Average   OBJ: Vocabulary

Essay

17. Students may mention that "Emancipation" tells about the events and emotions that led up to Lincoln's signing of the Emancipation Proclamation. "Brown vs. Board of Education" describes the people and circumstances surrounding the Supreme Court decision to declare segregation unconstitutional. Both essays, therefore, concern landmarks in the history of African American equality in the United States. Both authors have as their purpose to narrate a historical event and make it interesting to readers. "Emancipation" seems to have a single tone—seriousness—which comes across in the respect shown by the author for Lincoln throughout the essay. While "Brown vs. Board of Education" is also serious—notably, again, in the respect the author shows for Marshall—it has a secondary tone of informality and familiarity. This brief secondary tone comes across with the author's mention of young Marshall's "frequent scrapes" and of his reputation "as a young boy who couldn't be trusted to get along with the white folks."

Difficulty: *Average*

Objective: *Essay*

18. Students may mention that Lincoln was influenced by members of his cabinet, who were advising him about emancipation for the slaves; by congressmen, whom he did not want to alienate, in the border states; and by the abolitionists, who made ending slavery a goal. All these influences led to how and when Lincoln issued the Emancipation Proclamation. Students may note that white people who criticized young Marshall influenced him; that his mother's profession as a teacher and his father's belief in the importance of education may have influenced him; and that law professor Charles Hamilton Houston influenced Marshall by stressing the need for outstanding lawyers to help African Americans. The people who influenced Lincoln and Marshall continue to have an impact on daily life today in the United States, where full equality for African Americans remains the law of the land.

Difficulty: *Average*

Objective: *Essay*

19. Students should recognize the various influences on Lincoln's decision (abolitionists, northerners who supported slavery, the border-state congressmen, and the Republican congressmen) and the various influences on the Supreme Court decision (Marshall's argument, Kenneth Clark's evidence, and the Court's recognition that public education had changed since the time of the *Plessy* decision). Most students will say that both essays succeeded in providing the information necessary to understanding those decisions. Students who

feel that not enough information was presented should clearly describe what they did not understand.

Difficulty: *Average*

Objective: *Essay*

Writing Workshop

Editorial: Integrating Grammar Skills, p. 223

A. 1. <u>and</u>; compound subject; 2. <u>because</u>; complex sentence; 3. <u>as soon as</u>; complex sentence; 4. <u>whenever I can</u>; complex sentence

B. Answers may vary.
1. Gymnastics and weight lifting build muscles.
2. The competition is Saturday, but Harry didn't qualify.
3. He hopes to make the finals next year because he plans to practice.

Vocabulary Workshop—1, p. 224

Sample Answers

1. fog
2. tip
3. coast
4. plate
5. train
6. review

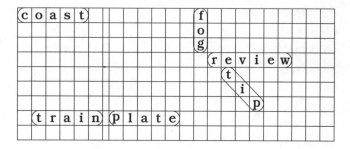

Vocabulary Workshop—2, p. 225

Noel couldn't **bear** the thought of seeing another **bear**. It was not in her **nature** to tolerate enormous, wilderness beasts that **might** or might not have her for lunch. Noel **leaned** against a tree and sighed. The camping trip had been Claudia's idea. Noel would have preferred a lush breakfast with toast and **jam** instead of canned beans over the campfire, lit with small branches instead of a **match**. Claudia was Noel's best friend and loved nature, so she tried to match her enthusiasm and stay **positive**. She mustered all of her courage and **might** to venture out into the woods that evening in search of more kindling. What would she do if she saw the bear again? Noel had learned that the important thing was to avoid surprising a bear. She shoved her cell phone in her pocket and set out honking a bicycle **horn** as she walked noisily through the forest. Noel felt nearly **positive** that a bear would find her too **lean** to make a decent meal anyway. She continued on, lost in her thoughts, and accidentally fell upon the long, curved **horn** of the lake. It was beautiful under the setting sun, and for the first time all week Noel felt happier in the woods than being stuck in a traffic **jam**.

Benchmark Test 6, p. 227

MULTIPLE CHOICE

1. ANS: B
2. ANS: D
3. ANS: A
4. ANS: B
5. ANS: C
6. ANS: B
7. ANS: A
8. ANS: C
9. ANS: D
10. ANS: B
11. ANS: C
12. ANS: B
13. ANS: D
14. ANS: D
15. ANS: B
16. ANS: A
17. ANS: B
18. ANS: A
19. ANS: B
20. ANS: A
21. ANS: D
22. ANS: C
23. ANS: C
24. ANS: B
25. ANS: B
26. ANS: C
27. ANS: D
28. ANS: D
29. ANS: A
30. ANS: A
31. ANS: A
32. ANS: D
33. ANS: C
34. ANS: D

ESSAY

35. Students' editorials should include a clear statement of the issue, credible support, and a response to opposing arguments.
36. Students' responses should include a statement of the idea and supporting reasons for agreeing or disagreeing.
37. Students' evaluations should include a description of the commercial, the persuasive techniques used, and an evaluation of the commercial's effectiveness.

Vocabulary in Context 3, p. 233

MULTIPLE CHOICE

1. ANS: A
2. ANS: B
3. ANS: A
4. ANS: D
5. ANS: C
6. ANS: D
7. ANS: A
8. ANS: C
9. ANS: C
10. ANS: A
11. ANS: B
12. ANS: D
13. ANS: B
14. ANS: A
15. ANS: C
16. ANS: A
17. ANS: D
18. ANS: C
19. ANS: B
20. ANS: C